Malcolm Hulke Studies

in Cinema and Television

Number Two

ISSN 0884-6944

Masters of EVIL

A Viewer's Guide to Cinematic Archvillains

by

Georgette S. Fox

R . R E G I N A L D

The Borgo Press

San Bernardino, California □ MCMXCVIII

THE BORGO PRESS

Publishers of Fine Books Since 1975
Post Office Box 2845
San Bernardino, CA 92406
United States of America

* * * * * * * *

Library of Congress Cataloging-in-Publication Data

Fox, Georgette S. (Georgette Sheila), 1950-
  Masters of evil : a viewer's guide to cinematic archvillains / by Georgette
S. Fox.
  p. cm. -- (Malcolm Hulke studies in cinema and television, ISSN 0884-
6944 ; no. 2)
  Includes bibliographical references (p.) and index.
  ISBN 0-8095-0003-5 (cloth). — ISBN 0-8095-1003-0 (pbk.)
  1. Villains in motion pictures. 2. Evil in motion pictures. I. Title. II.
Series.
PN1995.9.V47F68 1998   96-41059
791.43'6520692—dc20   CIP

FIRST EDITION

CONTENTS

INDEX

DEDICATION

With love to my husband, Steven, and my son, Paul;

In loving memory of my mom and dad;

And in memory of Rita Davenport, a true friend who encouraged me to keep writing.

ACKNOWLEDGMENTS

"Now I am the master."
"Only a master of evil, Darth."

—George Lucas, *Star Wars*

I want to express my gratitude to Daryl F. Mallett for his interest in my writing. Also, I am grateful to both Robert Reginald and Mary Burgess for their patience and valued advice. Thank you also to:

Ray Bradbury, whose story "Asleep in Armageddon" inspired me to want to become a writer;
Stephen R. Donaldson for being a person who cares;
George Lucas for becoming a writer and director of films;
Dr. John Pederson for allowing my imagination freedom and for being so much like Dr. Elwin Ransom;
Charles I. Jones with gratitude for his regard and support of my work;
The Public Library System, an indispensable part of my life.

Finally my special apprecation to all the actors who responded to my letters and wished me well, and especially to the following who have so successfully horrified me:

> Malcolm McDowell
> Robert Englund
> Jack Nicholson
> Michael Des Barres
> Russell Crowe
> Sam Neill
> Adrian Pasdar
> Jeremy Northam
> Bruce Campbell
> Edward Norton

And in memory of the late Warren Oates and Sir Michael Redgrave.

And I keep in mind *Revelations* 3:8.

INTRODUCTION

"Evil needs to be pondered just as much as good," according to Carl Jung, "for good and evil are ultimately nothing but ideal extensions and abstractions of doing, and both belong to the chiaroscuro of life."[1] If we accept this idea as valid, then a tangible representation of it can be found in the person of the invented archvillain, the paradigm of evil. On film the negative, malevolent aspects of human behavior presented in the imaginary archvillain take on an extra dimension.

This book is an examination of the methodology of the archvillain through his or her actions on screen, exploring only the characters whose desire, inclination, and preference have drawn each of them into a maelstrom of evil. If, as in the instance of Norman Bates in Alfred Hitchcock's *Psycho*, the character functions as a victim living out his or her inner torment, such an individual remains outside the scope of this study.

The theoretical duality of human conduct provides an additional focal point. Along with diverse psychologists and philosophers, many authors, notably Robert Louis Stevenson and Edgar Allan Poe, have espoused this idea in their writings. "The basest motives in man," as stated in a critical analysis of the novels of Dostoevsky, "exist side by side with the utmost sincerity and purity."[2] Emphasizing the significance of this dichotomy in personality development, this book concentrates on the decisions made and courses of action taken by the inexorable and unrelenting archvillain. Also, a distinction is made between the protagonist and antagonist which proposes a dissimilarity in the situational responses of each character.

We often detect a fragment of ourselves in the person of the archvillain. Through the archvillain we experience a cathartic release, one needed, at times, for our own mental balance. What we see on film is meant as an entertainment, yet it can just as readily supply us with personal insight.

The destructive behavior with which we are surrounded in reality seems far worse than the misdeeds of the archvillains imprisoned on celluloid. Each deed is but a mere reflection of actual evil, thus we are free to shrug off their fiendish ways and go about our business once the screen goes dark. We find ourselves in the light again, hoping our acts will prove to be the opposite of those of the archvillain on the screen.

—Georgette S. Fox

Aaron/Roy Stampler

Film Source: *Primal Fear*
Release Date: 1996
Director: Gregory Hoblit
Production Company: Paramount Pictures
Color
Running Time: 130 minutes
Performed by: Edward Norton
Additional Performers: Richard Gere (Martin Vail); Laura Linney (Janet Venable); Stanley Anderson (Archbishop Rushman).

Physical Description: Aaron Stampler is blessed with the face and demeanor of a true innocent. His wide-eyed gaze accentuates his angelic features, and his ingratiating smile, southern drawl, and conventionally short hair are a novelty in the big city. He has put these assets to good use in his role as altar boy and choir member at a church-run shelter for runaways. Aaron presents a non-threatening face to the world, but his most unusual characteristic is a pronounced stutter—which completely disarms the casual observer. Hidden within Aaron's psyche, however, is a being which can traverse great distances any time it splinters into "Roy," an alternate personality who seemingly inhabits Aaron's inner soul. Although lean in build, Aaron displays an inordinate amount of strength and vigor when he becomes Roy. An insidious sneer and unimpeded diction are clues that he is undergoing transformation.

Character Analysis: A time-honored fable relates how a turtle, after much hesitation, agrees to help a scorpion cross a stream. The scorpion promises no harm will come to his benefactor, but stings the turtle fatally before they can reach the shore. As they sink beneath the water, the turtle pleads with the scorpion for an explanation of his vile deed. The scorpion replies, "I couldn't stop myslf from being what I am." Aaron, is the embodiment of the scorpion in the fable. In reality, he is not "Aaron" at all, but a cunning sociopath who has slain his own supposed benefactor, Archbishop Rushman, by stabbing him to death and mutilating his body. It is *not* the Archbishop, however, who plays the part of the turtle in Aaron's devious scenario, but Martin Vail, the famous criminal lawyer who has undertaken Aaron's defense, partially to feed his own vanity. Vail is led to uncover facts in the case which provide motivation for Aaron's behavior. Rushman has forced Aaron to become a reluctant performer in pornographic sex videos made by the

Archbishop to appease his own self-doubt and unfulfilled desires. The rationale is that Aaron has finally snapped, and in a moment of desperation has killed his abuser. In reality, however, Aaron has devised a foolproof scheme which has resulted in the premeditated murders of both the Archbishop and Aaron's former girlfriend. All the killer needs is one element to insure his success, a "true believer" of Vail's reputation and caliber. So flawless and believable is Aaron's transition from one personality to another, first in front of the psychologist examining him, then in front of Vail, that both are convinced of its validity. In fact, Vail has no difficulty in accepting "Roy" as his client's response to an abused childhood and a vicious father, the real Roy. Vail places Aaron on the stand at his trial, and deliberately goads him into another transformation. When "Roy" appears, he viciously attacks the prosecuting attorney, giving the performance of his life. His violent outburst, as Vail has anticipated, earns Aaron a reprieve from the death penalty. Visiting his client later in an institution for the criminally insane, Vail is first bewildered, then infuriated, when Aaron mocks him for not having guessed his game. Vail shrinks in horror from the monster he has helped create. With Aaron's taunts in his ears, Vail turns away from the cameras and congratulatory newscasters awaiting him outside the prison. For now, he will relinquish the limelight and ponder the dreadful burden he will be forced to carry under attorney-client privilege. In his cell Aaron grins contentedly, patting himself on the back for a job well done. His vanity overshadows Vail's, as he recalls his savage mutilation of the Archbishop as "artwork," and his brutal killing of his former girlfriend as nothing more than a demonic "joke." Although he may have had reasonable justification for his anger, Aaron, as Roy, has transformed himself into an unreasonable monster. Even the real "Roy" might blanch at the true self of his inventor.

AARON: SEE: TONY AARON

ABBOTT

Film Source: *The Man Who Knew Too Much*
Release Dates: 1934; 1956
Focus: 1934 film version
Director: Alfred Hitchcock
Production Company: A Gaumont British Production
B&W
Running Time: 72 minutes
Performed by: Peter Lorre
Additional Performers: Leslie Banks (Mr. Lawrence); Edna Best (Mrs. Lawrence); Nova Pilbeam (Betty Lawrence).

Physical Description: Abbott is a small man who gives the impression of being much larger. A lock of hair falls across his forehead, emphasizing his boyish demeanor. His accent is unidentifiable, leaving the question of his origin in doubt. Corpulent and inclined to slouch, he looks uncomfortable in his clothes. His range of expression varies from a mischievous grin to an unexpected angry scowl.

Character Analysis: Abbott is a careful planner, possessing the unswerving determination so often seen in the leaders of saboteurs. He scrutinizes each detail of his plot to assassinate a diplomat, and is utterly convinced of the correctness of his actions. His dedication to such an extreme political cause doubtless reflects an unflinching zealotry founded in his youth. His biting, sardonic humor quickly changes to rage when his authority is challenged. Convinced his plot is destined to succeed, he foolishly kidnaps a child to embellish his scheme, completely underestimating the father's equally unswerving devotion to his child. This lapse proves to be Abbott's undoing, and he is shot and killed during a penultimate gun battle with the police.

ALEX

Film Source: *Pink Cadillac*
Release Date: 1989
Director: Buddy Van Horn
Production Company: Warner Bros.
Color
Running Time: 121 minutes
Performed by: Michael Des Barres
Additional Performers: Clint Eastwood (Tom Nowak); Bernadette Peters (Lou Ann McGuinn); Timothy Carhart (Roy McGuinn).

Physical Description: Alex illustrates the axiom that size has nothing to do with a forceful presence. His lean form is muscular and indomitable, and his booming, rasping voice is suggestive of a charismatic lead vocalist with a rock band. Alex resembles a Rabelaisian nobleman, with his hair pulled back in a ponytail, and clad in black boots, jacket, vest, and open-fingered gloves. He seems older than his thirty-something years might indicate, but one facial feature seems out of place with the rest of his persona: his dimples.

Character Analysis: Alex has excellent organizational skills, a clever, agile mind, and much determination. He is furious at everyone who is not, in his opinion, a "real American." Alex's anger possibly springs from the fact that he has been in the penitentiary twice, and is determined never to be incarcerated again. Alex is now the leader of a white supremacy group, "The Birthright." Using illegal activities, wild extremism, and outrageous violence, he has built an armed camp in a mountain retreat, stockpiled with automatic weapons and explosives. The men in his service are fighting machines, and the women (known only as "females") are objects to be controlled by him. Alex expects absolute loyalty from his followers, and he relishes his power over others. He adheres to a strict political doctrine untenanted by any modicum of sensitivity or humanity, being addicted to the use of violence (which he may have been forced to use for survival during his years in prison). Like a child building a house of blocks, one atop the other, Alex is training his army of "warriors" to lead "The Day of the Great Uprising." He longs for revenge against those in a position of power or upon whom his severe prejudice falls, and plots reprisals beyond even the most nightmarish of imaginings against those he blames most for his suffering and loss, the ones at whose hands he feels he has been irretrievably wronged. In order to finance his paramilitary group, Alex has counterfeited a large sum of money, but discovers that Lou Ann, the wife of Roy McGuinn, one of his followers, has run off with it. To penalize Roy for failing to control his wife, Alex tortures the man. Into the midst of this debacle wanders Tom Nowak, a skip-tracer assigned to pick up Lou Ann and return her to the authorities for a crime she insists she did not commit. Tom is drawn into rescuing Lou Ann when her baby is kidnapped by Alex's followers. Under the right circumstances, Tom might have become as warped as Alex, but unlike Alex, who would not hesitate to kill anyone who stands in his way, Tom has a strong regard for the sanctity of life, and respect for humanity in general. Alex mocks Tom for his "weakness," but is run off the road in a final showdown with Tom (although there is some doubt as to whether or not he is killed or survives). Alex is not just some "little man," seeking to control and influence others through the skillful use of viciousness and fear, but he *is* a person with a distorted design for the future—and a hideous outline of destruction and despotism. Such people may seem ridiculous at first, but, on closer scrutiny, they often have become some of history's most frightening individuals. Had Alex written a book he might well have entitled it *My Struggle*, as a nod to a well-known treatise written by a man incarcerated in a German prison during the 1920s who became a real-life archvillain.

ALEX

Film Source: *Bad Influence*
Release Date: 1990
Director: Curtis Hanson
Production Company: Epic Productions, Inc.
Color
Running Time: 99 minutes
Performed by: Rob Lowe

Additional Performers: James Spader (Michael Boll); Christian Clemenson ("Pismo" Boll); Tony Maggio (Patterson); Rosalyn Landor (Britt); Kathleen Wilhoite (Leslie); John de Lancie (Howard).

Physical Description: Alex's stylish wardrobe is secondary only to his phenomenal good looks. He may be *too* handsome, if possible, for if the editor of a men's fashion magazine spotted Alex at a party, the cover of the upcoming issue undoubtedly would be scrapped and a photo shoot featuring Alex would be arranged as quickly as possible. Alex's wavy hair, piercing eyes, attractive physique, and charming voice are not, however, the sum total of the whole man. Alex exploits his attributes in the same way a greedy entrepreneur might plunder a natural resource. A young man, not yet out of his twenties, he has the bearing of someone older and more seasoned.

Character Analysis: "People are *such* hypocrites," Alex tells Michael Boll, a naive young executive he has befriended. No one is innocent, he insists, especially those who believe they are. The ingenuous Michael is inevitably drawn into the flashy, exotic lifestyle Alex spreads before him. At their first meeting Alex easily gains an advantage over Michael by stealing his forgotten wallet from a bar. He then introduces Michael to Britt, surreptitiously films them during love-making, then informs Michael he "gave" him Britt. Michael's scheming business colleague steals one of his computer programs and Alex beats the man up, stating that he is just "giving" his friend what he wants. Alex is convinced that granting wishes through illicit and socially unacceptable acts is his right, and is likely an outgrowth of a lifetime of gaining attention by acting out in negative ways. Alex's questionable behavior escalates when he gets Michael drunk, gives him cocaine, and takes him on a reckless spree of late-night robberies. He then arrives unannounced at a family dinner party where he plays the video of Michael and Britt making love for Leslie, Michael's fiancée, and their horrified parents. Michael, at last repelled by Alex and his actions, throws him out, thus placing himself in a precarious predicament. Alex has systematically acquired a volume of information and identification on Michael, and sets about to destroy his "friend's" life. He burglarizes Michael's apartment, murders Britt (with whom Michael has fallen in love), videotapes the murder, and plants incriminating evidence. Michael's brother, Pismo, helps him dispose of Britt's body, but Alex, anticipating their actions, calls the police and leads them to it. The two brothers trick Alex into taping a confession and, in a final confrontation, Michael shoots Alex, a justifiable homicide. Alex stated that all "people are hypocrites," yet he himself was no less one. His "friendship" with Michael was actually a perversion of his declared objective of giving "favors" and granting "wishes," motivated by his own sick gratification. Alex's life was based upon doing what he pleased, to whom he pleased, whenever he pleased. His "no one is innocent" justification was a hollow excuse for his excesses. Michael, though willing to accept Alex's "favors," genuinely cared about his brother and loved Britt. He eventually renounced Alex and his "favors," once he comprehended the price demanded. Alex only cared about Alex; and in the end he was the only one who did.

ALEX D

Film Source: *A Clockwork Orange*
Release Date: 1971
Director: Stanley Kubrick
Production Company: A Stanley Kubrick Production
Color
Running Time: 137 minutes
Performed by: Malcolm McDowell

Physical Description: Alex D, clad all in white, and sporting a black bowler hat, boots, and cane, has drawn a strange enigmatic false eyelash around his left eye. Physically capable of "mashing" the toughest member of the gang of young delinquents he leads, Alex resembles nothing so much as a playful elf gone totally mad in the futuristic world he and his cohorts inhabit.

Character Analysis: Alex D, while remarkably intelligent, possesses not one gram of compassion or human decency. His outrageous, bestial lifestyle includes kicking and beating vagrants in alleys and raping and torturing a middle-aged couple in their own home. Incarcerated for murder, he opts for a (to him) distasteful rehabilitation in order to gain his freedom. Alex, brainwashed to shed his vicious personality, falls into the hands of his former companions. Since it was his own ferocious behavior that made thugs of his gang, it is only poetic justice that Alex now finds himself the tormented rather than the tormentor. Alex stumbles once more into the home of the man whose wife he had raped, and attracts yet more trouble. Learning nothing from what has befallen him, Alex welcomes the government's offer to return him to his old self, and sneers at the thought the government will study his malicious behavior for its own questionable ends. Kubrick's violent future world is based on the disturbing novel by Anthony Burgess, where corruption is not merely acceptable, but in demand. Alex's contempt for everyone and everything about him accurately reflects the corruption of those in power.

ALEXANDER: SEE: BOB ALEXANDER

ALEXANDER THORKEL

Film Source: *Dr. Cyclops*
Release Date: 1940
Director: Ernest B. Schoedsack
Production Company: Paramount Pictures
Color
Running Time: 76 minutes
Performed by: Albert Dekker
Additional Performers: Charles Halton (Dr. Bulfinch), Paul Fix (Dr. Mendoza).

Physical Description: Dr. Alexander Thorkel wears a permanently-wrinkled khaki suit. Although moustached, he either has shaved his head completely bald, or he has experienced pathological hair loss as a result of radium exposure during his exeriments. Advanced myopia obliges him to use lenses with a strong prescription. His diction borders on perfection—unless he is irritated.

Character Analysis: Alexander Thorkel is an eminent biologist whose self-assurance and resolution have deteriorated into an all-consuming fixation on his own omnipotence. Dr. Mendoza, a former student, invites Thorkel to his laboratory in the Amazon where together they will found the "Thorkel Institute" as a "palace of healing." Thorkel accepts the invitation, but ignores Mendoza's recommendations on the direction of their research. Instead, he uses the facilities for his own nefarious schemes. Horrified, Mendoza insists Thorkel halt his experiments and destroy his notes, declaring that Thorkel is "tampering with powers reserved to God." They quarrel and Thorkel irradiates Mendoza, thus assuming control of the valuable radium deposit unearthed by him. At Thorkel's invitation, Dr. Bulfinch, a famous scientist, selects a team of experts, and together they make the long journey to the institute, against the advice of a colleague. The new arrivals are shocked when Thorkel accepts the information he requires from them, then asks them to leave immediately. Their curiosity aroused, the group decides to stay on against Thorkel's will, and he responds with a menacing threat. They discover the radium deposit and Thorkel's notes and, convinced of his madness, they set about to seize him. Thorkel makes a crafty plea for their forgiveness and leads them into his experimental chamber where he locks the door. He starts up his miniaturizing machine with no regard for the effect his invention will have on the humans. "Now I can control life absolutely," Thorkel congratulates himself, as he settles down for a nap. While he is asleep, however, the miniaturized captives escape into the jungle. Thorkel then makes the chilling discovery that Dr. Bulfinch is growing, and will soon attain full stature again. He tracks down his fellow biologist and murders him without delay, while he is still vulnerable. Thorkel follows the rest of the team to their jungle hiding place, where he informs them of Dr. Bulfinch's death. Failing to flush them out of the tall grass, he resorts to more drastic methods by setting the compound on fire. In a final savage attack, Thorkel shoots his own miniaturized servant, Pedro, as the man attempts a diversion so the others can escape. The group makes a courageous stand against the biologist by smashing his glasses, and he is left with a single unbroken lens. Like some mythological "Cyclops," Thorkel pursues his prey into the topmost portion of the radium excavation, where he loses his balance and plummets to his death in the abyss below. Thorkel's failing eyesight was a physical imperfection, readily overcome by corrective lenses, but no prescription could remedy his emotional deficiencies. Blinded by conceit, Thorkel failed to heed Mendoza's warnings in time. His scientific discoveries had potential for both benefit and harm, but were warped by his exaggerated desire for fame and authority, and his lack of concern for the safety and well-being of others.

ANGEL

Film Source: *Street Hunter*
Release Date: 1990
Director: John A. Gallagher
Production Company: 21st Century Film Corporation
Color
Running Time: 96 minutes
Performed by: John Leguizamo
Additional Performers: Steve James (Logan Blade); Valarie Petriford (Denise); Reb Brown (Colonel Walsh); Frank Vincent (Don Romano); Tom Wright (Riley).

Physical Description: Diminutive Angel compensates for his lack of height with his powerful, albeit high-pitched, voice, with the further advantage that he speaks both English and Spanish fluently. His luxurious dark hair and riveting eyes demand undivided attention from those around him. He wears fancy suits, several rings on the fingers of both hands, and a tiny earring in his left ear. He is still in his twenties and his smooth, broad-featured face, marred only by a small scar near his right eyebrow, emphasizes his youth.

Character Analysis: Angel is a "street-wise" cocaine addict, whose link to the Colombian drug cartel assures his future as a major figure in the underworld of big city crime. A person more accustomed to giving orders than in taking them, he handles people the way he always has since his childhood—if what he had could be interpreted as "childhood." He either kills outright those who stand in his path—or plots to do so as soon as possible. Under his seething exterior lies more than a "street punk" mentality, for Angel has big dreams. Just as his behavior is the natural outgrowth of his lust for power and money, it is also an exercise in violence. A Mafia Don's son catches him stealing the Don's cocaine, and he forces the mobster's heir into a degrading plea for mercy before shooting him in the head, taking on the role of both judge and executioner at such close range that he is splattered with blood. Captured by bounty hunter Logan Blade, Angel shouts obscenities, threatening both the officers and their families as he is jailed. Angel's hired "soldiers," led by a brutal madman, Colonel Walsh, free him, and he sets out to fulfill his claim to the late Louis Romano's statement that "This city is mine." His men capture Logan, along with Denise, the woman Blade loves. Like a pesky mosquito on a humid day, Angel takes immense pleasure in irritating and tormenting his opponents. He intentionally tries to pique Logan by sitting on Denise's lap and kissing her until he extorts the desired response from his adversary. Logan succeeds in recapturing Angel, and is relieved to turn his unwilling charge over once more to the police. Angel does not in any way reflect the positive qualities of the name he has been given, but boasts of his own recidivism with gusto. Some hardened criminals *do* have the will to build new lives for themselves, but Angel likes himself just the way he is, making any change in his present behavior more than doubtful.

ANTHONY: SEE: BRUNO ANTHONY

DR. ANTON ARCANE

Film Sources: *Swamp Thing; The Return of Swamp Thing*
Release Dates: 1982; 1989
Directors: Wes Craven; Jim Wynorski
Production Companies: DeLaurentis Entertainment Group; Lightyear Entertainment
Color
Running Times: 91 minutes; 87 minutes
Performed by: Louis Jourdan
Additional Performers—*Swamp Thing*: Ray Wise (Dr. Alec Holland); Nannette Brown, (Dr. Linda Holland); Adrienne Barbeau (Alice Cable); Nicholas Worth (Bruno); Ben Bates (Arcane Monster).
Additional Performers—*Return of Swamp Thing*: Dick Durock (The Swamp Thing); Heather Locklear (Abby Arcane); Sarah Douglas (Dr. Lana Zurrell).

Physical Description: Dr. Arcane is a man of impressive physical characteristics who chooses his attire with an emphasis on style. His

French accent adds an elegant and charming touch to his baritone voice. Although he is quite possibly nearing fifty, his dark hair and eyes, and slim physique favor him with a youthful appearance.

Character Analysis (*Swamp Thing*): Arcane, whose surname is fitting, is a furtive person who keeps himself, his location, and his designs all well concealed. Dr. Arcane has stalked his Machiavellian dream of limitless power as a tiger stalks its prey. Machiavelli, however, was a creative man, while Arcane, although a genius in many ways, is not. Arcane dreams singlemindedly of stealing the discoveries made by scientists Dr. Alec Holland and his sister, Linda. Arcane has always considered himself to be a minor deity, and since he believes himself to be an even greater individual than Alec Holland, he concludes that Alec's work is destined to become his sole property. He and his mercenary army dispatch the Hollands; but their notebook records are not complete. Learning that Dr. Holland has been transformed into "Swamp Thing," a giant plant-like creature, while yet retaining his mental faculties, Arcane becomes obsessed with the idea of imbibing the formula himself. Arcane is convinced that his own evolution will be even more miraculous than Holland's. Arcane retrieves the indispensable last notebook from Alice Cable, whom Alec loves. Before using the formula himself, Arcane slips the drink to Bruno, his burly guard, during a stylish dinner party. His terrified guests are not prepared for what happens to Bruno. Instead of growing larger and more powerful, Bruno changes into a miniscule troll, who condemns Arcane's biting deception. Chained in a dungeon in Arcane's mansion, Alec explains to his perplexed captor that the formula only magnifies those qualities which the individual already possesses. Arcane deduces that the formula has translated Bruno's timid, childish personality into his current physical self. Arcane has lived his whole life in pursuit of ultimate power, convinced of his own perfection, both physical and intellectual. He assumes that the formula will only enhance those qualities in himself. When he takes the formula, however, it exaggerates the *evil* within his mind, rather than his genius and his handsome physical appearance. He witnesses his own transformation into a hideous monster—and has but one thought—the murder of Alec.

Character Analysis (*Return of Swamp Thing*): Arcane, although unsuccessful in killing Alec, has no interest in letting the matter go. He possesses the same insatiable cravings he exhibited both before and after his rescue from the swamp by his subordinates. Returning to a somewhat normal existence, and reinstated into a semblance of his previous life, Arcane sets about in his quest for Alec once more. Arcane had married, but his wife lost her life in the act of saving his. Now their grown daughter Abby arrives at the exact time he requires another special "transfusion." Betrayed by his lover, Dr. Lana Zurrell, Arcane shoots her, then attempts to transfer the "life force" from Abby to himself. Alec Holland saves Abby, leaving Arcane to die in a fiery explosion in his mansion near the bayou. At one time Alec had hoped his invention might increase the world's food supply. As the creature, "Swamp Thing," he still gives unstintingly of himself for the safety and benefit of others. In contrast, Arcane, whose intelligence *did* rival Holland's in some respects, used Alec's findings selfishly to enhance his own power. Arcane's scientific research, the pride of his life, leads to the creation, mutilation, and torture of monstrosities. Disinterested in the needs and hardships facing humanity, Arcane's view of the world was a narrow one. Looking through the small end of the glass, he focused entirely on himself.

ANTON BARTOK

Film Source: *The Fly II*
Release Date: 1989
Director: Chris Walas
Production Company: Twentieth Century Fox
Color
Running Time: 104 minutes
Performed by: Lee Richardson
Additional Performers: Eric Stoltz (Martin Brundle), Daphne Zuniga (Beth Logan), Saffron Henderson (Ronnie).

Physical Description: Anton Bartok's clothes, bearing, and speech are a textbook definition of the corporate executive. Tall, stout, and robust, his twinkling eyes, ingratiating smile and deep, melodic voice are winning assets. Bartok has reached the pinnacle of his career and late middle age at the same time, but he still possesses a look of raw strength and stamina which win those about him over to his desires.

Character Analysis: Anton Bartok, in the act of playing God, sets in motion a series of events leading to catastrophe. As the enduring power behind Bartok Industries, he demands that those in his employ must follow the most rigid guidelines conceivable. Bartok had supported the work of genius physicist Seth Brundle, but he is aware of the tragic outcome of Brundle's teleportation experiments. Bartok convinces Seth's pregnant lover, Ronnie, to have her baby at Bartok Industries under his charge, in the hope her offspring will be as "non-human" as the tormented Brundle himself became. Mr. Bartok is thrilled when Martin, Seth and Ronnie's son, is born, for it appears that the flawed gene has been passed. Bartok, resolved to avoid any future interference from the child's mother, allows Ronnie to die. He establishes a "chain of command" regarding the treatment and upbringing of Martin, whose mutation he awaits in patient wonder. He himself is at the apex of his microcosmic world. "From God's mouth to your ears," he instructs his staff. Martin, who grows at an accelerated rate, is told almost nothing of his father's true dilemma. Bartok, who knows from videotapes made by Seth Brundle how the scientist became linked at the genetic level with a fly while using his "telepod" devices on himself, scrutinizes young Martin like a laboratory animal. Although he lavishes birthday parties, gifts, and a vast education on the child, presenting himself as a loving, substitute parent, his affection is a all a sham, and Martin is kept a virtual prisoner in the bowels of Bartok's headquarters. Martin naively loves and trusts his surrogate father, but Bartok uses Martin's devotion to his own advantage, overlooking the pitfalls inherent in such a monumental deception. A single underlying theme motivates Bartok's relationship with Martin: his desire for power, long noted for its corruptible attributes. Bartok, who has always taken what he wanted, regardless of the consequences, has forgotten the value of compassion and respect for other human beings. Then an event takes place which is even more foreboding. Martin has made a pet of a laboratory dog, and is devastated when the animal is mutilated in a botched telepod experiment. Although Bartok tells Martin the dog is dead, Martin discovers his friend is still alive, though suffering, and is being kept under surveillance in a special room. In a confrontation, Bartok tells the horrified, anguished Martin that his desire is to "control the form and function of all life on earth." Martin, now fully mutated into the fly creature, cannot forgive Bartok's deception, and turns on him in terror and despair. Bartok threatens to kill both Martin and Beth Logan, whom Martin loves, but Martin's response is not what he anticipates. Martin has indeed discovered the secret of the telepods, just as Bartok had hoped he would. Realizing that the only way he can make himself human again is by using another human being during transfer, Martin forces Bartok into the telepod with him. Martin is fully restored, but Bartok becomes a mutated creature like the dog Martin loved. Unlike the dog, however, which Martin has had put out of its misery, the "new" Mr. Bartok is kept alive and imprisoned in the same room as the dog had inhabited. In the end, Bartok, who "played God" with other peoples' lives has become a victim of his own hubris.

ARI KRISTATOS

Film Source: *For Your Eyes Only*
Release Date: 1981
Director: John Glen
Production Company: MGM-UA
Color
Running Time: 127 minutes
Performed by: Julian Glover

Additional Performers: Roger Moore (James Bond), Carol Bouquet (Melina), Topol (Milos Columbo).

Physical Description: Ari Kristatos is tall, with a magnetic gaze, a graying beard, and is aristocratic and charming in manner. His mellow baritone voice is enhanced by a Greek accent. He appears younger than he is, in his sixties.

Character Analysis: Ari Kristatos, a World War II hero to the British, is not what he seems to be. He served as a double agent during the war, working for the Axis powers against Greece. He has also worked for the Soviet Union before the fall of communism, and has posed as an anti-communist as well. He smuggles heroin on the side. He murders the parents of a half-Greek woman, Melina, when they stand in his way, and she then allies herself with British agent James Bond to stop Kristatos. Kristatos catches Bond and Melina at the site of a wrecked British ship equipped with an indispensable intelligence device, explaining at gun point that he must make good on his deal with the Russians. He then has them tied up and thrown overboard into shark-infested waters. Devoid of all scruples, he is amused by their plight. Bond and Melina outwit him, returning to face him again, but it is Milos Columbo, who knows him as a traitor and drug smuggler, who eventually kills Kristatos as they do combat with knives. An inflexible, unfeeling man, he shows less interest in people than in things and satisfying his own desires. His double agent status has carried over into every part of his life. Mendacious and greedy, he learned his trade well, resisting no temptation set before him.

ARCANE: SEE: DR. ANTON ARCANE

ASHTON: SEE: MADELINE ASHTON

AURIC GOLDFINGER

Film Source: *Goldfinger*
Release Date: 1964
Director: Guy Hamilton
Production Company: United Artists
Color
Running Time: 108 minutes
Performed By: Gert Fröbe
Additional Performer: Sean Connery (James Bond).

Physical Description: Auric Goldfinger is blond, dapper, stout, and over forty. He provides his exhausted tailor with a lucrative trade. A continental accent and robust laugh do not mask the dire countenance underlying Goldfinger's suave appearance.

Character Analysis: Auric Goldfinger's actions speak louder than his words. When he learns that his secretary has been seen with British agent James Bond, Goldfinger (whose love of gold borders on worship) has her body painted with gold, and the toxicity kills her. This violent response is motivated by egoism and jealousy, a perfect expression of Goldfinger's philosophy that his ownership extends to people, as well as objects. Determined to monopolize the world's gold market, he arranges for the irradiation of the supply in Fort Knox. Casually he assembles a group of underworld figures at his Kentucky farm, where he slays them with nerve gas. He is just as casual about killing Bond—until he thinks the agent's death might risk his chance for unlimited wealth. After his plans for Fort Knox fail, Goldfinger stows away on the plane carrying Bond. He dies when he accidentally fires his gun through the plane's window, depressurizing the cabin. His vast supply of gold is surpassed only by his arrogance and insensitivity. Goldfinger is a man who idolizes winning and abjures defeat. His greed costs him all he has acquired—including his life.

MR. BARNABY

Film Sources: *Babes in Toyland*
Release Dates: 1934; 1961
Focus: 1961 film version
Director: Jack Donohue
Production Company: Walt Disney Pictures
Color
Running Time: 105 minutes
Performed by: Ray Bolger
Additional Performers: Annette Funicello (Mary, Mary); Tommy Sands (Tom); Ed Wynn (The Toymaker).

Physical Description: Mr. Barnaby resembles nothing so much as a stylish viper, dressed in black hat, cape, and suit. His slick black hair and moustache are attractively groomed. Tall and gaunt, he completes his ensemble with a walking stick.

Character Analysis: Mr. Barnaby's snicker demonstrates both his contempt and his disregard of others. He schemes to make sweet Mary his bride when he learns she will inherit a fortune. There is a sense of the clownish rogue in Mr. Barnaby when he dances and sings about the castle he plans to give Mary if she succumbs to him, but he is so controlled by greed that he becomes foolhardy in his efforts. He abducts

Little Bo Peep's sheep in order to ruin Mary financially, and then employs henchmen to dispose of Tom, Mary's suitor, and his rival for her affections. When this plot is foiled, he connives to use a shrinking device to reduce Tom in size, and thus force Mary to agree to be his bride. Barnaby is defeated by Tom when the miniaturizing toy explodes. Mr. Barnaby embodies the artful smoothness of a mountebank for whom treachery and cunning represent desirable attributes. He remains untouched by the goodness of those around him. Foiled by his own impatience and thoughtlessness, he founders in a mire of his own design. Disney interpretation of Victor Herbert's charming operetta.

MR. BARTHOLOMEW

Film Source: *Rollerball*
Release Date: 1975
Director: Norman Jewison
Production Company: United Artists
Color
Running Time: 128 minutes
Performed by: John Houseman
Additional Performer: James Caan (Jonathan E).

Physical Description: Mr. Bartholomew carries his vigorous, sound, six feet well, despite the fact he is in his sixties, gray and balding. His voice rumbles and purrs at intervals in near-bass tones. He wears executive business suits, tailored in the accepted conservative mode, but there is a dark storm brewing behind his magnetic eyes.

Character Analysis: In his exemplary poem, "Ozymandias," Percy Bysshe Shelley speaks satirically of a ruler whom the poet compares to a lone sculpture erected in the king's honor which is now all but consumed by time and desert sands. Shelley's comments on the fleeting nature of fame and temporal power *have* stood the test of time, and are appropriate here. In a near-future world, "Energy" is a vast conglomerate of leading businesses gathered under one corporate umbrella; Mr. Bartholomew is the current titular head of "Energy, " and his office is a fabulous kingdom in itself, equipped with every luxurious device imaginable. To keep the partners of the "Corporation," as it is known, from tearing each other (and their subject populations and constituents) apart in the so-called "Corporate Wars," a new sport has been invented as a surrogate for violence and war. The game—which the Corporation calls "Rollerball"—is a combination of basketball, hockey, and roller derby played in such a violent manner that the lives of its players are at risk each time they appear on the huge court. Since the games are televised worldwide by satellite, they have become a fiercely popular, albeit "safe," outlet for venting aggression and frustration amongst the general populace. Under Mr. Bartholomew's direction the world business machine runs with clockwork-like precision. Bartholomew is a cold man who displays rare emotion, hugging and kissing his elitist associates and friends at parties and corporate gatherings, in a superficial demonstration of feeling—playing a role which is a combination of winsome grandfather and sophisticated businessman. For all his subtle charm and obvious intellect, there is a slimy quality about him which is most noticeable in his underhanded dealings with veteran Rollerball star athlete Jonathan E. Jonathan is an assertive individual, and Bartholomew completely misreads him by attempting, unsuccessfully, to buy or blackmail him into allegiance to the cause. Jonathan, whose popularity has become too great for the Corporation's collective comfort, refuses to retire on his own. Control being paramount to both Bartholomew and the Corporation, since without it their whole house of cards might tumble—the Corporation must force him out. Bartholomew, in collusion with the other corporate heads, begins subtly to alter the rules of the game, hoping to force Jonathan's team into defeat. In the meantime, a series of incidents has turned Jonathan against the "utopian" society which has "removed" his wife from his life, and which has thrown his best friend, another Rollerball player, into a deep coma following a serious game injury. The Corporation sends Jonathan a new beautiful "replacement" woman every six months, but each one is a tormenting reminder of the woman he has loved and lost. Jonathan's team, however, keeps on winning. In the final championship game of the season a frustrated Bartholomew tosses out *all* the rules in the hope of destroying Jonathan completely, once and for all. Jonathan, contrary to expectations, defeats everyone on the circular rink and makes the winning point. The fans chant Jonathan's name over and over, undoing all the years of delicate authority the Corporation has set up for itself. Bartholomew, visibly angry and shaken, has witnessed in one man the unmistakable spirit of independence he and the Corporation have sought so long to suppress. Rollerball—the mechanism for quelling freedom and independence—conquers those who created it through the talent and tenacity of a single individual. Mr. Bartholomew and his fellow executives crumble beneath the will of Jonathan. Like the proud, unyielding Ozymandias, the self-assured, imperious head of "Energy" is swept away by the winds of his own foolish over-estimation of himself and the Corporation he serves.

BARTOK: SEE: ANTON BARTOK

QUEEN BAVMORDA

Film Source: *Willow*
Release Date: 1988
Director: Ron Howard

Production Company: Metro Goldwyn Mayer Productions
Color
Running Time: 125 minutes
Performed by: Jean Marsh
Additional Performers: Warwick   Davis   (Willow),   Val   Kilmer
(Madmartigan), Joanne Whalley-Kilmer (Sorsha), Ruth and Kate Green-
field (Elora Danan), Pat Roach (General Kael), Patricia Hayes (Raziel).

Physical Description: Queen Bavmorda wears a thorny crown of met-
alic laurel leaves. Draped from head to toe in black and white robes,
her face and hands are all that is visible of her. Hard eyes and a
crooked mouth lend a cold demeanor to her visage. Her powerful
speech and grating laugh are unpleasant to the ear. She is much older
than she seems, but uses sorcery to maintain an appearance of youthful
robustness. She resembles an old tree, tall and slender—and unwilling
to bow in the wind.

Character Analysis: Bavmorda, her ashen face reflecting her dark and
dreary surroundings, has closed herself off from all decency and human
kindness to live in isolation in her castle fortress. No one, not even her
own daughter, Sorsha, is exempt from Bavmorda's overwhelming desire for power. Sorsha, who longs for more out of life than her warrior's lot as her mother's enforcer, betrays Bavmorda who turns on Sorsha and nearly kills her. Sorsha is saved by the good sorceress Raziel,
and looks forward to a much different future with her handsome young
lover Madmartigan. Ultimate power continues to elude Bavmorda, although it is—and always has been—her single-minded pursuit. Now,
in the truest of ironies, it is a baby, Elora Danan, who stands between
Bavmorda and her goal. Devoted to the darkest of sorceries, her most
pressing need is to kidnap Elora to use in a terrible ritual that will send
the child to the "Netherworld." Bavmorda is prepared to follow this
course, even if she destroys herself in the process. The Queen, however, foolishly discounts the wit, quickness, and determination of Willow, an elfen farmer who has taken on the formidable task of protecting
the helpless Elora from her enemies. Trolls, monsters, and vicious
dogs do not deter him and his band from caring for and rescuing Elora
from the Queen's hideous plan. Willow, a would-be sorceror, tricks
Bavmorda as he might his friends at a fair. Believing Willow has se-
creted Elora in a hiding place, the Queen attempts to use Raziel's magic
wand to bring her back. She misjudges its power, and is torn asunder
by lightning, becoming a pillar of red flame which is whisked into the
elements she called on to do her bidding. Her darkness is transformed
into light, and the diligence and love of the gentle little farmer set Elora
free. Instead of attaining the ultimate power she coveted throughout her
life, Bavmorda disappears entirely, leaving behind the delightful child
who will one day become the new Queen. By then, Bavmorda and her

tyrannical rule will have become northing more than a sad memory from the past.

BEETLEJUICE

Film Source: *Beetlejuice*
Release Date: 1988
Director: Tim Burton
Production Company: Warner Bros.
Color
Running Time: 92 minutes
Performed by: Michael Keaton
Additional Performers: Geena Davis (Barbara Maitland); Alec Baldwin (Mr. Maitland); Winona Ryder (Lydia).

Physical Description: Beetlejuice is the spirit of a plague victim. His eyes are rimmed in inky circles, his mouth is outlined in dried blood, and his complexion is reminiscent of melted candle wax. Patches of matted grayish hair sprout from his mottled head. A bloated paunch bulges from under his improperly fitting clothes. Beetlejuice wears a perpetual sneer in lieu of a smile, and his laugh is a brutish grunt. Having met his demise during the age of the Black Plague, he has had some time in which to master his manipulation of the living, while acquainting himself with all the bizarre rules of the noisome deathly region he now inhabits.

Character. Analysis: The Maitlands are a likeable young couple killed suddenly in an accident, and whose spirits seem doomed to haunt their beloved old New England home for eternity. The property is sold to an upscale family who proceed to remodel the house in a manner abhorent to its resident ghosts. The Maitlands begin to cast about for ways to rid themselves of the new tenants. Beetlejuice, a spirit of questionable motives, insidiously advertises himself to the unsuspecting Maitlands as a "Bio-exorcist," that is, a ghost who can exorcize unwanted humans. The unsavory Beetlejuice, who steals a passionate kiss from a nauseated Barbara Maitland, is irrational to the brink of disaster, and his desire to help the unassuming couple rid themselves of the new residents is not altogether an altruistic one. Beetlejuice wants to live again, but first he must satisfy one requirement—a living and willing bride—and he targets the melancholy and suicidal Lydia, teenage daughter of the new family, for the role. Beetlejuice, who is able to transform himself into whatever he chooses, horrifies Lydia and her parents in the guise of an enormous snake, and further threatens to annihilate the Maitlands through a hideous decomposition. Lydia acquieces to Beetlejuice's demands to save the Maitlands, but through ingenuity, they are able to stop Beetlejuice's mockery of a wedding. His craftiness ultimately backfires, sending him back to his own realm, where he awaits another turn at redemption. Beetlejuice selfishly puts himself first, using everyone else as a means to achieve his own deplorable ends. He delights in his frenetic behavior, and shows no inclination to change.

BELLOQ

Film Source: *Raiders of the Lost Ark*
Release Date: 1981
Director: Steven Spielberg
Production Company: Paramount Pictures
Color
Running Time: 116 minutes
Performed by: Paul Freeman
Additional Performers: Harrison Ford (Indiana Jones), Karen Allen (Marion Ravenwood), Ronald Lacey (Toth), Wolf Kahler (Dietrich).

Physical Description: Belloq is a handsome man in his mid-forties, with sparkling eyes and curly gray hair. He has a tight, pensive mouth, which is relieved by a disarming smile. Of medium height, and slim physique, his stylish clothes give him a debonair appearance. His French accent in no way detracts from his impeccable English grammar.

Character Analysis: Belloq has left a trail of pain and dead bodies along his path of questionable achievements as an archeologist. Belloq aspires to wealth, fame, and glory in his searches, while his longtime rival Professor Indiana Jones desires only that the museum-quality pieces he finds are preserved in the best manner possible. Belloq crosses paths with Jones during his quest for a golden idol belonging to an ancient South American tribe. Jones is chased by the Indians and nearly murdered when he takes possession of the idol. Pleased about his latest act of treachery, Belloq quips that he can take away "anything" Dr. Jones can "possess." His adventurous life has led to wish fulfillment of the most barbarous sort. He discards people like used-up tissues. His greatest quest now is for the fabled lost Ark of the Covenant. He truly believes that with this artifact he will be able to "talk to God." He is excited by the thought, but lacks any real understanding of what such power entails. His expedition is financed by the Nazis, who are interested in unleashing the power of the Ark to do Hitler's bidding. Meanwhile, Indiana and his old flame, Marion, daughter of Indy's mentor Dr. Ravenwood, track down Belloq on the trail of the Ark. Marion is captured by Belloq, and Indy takes part in some daredevil exploits to rescue her and secure the treasure. The dead bodies mount up, but Belloq's wish is fulfilled at last when the Nazis take the Ark out into the desert in order to examine it. Bedecked in a priest's robe, Belloq is at first thrilled at the ethereal beings which begin to emerge from the resting place of the Ten Commandments when it is unsealed. His initial glee turns to horror, however, when he realizes the dimension of power residing in the Pandora's box he has opened. The full wrath of God is unleashed upon Belloq and his companions, and in a final gruesome scene, they are utterly and completely destroyed. Quick-thinking Indiana Jones warns Marion to avert her eyes from the Ark until all has settled, and their lives are spared. Belloq who has no respect for the sanctity of the artifacts he has stolen over the years and has always taken for himself what he wanted, gets nothing for his trouble but his own destruction from his misuse of the Ark.

MR. BENEDICT

Film Source: *Last Action Hero*
Release Date: 1993
Director: John McTiernan
Production Company: Columbia Pictures
Color
Running Time: 110 minutes
Performed by: Charles Dance
Additional Performers: Arnold Schwarzenegger (Jack Slater); Austin O'Brien (Danny Madigan); Anthony Quinn (Mr. Vivaldi),; Tom Noonan (The Ripper); Art Carney (Frank).

Physical Description: Mr. Benedict is a classy dresser. He wears the best suits, in white, beige, or black. Bright, carrot-colored, hair peaks above his high forehead. His six-foot plus height is accentuated by a slim build, and his speech is perfect "stage"-style British. His most arresting feature, however, is a collection of different-colored glass eyes, including one which is inscribed with the words: "Vengeance is mine." He is heavily armed with knives, explosives (including one hidden in his artificial eye), and a long-barreled gun.

Character Analysis: Benedict is a "No nonsense" kind of guy. He is "the genuine article," according to his employer, drug kingpin Mr. Vivaldi, even though they are residing in an alternate universe—the world of films. When he meets "action hero" Jack Slater and his young charge Danny Madigan, Benedict understands he has, literally, a "ticket" out of his screen world (and Vivaldi's clutches) into Danny's real world. Danny has brought a magical "ticket" with him which can give Benedict a new universe to plunder. He first ponders how much he can steal without being caught, but soon comes to understand that the "ticket" can bring him unlimited power. Benedict is followed by Slater and Danny from screen fantasy into stark reality. Rather than shrinking from his new surroundings, Benedict thrills at the thought he can shoot a man and literally "get away" with murder by jumping back and forth between universes. He hatches a plot to bring the most evil characters from the film world into the real world and use them to carry out his nefarious schemes. He sets his design in motion by viewing films all over New York, in order to choose the most notorious characters he can find for his army of archvillains, He materializes The Ripper, a character from Jack Slater's film past who, although confused by his transformation, is willing to assassinate Jack at a premiere of the latest "Jack Slater" movie. Meanwhile, Jack and Danny have crossed over behind Benedict, and have begun a search for the vicious mastermind. When the Ripper fails to kill Jack, Benedict steps in. Slater is severely wounded, but is helped by Danny, who, faking a broken arm, jumps Benedict. Benedict's exploding glass eye, intended for others, now blasts its owner to bits. Benedict read the *Wall Street Journal* for tips on money-making ideas, but he is made vulnerable at the last because he could not "read" a little boy's mind. Dissatisfied in his make-believe world, he found great pleasure in a reality where, as he put it, "The bad guy can win." In the end, however, he was just another "bad guy" who lost it all.

BILL SIKES

Film Source: *Oliver Twist*
Release Dates: 1922, 1933, 1948
Focus: 1933 film version
Director: William Cowen
Production Company: Herbert Brenon/Monogram
B&W
Running Time: 77 minutes
Performed by: William "Stage" Boyd
Additional Performers: Dickie Moore (Oliver Twist), Irving Pichel (Fagin), Doris Lloyd (Nancy).

Physical Description: Bill Sikes is a thick-set man of above average height, who assumes a façade of dignity in his garish suit, high hat, and walking stick. His long, black sideburns accentuate his leaden countenance. He dispenses words in a coarse, splenetic fashion. While he appears older due to a life of heavy drinking and violent crime, Sikes must be no more than in his middle twenties. (Note: This is *not* the William Boyd who played "Hopalong Cassidy" in Westerns!)

Character Analysis: Bill Sikes exudes an aura of deliberate perniciousness through his gruff rancor, and the use of brute force on his colleagues. Anyone who offends Sikes is subject to a swift rebuke or worse. Fagin, the aged thief who took Bill in and taught him his larcenous craft, deals with his former apprentice in a most prudent manner. In fact everyone, even Bill's "wife" Nancy, cringes before his drunken outbursts. Bill informs Fagin, in Nancy's presence, that he will kill her if she betrays any of their band. Oliver Twist is a waif plucked from Fagin's grasp through the auspices of a rich gentleman. His plight arouses Nancy's compassion and sympathy, which results in her exposure of Fagin and his pickpockets to the authorities. Fagin apprises Bill of Nancy's betrayal, and he beats her to death, even though she denies having implicated Bill. Fagin is captured and, as the authorities surround Fagin's house, Bill goes to the roof where he attempts to escape with a rope. He slips, and accidentally hangs himself, ironically meeting his end in a noose of his own devising. In nineteenth-century England, orphans and children of poverty either faced life in the workhouse, a dismal institution often run by corrupt officials, or braved a perilous existence on the streets. Bill Sikes was such a child and, weighing the alternatives, robbing for Fagin must have seemed a marvelous solution. A life of crime was the only "school" available to Bill, and it became a natural way of life for him. His alcoholic binges magnified his already violent manner. Always dubious of others, he preferred their fear to their respect or affection for him. Only Nancy was allowed the intimacy he so persistently shunned in everyone else. When he thought he could no longer trust Nancy, Bill's feelings for her failed to deter his defensive tendencies. Bill Sikes had none of life's favorable advantages as a child, and, in the end, his decisions as an adult remained true to form. Based on Charles Dickens' classic novel.

THE BISHOP

Film Source: *Ladyhawke*
Release Date: 1985
Director: Richard Donner
Production Company: Warner Bros.
Color
Running Time: 121 minutes
Performed by: John Wood
Additional Performers: Rutger Hauer (Navarre); Michelle Pfeiffer (Isabeau); Matthew Broderick (Phillipe); Leo McKern (Father Imperius).

Physical Description: The Bishop is bedecked in sparkling white vestments and a towering headpiece of the same hue accentuates his impressive height. Near or past fifty in age, he has kept himself in fine health. His brilliant eyes and rich, baritone voice seize the attention of anyone to whom he speaks.

Character Analysis: The Bishop has alienated even the hierarchy of Rome, and the people from whom he demands huge taxes despise him. How does he hold his office? He keeps his people under heel in this medieval world through fear—and he deals it out as easily as cards are dealt from a deck. He does not hesitate to send his army or hired assassins against anyone who opposes him. Navarre, the Bishop's former Captain of the Guard opposes the Bishop with good reason. Isabeau, the woman Navarre loves, was wrongfully desired by the Bishop, who called upon "the Evil One" for help. From this inhuman sorcery the Bishop has cast a dreadful spell upon Isabeau and Navarre. By day Isabeau is transformed into a hawk, while by night, Navarre exists as a wolf—but they can never be human together. Had it not been for the drunken Father Imperius, the jealous Bishop might never have learned of their love, and Isabeau and Navarre would have been safe. Because he takes the blame for their condition, Imperius assists them, and with the connivance of a sympathetic young renegade, Phillipe, they regain their true forms as they stand before the Bishop during a solar eclipse. He shudders at the sight of the reconstituted Isabeau, fearful of the retribution his own handiwork will undoubtedly bring. Covetous and vindictive until the end, the Bishop has no intention of letting Isabeau out of his grasp. He lunges at her, shouting that none will have her but him, but before he can deliver the death blow, Navarre slays him. Not at all the man of God he appeared to be, the Bishop misused those entrusted to his care. Carnal pleasures ruled him, and he, in turn, ruled over people in the harshest possible manner. The Bishop chose self-indulgence over compassion, in direct contradiction to both the teachings of his faith and the dictates of his office.

BLEAK

Film Source: *Adventures in Babysitting*
Release Date: 1987
Director: Chris Columbus
Production Company: Touchstone Pictures
Color
Running Time: 102 minutes
Performed By: John Chandler
Additional Performers: Elisabeth Shue (Chris Parker); Calvin Levels (Joe Gipp).

Physical Description: Bleak's glaring eyes peer out from under heavy eyebrows. His high forehead and long face accentuate his gaunt form, endowing him with a predatory mien. Bleak's grating voice suits his surly manner of delivery. His executive "look," in dark suit and overcoat, and black gloves, is deceptive.

Character Analysis: Bleak's name, meaning "harsh and desolate," is appropriate. His icy gaze and unchanging scowl hint at a bellicose disposition. Through a series of mishaps, young Chris and the children she is babysitting are treated to Bleak's derision and animosity during an unplanned "visit" to his back alley warehouse. Bleak first insults the youngsters—then slams his fist on a table to frighten them. His illicit business has first priority for Bleak—people and their legitimate concerns occupy a rung far down on the ladder. As they leave, Chris and the children inadvertently take along a magazine containing hidden orders for stolen cars, and Bleak sends a young thief, Joe Gipp, after them to recover his property. The roguish Gipp is a decent sort, however, and becomes concerned with the safety of Chris and her young charges. Bleak tracks them down and orders Joe to hand over the magazine and depart, since he plans to leave no witnesses. Bleak assumes that Joe will obey his command without question, but Joe takes Bleak by surprise and frees his new friends. Bleak's pervasive enmity in his relationship with others constructs for him a personality suited to his illicit occupation. Unlike Joe Gipp, who cares about others as much or more than himself, Bleak persists in his cruelty until it defeats him.

MR. BLIFIL

Film Source: *Tom Jones*
Release Date: 1963
Director: Tony Richardson
Production Company: Woodfall
Color
Running Time: 127 minutes
Performed by: David Warner
Additional Performers: Albert Finney (Tom Jones); Susannah York (Sophia Western); George Devine (Squire Allworthy).

Physical Description: Mr. Blifil, the good Squire Allworthy's young nephew, emulates the landed gentry of eighteenth-century England. His wig and clothes are in place, his speech is careful, and his elocution grand. Blifil is not, however, an appealing figure of manhood, being as ungainly as he is tall, with a prominent nose, thin lips, and an acne-ravaged complexion. He gives his handsome adopted brother, Tom Jones, little competition.

Character Analysis: Mr. Blifil is introduced as a well-respected member of Squire Allworthy's household. While those around him believe he is an admirable young gentleman, it soon becomes obvious that Blifil is in reality an unprincipled scoundrel who hates Tom Jones, his rival for the Squire's wealth and affection. In addition, Blifil makes no effort to conceal his lust for Tom's friend, Sophia Western, the lovely daughter of a neighboring Squire, and forces himself on her. So intense is his animosity toward Tom that Blifil uses every means available to discredit the young man. Blifil's mother is killed and the Squire, her brother, is badly injured in an accident. Blifil is adept at feigning concern for those he wishes to use for his own gain, and now uses his wiles to convince the world of his worry over his uncle's condition, and to force Tom away from the only home he has known. Blifil's mendacity ruins him in the end, however, when a former servant tells the Squire the truth about Jones's birth. Blifil has known since his mother's death that Tom is actually his half-brother. Having concealed the letter that verifies this fact, Blifil is terrified when the Squire interrupts his malicious plans. The twin evils of avarice and envy are often companions in human personality. Here they govern Blifil's actions until his weaknesses, inevitably, discredit him. Oscar-winning screenplay by John Osborne based on Henry Fielding's rollicking novel.

BLUTO

Film Source: *Popeye*
Release Date: 1980
Director: Robert Altman
Production Company: Paramount/Disney
Color
Running Time: 114 minutes
Performed by: Paul L. Smith
Additional Performers: Robin Williams (Popeye); Shelley Duvall (Olive Oyl); Ray Walston (The Commodore).

Physical Description: Bluto's gargantuan size is his most significant physical characteristic, and Olive Oyl, his intended bride, and her friends discuss that fact in song. Bluto huffs and puffs like the big, bad wolf, resembling nothing so much as a destroyer releasing a depth charge. His moth-eaten shirt and torn suit complement his shabby, black cap. Flies buzz around his dense beard and moustache, adding to Bluto's repugnance.

Character Analysis: Bluto is virtual dictator of the port town of Sweethaven, and uses his pull with the mysterious Commodore as his foundation of supremacy over the residents. Virulence is an intrinsic part of his personality, and he always has a caustic remark or a growl for any person he meets. It surprises no one at his engagement party then, when he announces that he is "mean." Furious that his fiancée Olive has not joined the group, Bluto demolishes the Oyl family dining room. Aware of Popeye's concern for Sweetpea, the foundling who can predict horse race winners, Bluto kidnaps the baby for his own greedy advantage. When Bluto's strength is successfully challenged by an indignant Popeye, he demonstrates his cowardice by running away. Since Bluto is little more than a bully, nothing more can be expected of him. Based on the popular Fleischer Brothers cartoon series.

31

BOB ALEXANDER

Film Source: *Dave*
Release Date: 1993
Director: Ivan Reitman
Production Company: Warner Bros.
Color
Running Time: 110 minutes
Performed by: Frank Langella
Additional Performers: Kevin Kline (Dave/Bill Mitchell); Sigourney Weaver (Ellen Mitchell); Ben Kingsley (Vice President Nance); Kevin Dunn (Alan Reed).

Physical Description: Bob Alexander is set apart from the rest of the crowd by his brisk gait, fine physique, and near-perfect elocution. Well-groomed, he wears his impeccably tailored suits with panache. His piercing gaze and trim hair complete the picture of a man on the rise.

Character Analysis: Bob Alexander has made it from the Senate nearly to the top, but he wants to be much more than Chief of Staff, the position he presently holds—he wants to be President. His chance comes when Bill Mitchell, the real President, while in the arms of his lover, suffers a near-fatal stroke which leaves him in a vegetative state. Alexander masterminds the "temporary" removal of Mitchell to an iso- lated, well-guarded, hospital room in the bowels of the White House, unbeknownst to Mitchell's estranged wife, Ellen, or to the public in general. To maintain the fiction, he handpicks an average citizen, Dave, a "look-alike" who is called upon to serve as the President's double as his "patriotic duty." Bob plans to use Dave for his own con- niving purposes, but Dave nervously and naively accepts his role in good faith. At the same time, Bob also hopes to discredit Vice Presi- dent Nance, a decent man, who is conveniently out of the country. Although the unsuspecting Dave becomes a pawn in the power play, he is not the fool Bob takes him for, and gradually he begins to assert him- self, to Bob's chagrin. With Ellen's encouragement, Dave takes charge. Unlike the real Mitchell, who cared nothing about the nation's well-being, Dave proposes a full employment program and help for the homeless. At the same time he publicly calls for Bob's resignation. In- furiated, Bob resurrects an old lie about Nance's supposed involvement in a savings-and-loan scandal, this time implicating Dave. Even Bob's second-in-command, Alan Reed, warns his boss against such a move, but Bob feels he has waited too long to give up his bid for real power now. Instead of assassinating Dave, Bob plans to ruin him. Realizing Bob has gone too far, Alan gives Dave proof of Bob's own guilt in the scandal. Dave apprises Nance of the scheme, and they unite to oppose Bob, discrediting him in the process. Vulgar, mean-spirited, lowest of the low, Bob had high aims he could not hope to achieve by honest means. Dave resigns and Nance, a decent man, assumes the presidency. Bob is the kind of politician who gives all elected officials a bad name. Justice triumphs when he is forced to trade his illegally-won power for an indictment and, very likely, tenure in prison rather than in the White House.

BODDICKER: SEE: CLARENCE BODDICKER

BODHI

Film Source: *Point Break*
Release Date: 1991
Director: Kathryn Bigelow
Production Company: Largo Entertainment Productions
Color
Running Time: 120 minutes
Performed by: Patrick Swayze
Additional Performers: Keanu Reeves (Johnny Utah).

Physical Description: Bodhi is a handsome young man in his thirties, with long sun-bleached hair and the tanned body of an athlete. His clothes are "surfer" casual, and he speaks with a melodic baritone voice. He is a natural leader, and is personable and well-liked by his cohorts.

Character Analysis: Bodhi lives for all the freedom and excitement he can cram into life. Unfortunately, the method he and his gang of thrill seekers use to reinforce this lifestyle is bank robbery. F.B.I. agent Johnny Utah is assigned the task of infiltrating this den of thieves and surfers. Johnny finds the outrageous Bodhi likeable, and, as a result, turning him in to the authorities will be difficult. Bodhi's exploits have always been non-violent confrontations. But when his masked "Ex-Presidents" are cornered at the scene of yet another robbery, shooting starts and blood is spilled. Bodhi escapes to Australia to catch a fabled wave. Johnny tracks him down, but when Bodhi begs for one last chance to ride the surf, Johnny relents. They both know that Bodhi won't be coming back. Freedom means too much for him to let it slip away, so he chooses death over prison. Living for pleasure, he dies in the midst of his dream of catching the biggest wave of all.

BOLIN: SEE: KRIS BOLIN

BOOTH: SEE: FRANK BOOTH

BREWSTER: SEE: JONATHAN BREWSTER

BRUNO ANTHONY

Film Source: *Strangers on a Train*
Release Date: 1951
Director: Alfred Hitchcock
Production Company: Warner Bros.
B&W
Running Time: 101 minutes
Performed by: Robert Walker
Additional Performers: Farley Granger (Guy Haynes); Marion Lorne (Mrs. Anthony); Jonathan Hale (Mr. Anthony).

Physical Description: Bruno Anthony is a smart dresser, but his youthful good looks are marred by a facial expression of nearly unwavering cynicism. His speech though faultless, is pretentious, and a loud, callous laugh further detracts from the impression he is trying to make. He is *too* neat, if possible, and too well-manicured. Shoes with spats set off his wardrobe of expensive suits and hats.

Character Analysis: Bruno Anthony is verbose and audacious, exhibiting few of those qualities that promote close, personal relationships. His spoiled, condescending attitude toward others is rooted in the loathing he feels for his overbearing father and an unnatural fondness for his doting mother. Stemming from this unhealthy relationship with his parents, Anthony has developed into a self-serving daredevil, whose philosophy is that no experience in life should be avoided. Anthony's chance meeting on a train with tennis pro Guy Haynes leads to a hypothetical (so Haynes believes) discussion of murder. Haynes, thinking Anthony harmless, though quirky, is later stunned to discover that Anthony has murdered Haynes' estranged wife. Anthony tells Haynes he has only "helped" him out of an unhappy marriage, but once the murder is committed, he expects Haynes to reciprocate by killing Anthony's father. By prearrangement Anthony meets Haynes at an amusement park, but, finding himself betrayed, Anthony inadvertently drops the incriminating piece of evidence, Guy's cigarette lighter, through a grate. He exerts himself with mulish determination until he clutches the object in his hand, then holds on to the lighter with which he had hoped to force Haynes into cooperation. Anthony dies still grasping the lighter in his hand, and Haynes is able to retrieve the proof of his innocence. Bruno Anthony lived his whole life in the shadow of a father whom he despised and endured the pampering of a mother whom he adored, but his immature viciousness and compulsive brutality were all his own. Beneath his callous exterior he longed for real companionship, but he never learned how to get along with people—only how to use them. He forfeited his life still trying to have his own way in everything. This Hitchcock classic was recast as a hilarious comedy, *Throw Momma from the Train* (1987), starring Billy Crystal, with Danny DeVito (who directed) as the villain who beleaguers him.

GENERAL BULLMOOSE

Film Source: *Li'l Abner*
Release Date: 1959
Director: Melvin Frank
Production Company: Paramount Pictures
Color
Running Time: 114 minutes
Performed by: Howard St. John
Additional Performers: Peter Palmer (Abner Yokum), Billie Hayes (Mammy Yokum), Stella Stevens (Appassionata Von Climax).

Physical Description: General Bullmoose, in all his executive finery, is the best-dressed millionaire in Dogpatch. Past fifty, with strong, hard, facial lines, and a coarse voice, he is a person accustomed to giving, not taking orders.

Character Analysis: General Bullmoose could give Midas lessons in avarice, since no one places more value on finances than he does. A bombastic tyrant from whom everyone shrinks and over whom everyone fawns, he has absolutely no interest in the needs and desires of others. His greediness is stimulated when he realizes there is a fortune to be made from Mammy Yokum's Yokumberry elixir. Bullmoose calls on his libidinous associate, Appassionata von Climax, to ferret out the secret formula from L'l Abner Yokum. She fails and Bullmoose calls in another henchman with mesmerizing talents to attain his goal. Mammy Yokum rescues her son by turning Bullmoose's reprehensible plot back on the general himself. Bullmoose's treachery is at last uncovered, and his unrestrained power and greed culminate in his disgrace and defeat. Because he is so sure that he cannot fail, Bullmoose ensures his own downfall. Musical based on Al Capp's comic strip.

BURKE: SEE: CARTER J. BURKE

CADY: SEE: MAX CADY

CANDYMAN

Film Source: *Candyman*
Release Date: 1992

GEORGETTE S. FOX

Director: Bernard Rose
Production Company: TriStar
Color
Running Time: 98 minutes
Performed by: Tony Todd
Additional Performers: Virginia Madsen (Helen Lyle), Xander Berkeley (Trevor Lyle), Kasi Lemmons (Bernadette Walsh), Latesha and Lanesha Martin (Baby Anthony McCoy), Vanessa Williams (Anne Marie McCoy).

Physical Description: Candyman is the ghost of a nineteenth-century artist. Outwardly he is a handsome, young Black man of immense height, yet under his long fur-lined coat something bizarre is present. Candyman has a hive of bees in his chest. His bass voice reverberates with their humming as he speaks. Clothed in checked pants and leather shoes, he was a person of means during his lifetime. He has a hook in place of his right hand and can float in the air. Beyond this, he has supernatural might and can appear and disappear at will.

Character Analysis: Candyman was not an evil man during his lifetime, yet in death he has become a fiendish spirit, avenging himself on the innocent rather than the guilty. He is an "urban legend" who may be summoned by saying his name five times while looking into a mirror. Helen Lyle, who is basing her doctoral thesis on urban legends, makes the hasty mistake of repeating his name as she stares into her own bathroom mirror. He obliges her, appearing out of nowhere and tells her his story. Candyman, the son of a freed slave, fell in love with the daughter of a wealthy white man, and died at the hands of thugs hired by her vengeful father. His background as an artist lifts him above some of his violent behavior, but he still kills out of thwarted desire. He forces Helen, who is powerless to defy him, to kidnap a baby, Anthony McCoy. Matters escalate when Candyman murders Bernadette Walsh, Helen's best friend and implicates her. Acknowledging his motive for taking the baby, Helen "surrenders" to him but is lured into a trap. Under a pile of debris Candyman holds her and the baby prisoner. Nearby apartment dwellers are setting fire to the junk, and the three are doomed to be burned to death, ensuring that they will exist in the afterlife together forever. Helen escapes with Anthony in her arms. Charred and dying, she hands the baby over to its mother's waiting arms. Shouting for her to return to him, Candyman is consumed in flames as Helen turns back toward him. His hook is tossed into Helen's coffin at her funeral, and she takes on Candyman's characteristics, returning to kill her faithless husband, Trevor, with the fatal implement. Runaway desire and brutality were Candyman's undoing. His need for love, directed toward the unsuspecting Helen and the innocent Anthony, draws him into a blind alley of his own design. The resurrected

Candyman charts a course of vengeance and murder every bit as profane as the way he met his own demise. Based on Clive Barker's chilling story, "The Forbidden."

CARTER J. BURKE

Film Source: *Aliens*
Release Date: 1986
Director: James Cameron
Production Company: Twentieth Century Fox
Color
Running Time: 138 minutes
Performed by: Paul Reiser
Additional Performances: Sigourney Weaver (Ellen Ripley), Carrie Henn (Newt).

Physical Description: Carter J. Burke is a man of small stature, but trim and well-built, with sparkling eyes, and wavy hair. His speech is precise and clipped, but he is boyish-looking in his proper business suits or combat attire. Burke is "thirty something" at the the time of his space voyage to Planet LV426. He is diffident, and has grown to revere power and money much more than he respects the life and well-being of his human companions. He is, quite simply, disinterested in such matters.

Character Analysis: Burke will lie and kill to achieve his purpose of getting to the top. He seems reasonable so long as no one objects to his methods; but once pinned down he can turn deadly. If the Company for whom he works discovers that Burke has sent at least sixty colonist families to planet LV426 without the slightest regard for their personal safety, he will soon find himself in prison. Now an expedition has been mounted to return to the planet to search for survivors. Former Company ship crew member Ellen Ripley heads the expedition, and Burke joins the group with the sinister intention of acquiring one of the alien creatures, which has transplanted to LV426 from far off space, for biological weapons research. When Ripley learns of his sinister plot, she cannot imagine how he plans to get it through quarantine, and tells Burke she will inform the Company of his subterfuge. Burke responds by locking Ripley and the child Newt (the one remaining survivor of the colony) in a specimen room with a "facehugger" form of the alien, which deposits its embryos into living beings. Ripley saves the child, but Burke, terrified once the aliens attack, abandons Ripley, Newt, and the small expeditionary force and attempts to escape the planet in the one remaining space shuttle. The exchange of others' lives for his own is an equitable one to Burke, but he pays a price for such cowardice. He had anticipated the rewards he would realize by capturing one of the aliens to take back to Earth, but Burke receives a most incredible bonus. As he checks his shuttle for take off, he is ambushed by one of the creatures and loses his life in the process, a loss which far outweighs whatever he had hoped to gain.

CATHARINE

Film Source: *Black Widow*
Release Date: 1987
Director: Bob Rafelson
Production Company: TCF/Mark Laurence
Color
Running Time: 98 minutes
Performed by: Theresa Russell
Additional Performer: Debra Winger (Alexandra Barnes).

Physical Description: Catharine, as changeable as a chameleon, modifies her appearance as her situation dictates. Each disguise is skillfully drawn to appeal to the wealthy man she has chosen to marry and kill for his money. She may have shoulder-length blonde hair, dark brown hair pulled back from her face, or vermilion hair set in waves. Her immaculate wardrobe matches perfectly the personality she creates for each part. Her regular features lend themselves well to her dissembling nature, since they are both beautiful and easily altered with touches of make-up. Catharine's voluptuous figure is another asset she enlists in each of her meticulously planned seductions.

Character Analysis: Many paths lead to riches. Some are acceptable, others are ignominious. Often the dishonest pursuit of affluence cloaks an even greater yearning for absolute power over others. While Catharine evinces a desire for lavish wealth, she also relishes the full control she maintains over the men she lures into marriage then murders. She gives the outward appearance of feeling a very real grief at the death of each one of her husbands. At the same time, she puts her insidious, retentive mind and striking beauty at once to work on ensnaring the next victim on her list. Catharine lures a shy museum curator into wedlock. Quick to uncover useful information about her new husband, Catharine spots the medical alert chain that identifies his allergy to certain medications. As with her other husbands, an unopened wine bottle or toothpaste tube effectively conceals her murder weapon. Justice Department Investigator, Alexandra Barnes, her suspicions aroused, obtains official permission to enter Catharine's intricate world of duplicity and homicide. Alex trails Catharine to Hawaii, where the newly-bereaved widow is already stalking a new husband. Under cover, Alex initiates a friendship in order to apprehend Catharine. At the same time, she attempts to warn Catharine's new prey, a handsome islander, and finds herself falling in love with him. Catharine is "on" to Alex, but her vanity refuses to accept the fact that Alex is as resourceful and determined as she is. With the connivance of Catharine's victim and the local police, she is fooled into confessing her misdeeds to Alex, a private conversation which is overheard by the authorities. Too proud to believe that any other woman could be as shrewd as she is, Catharine commits the fatal mistake of complacency, and loses all for which she has striven in the balance.

CATWOMAN (SELENA KYLE)

Film Source: *Batman Returns*
Release Date: 1992
Director: Tim Burton
Production Company: Warner Bros.
Color
Running Time: 126 minutes
Performed by: Michelle Pfeiffer
Additional Performers: Michael Keaton (Bruce Wayne/Batman), Danny DeVito (Oswald Cobblepot/Penguin), Christopher Walken (Max Shreck).

Physical Description: Selena Kyle has soft blonde hair, pouting lips, and a deep, husky voice which demands attention. Her slim figure is acrobatic. Although she seems understated and mousy in her sedate business attire, she is sleek and sexy in the mask and suit she stitches together for her alter ego, Catwoman. She adds the finishing touch, matching black claws on each finger of her black gloves.

Character Analysis: Beneath the drab exterior of her secretarial identity, Selena Kyle is another person altogether. Aided by her feline friends, the cats, she manages to survive a near-fatal fall when she is thrown out of an upper-story window by her boss, business tycoon Max Shreck. Shreck has decided to kill her because she knows too much about his business operations. He underestimates her resilience, however, as she transforms herself into the slinky, iniquitous Catwoman, and returns to the scene to take her revenge. In her Catwoman garb she goes on a rampage against Shreck, blowing up one of his shops as Batman and her future partner, the Penguin, look on. She meets Bruce Wayne, who is also hiding a secret identiy and, in spite of her confusion and uncertainty, falls in love with him. She joins forces with the Penguin to stop Batman, but is betrayed and begins to operate on her own. Shot during a showdown with Shreck under Gotham City, she survives, crediting her "nine lives." Her feline ways do not keep Bruce Wayne from discovering her real identity, nor do his roses stop her from discovering his. Uncertain of herself, she clings to the Catwoman *persona*—even after her second near-fatal encounter with Shreck. Having once been caught defenseless, she craves the self-reliance she feels as Catwoman. She breaks the law for profit and fun and retaliation, feeling no remorse over her maelstrom of violence. After all, she reasons, this predatory behavior is her natural state.

CENOBITE LEADER

Film Sources: *Hellraiser*; *Hellbound: Hellraiser II*; *Hellraiser III: Hell on Earth*; *Hellraiser IV: Bloodline*
Release Dates: 1987; 1988; 1992; 1996
Focus: *Hellraiser* (Director: Clive Barker)
Focus: *Hellbound: Hellraiser II* (Director: Tony Randel)
Directors: Clive Barker; Tony Randel
Production Company: New World Pictures
Color
Running Time: 94 minutes, 97 minutes
Performed by: Doug Bradley
Additional Performers: Ashley Laurence (Kirsty Cotton), Sean Chapman (Frank Cotton), Kenneth Cranham (Dr. Channard), Imogen Boorman (Tiffany).

Physical Description: The Cenobite Leader known as "Pinhead," victim of a hideous mutilation, resembles a cadaver. His face, scalp, and body are stripped of hair, his skin is bleached. Truly, he is a lurid specter to behold. Intersecting gashes divide his face into sections from which enormous pins, about two inches in length, protrude in a sinister halo. The Cenobite's emaciated body, underscored by an imposing height, is clothed in a long robe of Stygian hue, the collar of which is wrapped around his neck, terminating in an elongated nail that pierces the back of his head. A chilling postscript to this macabre appearance is the Cenobite's impassive, bass voice, booming like a tympani, and ensuring the nearby listener of a shudder.

Character Analysis: The Cenobite leader was once an orderly, respected British officer who, upon solving the riddle of an ornate puzzle box, has been flung into the realm of the evil Leviathan. The monstrous physical transformation he undergoes results in a frightening personality change as well. Now oblivious of his former life and self, he has joined the select group known as Cenobites who dwell in the abyss of the Labyrinth, and has become their leader. The dictatorial sway he holds over his fellows attests to his previous command experience, and is further evidenced by his precise manner of speech and walk. Young Christy, while trying to save her dead father's soul, opens a puzzle box, and is threatened by the obdurate Leader and his companions. During this confrontation, the Leader demands she accompany them into their realm. The Leader, who regards torture and suffering to be ultimate forms of pleasure and gratification, explains to a horrified Christy, in sepulchral tones, that it is her flesh that interests the Cenobites. Even more detestable, he insinuates that Christy herself craves this repulsive existence. Christy learns of the Leader's former interest in phrenology, which compares an individual's skull with diagrams that map out character traits. She deduces that the Cenobite Leader has been disfigured as a perversion of his own fascination with this study. The trauma he underwent caused memory loss, as well as the loss all of his positive human qualities, while the evil Labyrinth exaggerated his negative attributes. His mind beclouded by his circumstances, the Leader thus became the servant of suffering and lust. Summoning her courage, Christy presents the Cenobite Leader with a photo of himself from his previous life, and his positive characteristics begin to surface. Newly motivated, he battles a recent convert, Dr. Channard, a psychiatrist obsessed with the puzzle boxes. Although the Leader is bested in his efforts, the contest enables the Leader to acknowledge his gratitude to Christy, affording both a moment of tenderness. His defiance of Leviathan gains the Cenobite Leader only agony, yet his opposition to Channard remains an act of uncommon bravery in the face of such insurmountable evil.

DR. CHARLES LUTHER

Film Source: *Runaway*
Release Date: 1984
Director: Michael Crichton
Production Company: Tri-Star
Color
Running Time: 100 minutes
Performed By: Gene Simmons
Additional Performers: Tom Selleck (Jack Ramsey), Kirstie Alley (Jackie Rogers), Chris Mulkey (Johnson).

Physical Description: Dr. Charles Luther's sensual, knowing eyes accent his thick lips and broad grin. He is tan, with dark wavy hair and a sinewy frame. He selects his wardrobe with painstaking attention to its effect on others. His voice is chilling and deep, like a turbulent river. His movements are sure and deliberate.

Character Analysis: Charles Luther is a scientific genius with an uncommon proficiency in the field of robotics. He enjoys taking risks, but he leaves nothing to chance. Jackie Rogers, his lover and cohort, understands this trait and calls him "evil"—but she is not sufficiently concerned for her own safety. A police search has uncovered numerous "bugging" devices on her person, as well as contusions from the beatings he has given her. She still believes he will not harm her while she conceals certain valuable items from him, but her belief is shattered when he stabs her to death in the neck. Johnson, another of Luther's cohorts, has planned treachery against Luther, but finds his wife and sister-in-law dead. Luther has tampered with Johnson's domestic robot in order to kill his associate, but Johnson's family members become the victims instead. A traumatized Johnson flees the scene before learning whether or not his baby has been rescued, but Luther corners and shoots him with a bullet-sized tracking missile. Luther, a sociopath, delights in the deaths he causes, taking pride in each and every one. Luther's nemesis is Officer Jack Ramsey, another robotic expert. Ramsey is a widower and devoted parent who averts the death of Johnson's baby. Luther, learning Ramsay suffers from vertigo, kidnaps his son, and takes him to a skyscraper under construction for their meeting. Ramsey offers Luther the templates he desires in exchange for his son's life. As Ramsey's son descends on an elevator, however, Luther advises the officer that there are tiny spider robots waiting to kill the child as soon as he steps on the ground. Ramsey's son is saved by his partner and friend, but Luther sends Ramsey rocketing to the top of the structure, then drops him suddenly down again. As they wrestle for Luther's gun, he asks Ramsey perversely if he liked the ride in spite of his vertigo. Ramsey defeats Luther who is trapped and injected with poison by his own metal "spiders." Even in the throes of death Luther reaches up and grabs at Ramsey for an instant. His predisposition for bestiality is rooted in the depths of his brilliant, but distorted, mind. The attainment of wealth and power are secondary to Luther, whose unquenchable longing to torture and kill produce the utmost gratification for him.

CLARENCE BODDICKER

Film Source: *Robocop*
Release Date: 1987
Director: Paul Verhoeven
Production Company: Orion Pictures
Color
Running Time: 103 minutes
Performed by: Kurtwood Smith
Additional Performers: Peter Weller (Alex Murphy/Robocop); Ronny Cox (Dick Jones).

Physical Description: "Chic" does not quite describe crime boss Clarence Boddicker. Yet he still creates his own idiosyncratic illusion of a dapper aristocrat on the town by folding and tying his neckties and scarves in a bizarre manner. His wire-rimmed glasses are worn for appearance, as well as necessity. Balding and slight, he is unimposing until his skills as a marksman and his greater-than-average strength are called upon. His voice raises to a whirring shriek when he is angry, and he commands an uneasy attention even in the midst of a relaxed conversation. Gentleness is not a part of Boddicker's life. His bitter laughter, his twisted grin, and his callous disregard for those around him, reflect graphically the boorish world he inhabits in his mind.

Character Analysis: Boddicker translates his lack of respect for others into a form of artistic expression. He arrives at the offices of powerful executive Dick Jones, sticks his chewing gum on the secretary's name plate, asks her for a date, and, upon being turned down, says she can "keep the gum." Disgusted when one of his cohorts burns the money in a stolen safe, Boddicker has him thrown from the escape vehicle into an approaching police car. "Can you fly, Bobby boy?," he laughs as the man smashes into the windshield of the pursuit car. Boddicker, who has committed almost every felony in the book, has a cold, restive antipathy towards everyone with whom he deals. Nowhere is this more apparent than in his taut partnership with Jones, whose company oversees management of the entire city. Boddicker has just ensconced himself in the position of chief racketeer when a former adversary resurfaces. Alex Murphy, the policeman Boddicker and his thugs nearly murdered, lives on as a cybernetic "Robocop." Murphy, in his old life, had a family he loved, and distinguished himself as an unflinching, incorruptible police officer. As Robocop he rediscovers his true identity, but lays aside personal despair and animosity out of a profound concern for the public he has sworn to serve. Jones pays Boddicker to murder an executive who has attempted to circumvent their plans for a series of inefficient, malfunctioning robot sentries. Boddicker shoots the man and blows up his apartment with a hand grenade. Jones then offers Boddicker new territory for the felon's illicit market of drugs, gambling and prostitution if he will eliminate Murphy's alter ego. Robocop confronts Boddicker during a narcotics deal in a warehouse. The crime boss attempts to plunge a metal rod into Robocop, but is stabbed in the neck by the disabled cybernetic officer. In the end, the pain Boddicker has caused others is more than matched by his own.

COBBLEPOT, OSWALD: SEE: THE PENGUIN

CODY JARRETT

Film Source: *White Heat*
Release Date: 1949
Director: Raoul Walsh
Production Company: Warner Bros.
Color
Running Time: 114 minutes

Performed by: James Cagney
Additional Performers: Edmond O'Brien (Vic Pardo), Margaret Wycherly (Ma Jarrett), Steve Cochran (Big Ed).

Physical Description: Cody Jarrett is past forty but, possessing youthful good looks, dresses himself in smart suits, hats, and ties. He has light hair and bright, energetic eyes. His blunt speaking style demands the attention of others. He suffers from chronic headaches since childhood, and only his beloved mother can ease the pain.

Character Analysis: Hotheaded Cody Jarrett exhibits his disrespect for human life by shooting a railroad engineer and his brakeman during a train robbery. Later, he settles with a fellow prison inmate who made an attempt on his life by locking the man in a car trunk, derisively inquiring whether or not he needs air, then shooting him through the closed trunk door. He wants to leave another gang member behind at the crime scene when the man is scalded by steam, then ordains the man's death as the police uncover the gang's hide-out. Jarrett surrenders himself to the police for a lesser crime than the train robbery to obtain a shorter stay in prison, where he develops a close friendship with Vic Pardo, an undercover agent posing as a convict. Pardo is aware that Cody's sole refuge during his chronic headaches is his doting mother, whom he idolizes to the exclusion of all others, even his own wife. Like Cody's mother, Pardo has the ability to ease the felon's pain, thus supplanting her as Cody's protector and *confidante*. When Cody discovers Pardo's true identity, he is shocked and humiliated more than angered. Cody nearly strangles his wife because he thinks she's involved with his accomplice, Big Ed, Knowing Cody's obsession with his mother, she shifts the guilt for his mother's murder from herself to Big Ed, and Cody goes berserk, shooting his cohort and kicking him down a flight of stairs. Finally cornered at the top of a gasoline tank during a robbery, Cody's mind shatters. He blows up the tank, yelling "Top of the world!," his mother's favorite phrase, as the flames rise up about him. As a child, Cody had pretended to have headaches for the attention it brought him. As a man, he is bent upon the ruthless control of everyone around him. His violent death is not solely an extension of this wish for absolute power, but is a deranged offering up of himself to the successful image his mother had demanded of him.

COHAGEN: SEE: VILOS COHAGEN

CONCANNON: SEE: ED CONCANNON

DARIAN FORRESTER

Film Source: *The Crush*
Release Date: 1993
Director: Alan Shapiro
Production Company: Morgan Creek Productions
Color
Running Time: 89 minutes
Performed by: Alicia Silverstone
Additional Performers: Cary Elwes (Nick Eliot), Jennifer Rubin (Amy Maddick), Kurtwood Smith (Cliff Forrester), Amber Benson (Cheyenne).

Physical Description: Darien Forrester is a mature young woman of fourteen who seems older than her years. Her long blond hair and bright eyes attract immediate attention. She is lithe, lissome and of medium height, with just enough of a tan to be noticed. Her voice is sweet and soft most of the time, but she can attain a high screech when she is angry.

Character Analysis: Darian Forrester is a teenager who thinks like an adult. A genius, she has been pushed ahead by her overbearing parents, yet inside she is still a child, frightened and lonely. She has never felt loved by her father, Cliff Forrester, so she searches for "love" in all the wrong places. She "falls" for a camp counselor who rebuffs her advances and, according to her friend Cheyenne, she poisons him in revenge. She gets away with this initial act of violence, and now proceeds to intimidate unsuspecting magazine writer, Nick Eliot. Her intelligence is more than a match for the hapless Nick, who must fight for his life and the lives of his friends before Darian is finished. Cheyenne tells Nick about the camp counselor, and Darien insures her friend's silence by loosening the cinch on her horse's saddle, severely injuring the girl. Darien then turns on Nick's lover, Amy, trapping the allergic photographer in her darkroom and stuffing deadly wasps into the fan ducts. She gets Nick arrested on false charges of molestation by bruising herself. Nick returns to Darien's palatial home, only to be attacked by her angry father. Cliff nearly strangles Nick, but Darian stops him with a near-fatal blow. Ambivalent, stressed, brilliant, Darien wants her Daddy's love—not the torrents of gifts and material possessions he showers on her. She looks for a love she can never have—in the camp counselor, in Nick, and, still later, in the doctor under whose care she is placed. She will not get what she wants, and her wish is doomed to go unfulfilled. More vindictive behavior is in store, it can be assumed, for the unsuspecting doctor upon whom she bestows her latest "crush."

MR. DARK

Film Source: *Somethinq Wicked This Way Comes*
Release Date: 1983
Director: Jack Clayton
Production Company: Walt Disney
Color
Running Time: 94 minutes
Performed By: Jonathan Pryce
Additional Performers: Vidal Peterson (Will), Shawn Carson (Jim), Jason Robards (Charles Holloway).

Physical Description: Mr. Dark is clad in apparel reflecting his name: black top hat, coat, vest, pants, and shoes. His hair, moustache, and beard match his ensemble. Only his bright eyes and white shirt offer a contrast. Lean and tall, Dark sports an ebony walking stick and gloves to complement his wardrobe.

Character Analysis: If our fondest wishes are granted with the sole intent of harming us, we have been accorded only shadow and deception. Two amazed friends, young Will and Jim, watch a midnight train bring the Pandemonium Carnival, Dark's troupe of lost souls, into the outskirts of their little town. The curious Mr. Dark himself presides over a spectral convocation devoted to the perdition of those who can be tempted. Will's father, town librarian Mr. Holloway, is also interested in these carnival people and their motives, and reads his own father's notation of one of their odious visits to Will and Jim. Alerted to Mr. Holloway's deductions, Mr. Dark first offers him renewed youth, then foreshadows the librarian's death in retaliation for Holloway's incorruptible perseverance. Unprepared for Mr. Holloway's tenacious spirit, Mr. Dark forfeits both Will and Jim, as a cloudburst rinses away the malefic Pandemonium Show. Mr. Dark admits that his carnival feeds on the afflictions of those it claims. The hall of mirrors that furnishes Mr. Dark with his chief instrument of enticement resolves a longstanding conflict between Mr. Holloway and his son, instead of its usual destructive effect. Furious and desperate, Mr. Dark puts the spellbound Jim on a merry-go-round that can advance or decrease a person's age as it runs. If he cannot have Mr. Holloway's son, Mr. Dark will substitute Jim, to whom he offers a partnership in his carnival. Mr. Holloway's newly discovered hope imparts the strength he needs for Jim's rescue from this carnival of lies. Mr. Dark is plunged forward on his magical carousel until he decomposes into a skeleton. Pandemonium, the habitation John Milton ascribed to demons in *Paradise Lost*, represents Mr. Dark's conduct, ideology, and, most of all, his actual residence when his carnival evaporates in the tempest. What he was before he ruled the carnival is uncertain, but the consequence of his acts have obscured and nullified any virtue he may once have enjoyed. While he takes pleasure in the enslavement of others, his own bondage to depravity and ruthlessness makes him the most subjugated member of his carnival. Screenplay by Ray Bradbury, based on his classic fantasy.

DARRYL REVOK

Film Source: *Scanners*
Release Date: 1981
Director: David Cronenberg
Production Company: Filmplan International
Color
Running Time: 102 minutes
Performed by: Michael Ironside
Additional Performers: Stephen Lack (Cameron Vale), Patrick McGoohan (Dr. Paul Ruth).

Physical Description: Darryl Revok, in his thirties, has brooding eyes, a flat nose, thin lips, and a most unappealing smile. He is not tall, yet his strong frame gives him a commanding appearance. His gravelly voice has an undertone of explosiveness. Rugged and formidable, Revok seems inappropriately dressed in his business suit attire. While in a psychiatric ward during his twenties, he had stopped what he felt were invading "voices" in his mind by drilling a shallow hole in his forehead. The startling scar from this self-mutilation is still visible.

Character Analysis: Darryl Revok cannot mask his antipathy toward others with any manner of emotional disguise. He has a special hatred for "normals," who do not share the incredible ability that makes him a "scanner." Revok has prepared himself to rule over ordinary humans in the future by contacting several individuals like himself in a bid for power. His father, Dr. Paul Ruth, is a researcher in the field of psychopharmacy, and his experiments on Darryl's mother have resulted in Revok's "scanner" traits. Having infiltrated a demonstration at the company where his father works as a research scientist, Revok uses his ability to disrupt the nervous system of a "scanner," until the man's head bursts, then he murders Ruth's security people and escapes the compound. Dr. Ruth sends Cameron Vale, another talented young "scanner," to intercept Revok, but during their confrontation, Revok informs Cameron they are brothers and Dr. Ruth, whom he condemns, is their mutual father. Revok is overjoyed when Ruth is killed by one of his conspirators, and makes plans to expand his father's program by producing a drug that will cause other unborn children to become scanners. Revok hopes to develop an army of people like himself and his

47

brother, but Cameron denounces the scheme for ultimate power. Their disharmony turns into a battle to control Cameron's mind. Revok's madness is manifested in his complete insensitivity. He is as unfeeling as his father. When assassins kill Kim Obrist's scanner friends, Cameron rushes her into hiding. As they talk, Kim calls Revok a "nightmare." His vengeful alienation from his father, who had accepted responsibility for the experiments, makes Revok a source of aversion for those who should be closest to him. Some of Revok's enmity is well-founded, yet, unlike Kim and Cameron, he repudiates any benevolent application of his talents. Even as he admits his need for his brother, Darryl clearly expects Cameron to acquiesce in the final step in consolidating their power. Revok forfeits the warmth they might have shared after a lifetime of separation for his goal of predominance. Kim finds "Revok" and realizes that he has been "inhabited" by Cameron, who has finally overthrown his evil brother. Revok could have reversed his joyless youth and tormented early adulthood, but he chose a path to supremacy and is, instead, obliterated by a self-imposed estrangement from gentleness and love. "Revok's" orbs now reflect the sorrow of loss felt by the brother who inhabits his body.

DARTH VADER

Film Sources: *Star Wars*; *The Empire Strikes Back*; *Return of the Jedi*
Release Dates: 1977; 1980; 1983
Director: George Lucas; Irvin Kershner; Richard Marquand
Production Company: Twentieth Century Fox
Color
Running Times: 121 minutes, 124 minutes, 132 minutes
Performed by: David Prowse, with the voice of James Earl Jones
Additional Performers: Mark Hamill (Luke Skywalker), Alec Guinness (Obi-Wan Kenobi), Carrie Fisher (Princess Leia), Ian McDermid (The Emperor).

Physical Description: Darth Vader towers above his cohorts like some formidable bronze warrior of ancient mythology. He is imposing, and completely masked in ebony helmet and armor. Black gloves cover his hands, black boots encase his feet. An intricate control panel rests on the chest plate of his armor. The mouthpiece of Vader's helmet is equipped with a voice amplifier, and crimson visors shield his eyes. His deep, stentorian voice demands obeisance from his underlings. He is an expert in the art of the lightsaber and the wielding of the "Dark Side" of the energy field known as the "Force." His inexhaustible stamina and strength conjure up a vision of an indomitable warrior. Relying on his proficiency in the use of the Force, Darth Vader is the epitomé of profound darkness and evil. Beneath this formidable façade. however, Vader's physical body is an incongruous repudiation of his outer strength. Mutilated from battles, prematurely aged, and without the capacity for maintaining his own life support, Vader's very existence depends on the artificial shell of his armor.

Character Analysis: Darth Vader, as talented, young pilot Annakin Skywalker, was taught the ancient use of the Force by his mentor, Jedi knight Obi-Wan Kenobi. But before he mastered what, for a millennium, had been the most revered philosophy in his galaxy, Annakin/Vader was lured to the Dark Side of the Force by the future Emperor, whose obsessive megalomania has propelled the galaxy into war and rebellion. Darth Vader's bold rashness provided the one ingredient needed most by the future Emperor, and under his rule the erstwhile Jedi knight of the once-peaceful Republic has gained increasing power over the military and, indeed, the entire galaxy. For his own aggrandizement he has abetted the Emperor in the destruction of the protectors of the galaxy and his former comrades, the ancient Jedi brotherhood, but Obi-Wan, now in hiding in a remote outpost on a desert world, has escaped him. Here, the old master has watched over Luke Skywalker, the son Vader has never known. Vader psychically detects the existence of his son and determines to take the young man alive to lure him over to the Dark Side. Obi-Wan responds to Vader's attempt to entice Luke by engaging his former student in a lightsaber duel to the death on the Empire's formidable "Death Star." Vader dispatches his former teacher, and Obi-wan acknowledges him as a master—of the Dark (or evil) Side. Vader had learned half of the "key" to the Force only, and still lacks maturity and self-realization. Now he will learn the other half from his son, after the imminency of Luke's death at the hands of the Emperor on the Death Star restores Annakin Skywalker from the fortified vault in Vader's mind. Years of anger and selfish design have all but consumed Vader. The worlds he has crushed, with the resultant legion of deaths he has caused, have pushed Vader further and further away from his own humanity. Now, faced with his son's death, Annakin recalls the sorrow of having tortured his own daughter, the rebel leader Princess Leia—who is, in reality, Luke's long-lost twin sister. All Vader's hatred and wrath are subsumed by Annakin's native integrity and altruism. Ironically, it has been through the act of seeking his son's allegiance to the Emperor and the Dark Side that Vader has set himself on the course that will enable him to resume his Jedi values. As Annakin he thanks Luke for his unshakeable confidence in his father's deliverance. Vader dies, and Luke envisions his father's spirit with those of Obi-Wan and Yoda, the ancient Jedi master who taught them all. As the grip of the Dark Side on Vader is released, Annakin Skywalker, for a brief interval, has cleaved to his son once more. At the same time the pain of unlocking the baseness of his actions has vanished with the loving acceptance of his son.

DAVID GREENHILL

Film Source: *Guilty as Sin*
Release Date: 1993
Director: Sidney Lumet
Production Company: Hollywood Pictures
Color
Running Time: 120 minutes
Performed by: Don Johnson
Additional Performers: Rebecca De Mornay (Jennifer Haines), Jack Warden (Moe).

Physical Description: David Greenhill is tall, exceptionally handsome, and a sight to behold. He is well-groomed, and well-built, with neatly-styled hair and a boyish grin. His tailored suits and designer ties do him justice. His rather raspy, high baritone catches the ear. In his forties at most, he is both charming and elegant. A real "lady-killer."

Character Analysis: No one can resist this charming man—yet under David Greenhill's pleasant exterior lurks a deadly serpent, lying in wait for any "Eve" willing to take the risk. His flawless orchestration of the murder of his wealthy wife is a result of careful detailed planning. For a year he has been watching and following attorney Jennifer Haynes, who is adept at winning her cases. In his warped mind, in fact, Jennifer has become his unwitting "accomplice." In the course of things David beats Jennifer's lover into a comatose state. He ransacks and destroys her office, killing her associate. He admits to murdering another woman and putting still another into a coma. Money is his ostensive motive. He uses it up, then goes on to his next victim. In reality, however, he is addicted to the feeling of power and enjoys abusing each one of his victims. An accomplished actor, he sets up his defense by pointing a finger of guilt at his wife's greedy relatives, and for further protection he forges his wife's signature to a letter stating she is in fear for her life from an unknown assailant. He then confesses all to his disgusted, angry lawyer, after everyone else has left the courtroom. But Jennifer, to his chagrin, is the one woman he cannot seduce. She has a final showdown with David in her high-rise apartment. She knows too much, and worse, will not hesitate to use what she knows against him, so he attempts to cast her off the side of the building. Underestimating Jennifer's resolve, David is killed when she fools him, causing him to fall instead. A woman has gotten the best of him—and that seems like the most fitting retribution of all.

DAVID JASON

Film Source: *Deep Cover*
Release Date: 1992
Director: Bill Duke
Production Company: New Line Cinema
Color
Running Time: 107 minutes
Performed by: Jeff Goldblum
Additional Performers: Laurence Fishburne (Russell Stevens, Jr.), Gregory Sierra (Felix Barbosa).

Physical Description: David Jason is an impressive sight. He is extremely tall, his dark hair is combed back smoothly, and he has piercing eyes and strong facial features. His warm baritone voice can become a growl when he is upset. In his forties, but still vigorous, Jason is powerful in appearance.

Character Analysis: "I want my cake and eat it too," explains David Jason. He is never satisfied: his wife and child are not enough. His shady legal practice is not enough. Under the surface is a man whose desires outweigh his common sense. He has a mistress on the side—and he makes a tidy amount selling cocaine. Felix Barbosa, his drug-dealing superior, nearly breaks his hand during an argument, so David shoots Felix in the hands for "pay back." Russell Stevens, Jr., an undercover police officer trying to infiltrate the drug ring, enters David's murky world. Once he meets David his success is insured, but at immense risk. David begins to trust Russell and invites him to become his partner in the promotion of a designer drug. This drug, David believes, will bring him millions. David's world, however, is crumbling. His time and attention are being eaten up with the constant demands of having and getting drugs. Although he speaks the language of an educated man, he also curses in vile abandon. He leads a double life of loving parent and husband on the one hand, and irresponsible lover and drug dealer on the other. All this seemingly has no effect on him, since he either has no conscience, or has lost what conscience he did have. A final confrontation between Russell and David takes place, and another police officer is wounded. Still clinging to his dream of future wealth to be made from the designer drug, he again invites Russell to join him. Holding his wounded colleague in his arms, Russell refuses the offer and shoots David instead. Temptation could not sway Russell from his duty, but David was its prisoner. On the surface David seemed vigorous and alive; underneath beat a cold heart. He may have "had" his cake at one time, but through greed, he lost his opportunity to "eat" it as well.

DAVID LO PAN

Film Source: *Big Trouble in Little China*
Release Date: 1986
Director: John Carpenter
Production Company: Twentieth Century Fox
Color
Running Time: 100 minutes
Performed by: James Hong
Additional Performer: Kurt Russell (Jack Burton).

Physical Description: David Lo Pan, wizened and confined to a wheelchair, is a "changeling," concealing his true self from the world. Cursed in a past life, he may present himself as an ancient Chinese god—when he so desires. At times his body may be covered by flowing crimson robes, at others he may be dressed in a gray business suit. His hair may be black one time, white another. He is capable of producing penetrating rays of light from his eyes and mouth that temporarily blind the beholder. His voice is a high-pitched twitter, sounding more like a bird's chirp than human speech. He is "master" of Chinatown, and no one dares to meddle with him.

Character Analysis: David Lo Pan, in the guise of a rich criminal, searches Chinatown for a Chinese woman with green eyes who will become his "perfect mate." He is thrilled when he finds *two* women with green eyes! He makes plans to marry both, then sacrifice one to appease the god who cursed him. He will be an even more dangerous adversary if he becomes fully human again, combining elements from the supernatural realm with the mortal world. Truck driver Jack Burton wanders into Lo Pan's domain, and he and another magician from Chinatown try to stop Lo Pan by rescuing the two women he has kidnapped, at the risk of destroying everything around them. Burton does not believe in ancient gods and Chinese magic initially, but Lo Pan creates diversions and other "difficulties" for those who would thwart him. With capricious malevolence he calls on the spirits of thunder, wind, and lightning. He captures Jack and his friend through magic, but cannot hold them. Under his dominion Chinatown has trembled, but still he underestimated the love and resolve of those about him. Jack and Lo Pan toss a knife back and forth, each attempting to confuse the other. Suddenly, Lo Pan is struck in the head, and dies. In spite of his ancient wisdom, he has foolishly attempted to recover his human side at all cost—an act which proves to be his downfall.

DE MERTREUIL: SEE: MERTREUIL

DEAGLE: SEE: MRS. RUBY DEAGLE

NURSE DIESEL

Film Source: *High Anxiety*
Release Date: 1977
Director: Mel Brooks
Production Company: Twentieth Century Fox
Color
Running Time: 94 minutes
Performed by: Cloris Leachman
Additional Performers: Mel Brooks (Dr. Thorndike), Harvey Korman
(Dr. Montague).

Physical Description: Nurse Diesel is as terrifying as an image out of Lovecraft or Poe. A caricature, she stomps about mechanically, stiff-necked and tight-lipped, her starched uniform as unyielding as a suit of armor. She barks her words as fierce commands, her speech coarse and guttural. Most electrifying is the sight of her formidable pointed breasts, encased as if in steel, rather than a softly feminine bosom.

Character Analysis: Nurse Diesel is the last person in the world one would want as a personal "caregiver." Diesel rules cruelly and despoti-cally over a sanitarium for the mentally ill. With the connivance of her lover Dr. Montague, the release of wealthy patients who no longer need treatment is blocked. Another doctor threatens to "spill the beans" about the nefarious goings on at the asylum and, fearing she will be displaced, Diesel engineers his death by blasting his ears with loud music while he is trapped in his own car. Aware of her tenuous position should the new director, Dr. Thorndike, discover foul play, Nurse Diesel uses all of her cunning to ruin him or have him murdered. Desperate to eliminate Thorndike, she tries to fling him over a parapet. Resembling the Wicked Witch from *The Wizard of Oz*, she makes a grotesque spectacle of herself, and ultimately falls to her own death. Her perverse relationship with the slavish Dr. Montague, her cruel incarceration of her patients, and her attempts to drive Dr. Thorndike mad or kill him, constitute a predisposition toward grandiosity and virulence. Nurse Diesel is an exaggeration of everything dreadful—and terrible to behold. See also: NURSE RATCHED, from *One Flew Over the Cuckoo's Nest*, the model for Diesel. Mel Brooks, through the vehicle of *High Anxiety* also pays clever homage to many Hitchcock thrillers, most notably, *Vertigo*, *North by Northwest*, and *The Birds*.

DILLINGER

Film Source: *Tron*
Release Date: 1982
Director: Steven Lisberger
Production Company: Walt Disney
Color
Running Time: 95 minutes
Performed By: David Warner
Additional Performer: Jeff Bridges (Flynn).

Physical Description: Dillinger, senior vice-president of a corporation known as ENCOM, rarely smiles. His polished voice, lean build and impressive height present a compelling figure, but his gelid stare and acrid delivery reflect a more nefarious image.

Character Analysis: Dillinger, a petty, conscienceless individual, has stolen a valuable computer disk from the talented young programmer Flynn. Dillinger is now the plenary control over the Master Computer Program at ENCOM, the vast complex which employs both Dillinger and Flynn. His office, like his internal self, is devoid of warmth and empty of human touches. He remains indifferent to the questionable steps he has taken to arrive at the top. Grasping at each rung on the ladder leading him to even further power, he focuses on himself and his future alone. Flynn, desperate to regain his stolen property, enters into the world of the Master Computer Program, and challenges Dillinger to a test of wills. Dillinger is outclassed and finds himself trapped within his own network of lies. As his empire crumbles around him, Dillinger is isolated through his own self-aggrandizement, unmindful of anyone's needs but his own.

DOYLE LONNEGAN

Film Source: *The Sting*
Release Date: 1973
Director: George Roy Hill
Production Company: Universal Pictures
Color
Running Time: 129 minutes
Performed by: Robert Shaw
Additional Performers: Paul Newman (Henry Gondorf), Robert Redford (Johnny Hooker).

Physical Description: Doyle Lonnegan is a well-groomed man in his fifties who wears the best clothes and hats the Roaring '20s have to offer. He sports a thin moustache, a full head of hair, and a mole on his left cheek as a distinguishing mark. He walks with a limp due to an old injury. His gruff Irish accent adds a special touch to his persona.

Character Analysis: Doyle Lonnegan lives in a fancy home and has entrenched himself in Chicago politics of the 1920s. In reality, he is a "con" artist and crime boss. With the politicians he holds in his pocket, he has fallen rather easily into the trap of believing his own publicity. The sides of this particular trap, however, are wide, and deep, and extremely slippery. Lonnegan. who does not always stop with the "con," can be vindictive, and he has made many fearful of his power. He has, in fact, committed murder (or ordered it done); but he never wastes time worrying about such deeds, just wants it over with as quickly as possible. Grifter Johnny Hooker's friend has become the target of Lonnegan's wrath. Rather than killing Lonnegan for revenge, however, Hooker and Henry Gondorf, another con artist, work out an elaborate scheme to deceive him. Lonnegan's love of horse racing proves to be his undoing when he loses $500,000 to Gondorf, Hooker, and their colleagues. No one has ever gotten the better of Lonnegan until now. These men, who themselves are often on the wrong side of the law, still have respect and some compassion for others. Lonnegan, however, is insulting, cold, and scornful of everybody. He has it made, and wants to keep it that way. His superior attitude and lack of imagination lead him straight into the trap set for him. Control, for him, is a narcotic, Now it is he who is controlled by others—when the last horse crosses the finish line. Oscar-winning ragtime score revived interest in Scott Joplin's music.

DRACULA

Film Sources: *Dracula, Horror of Dracula*
Release Dates: 1931; 1957; 1979
Focus: 1931 film version
Director: Tod Browning
Production Company: Universal Pictures
B&W
Running Time: 75 minutes
Performed by: Bela Lugosi
Additional Performers: Dwight Frye (Mr. Renfield), Helen Chandler (Mina), Edward Van Sloan (Dr. Van Helsing), Herbert Buntson (Dr. Seward).

Physical Description: Count Dracula's pale complexion, highlighted by dark hair and hypnotic, penetrating eyes, make this nobleman an eerie combination of charisma and the ghastly. His cultivated voice, both terrifying and seductive, catches one by surprise, as do his deliberate, mannered gestures. He wears fine clothing accentuated by an ancient medallion around his neck, perhaps a token from some medieval war. Elegant in top hat and tails while attending the opera, he can transform himself into other creatures, such as a wolf or a bat, at will. His ravenous expression while attacking a victim makes him the epitomé of bestiality.

Character Analysis: Count Dracula is a perplexing blend of the romantic and the horrific who devours and discards individuals in much the same way some might crumple up a tissue and throw it away. As one of the legendary "undead" he seems unaffected by the carnage demanded by his perpetual need for fresh blood supplies. Renfield, a visitor to Dracula's ancestral castle, becomes the vampire's slave, living on flies and spiders, and enduring the whims and torments of his master. On a voyage from his Transylvanian homeland to England the Count leaves the ship's crew, hired by Renfield, dead. Once in England, he settles in a crumbling abbey near the home of Dr. Seward, whose lovely daughter Mina, Dracula desires as his mate for all time. Confident of his invulnerability, Dracula bites Mina, mixing his blood with hers, in a bid to dominate her. Dracula's attentions bring Mina to the point of figurative consumption, alarming her father and friends. Dracula's self-assurance vanquishes him in the end, however. He is challenged by Professor Van Helsing, whose extensive research of the supernatural has accorded him full knowledge of Dracula's inadequacies, thus allowing him to counteract the vampire's exploitation of Mina. A tempting oppressor, Dracula, whose name has become synonymous with dread, is both abhorrent and bewitching. Even as the evil he represents unnerves and repels, it allows him to fully exploit the fears—and desires—of those he intends as his victims.

DUKE MANTEE

Film Source: *The Petrified Forest*
Release Date: 1936
Director: Archie Mayo
Production Company: Warner Bros.
Color
Running Time: 83 minutes
Performed by: Humphrey Bogart
Additional Performers: Leslie Howard (Alan).

Physical Description: Duke Mantee's brooding eyes are as impenetratable as the petrified forest in which he finds himself. A man who considers everything with great deliberateness, he walks stiffly hunched over with hands anchored in front of him, as if molded in concrete. His hair is slightly unkempt and he speaks crudely, through clenched teeth, in a manner that recalls the static-laden delay of a radio message sent over a transceiver—from a great distance away.

Character Analysis: Duke Mantee *does* have a conscience of sorts, he just prefers not to grapple with it. His concept of good and evil is questionable, however, since he first disdains a specific act of violence, then, almost at the same moment, employs it. On the barren desert, a place of desuetude and relentless winds, Duke encounters the one person whom he cannot regard simply as an impediment or as an object to be used. Faced with Alan, a contemplative drifter who offers his own life as a gift for the benefit of a talented young woman, Duke stares into the seeds of his own destructiveness. Duke, for whom death is a topic of sardonic humor, is an uneasy man. He leaps from his chair, his gun ready, when a gust of wind blows a door open behind him. Duke is overcome with fitful vacillation when his cohorts recommend a quick escape because they think his lover has betrayed him. Duke, a thief responsible for six murders, is convinced that breaking the law far exceeds upholding it. He confronts his own vulnerability, however, when Alan asks Duke to shoot him so that the young woman who loves him will receive the full benefit of his insurance policy. Alan's motive is as selfless as it is eccentric. Since Alan has lived only for himself up to now, he hopes this deed will bring a promising new artist her opportunity for distinction. Duke, having found the one person whom he can almost respect, resists the act which would be tantamount to being manipulated by another person. By pulling the trigger, Duke colludes with Alan by doing what he considers most estimable. The intent of it aside, it remains murder, and Duke mindfully accomplishes it. His capture, near the forest, as petrified as his soul, is inevitable, since Duke not only is a person overflowing with thoughts of death—he has been the cause of so many of them.

EARLY GRAYCE

Film Source: *Kalifornia*
Release Date: 1993
Director: Dominic Sena
Production Company: Polygram Films
Color
Running Time: 117 minutes
Performed by: Brad Pitt
Additional Performers: Juliette Lewis (Adele Corners), David Duchovny (Brian Kessler), Michelle Forbes (Carrie Loughlin).

Physical Description: Early Grayce, still in his twenties, has the appearance of a man with many more miles on his youthful body. Slender, and of medium height, he is strong, and moves in a graceful manner. Although not well-educated, his smooth voice has an enticing quality about it. Straggly blond hair, beard and moustache, together with an open shirt, t-shirt beneath, and baggy pants, lend Early an air of casual slovenliness. His fascinating eyes, his best feature, draw attention to an equally handsome face. Yet, for all their soulful quality, these are weary eyes, overflowing with life's burdens and sorrows.

Character Analysis: Early Grayce became disenchanted with everything long ago. Although youthful in years, he has been schooled in the harshness of life. Early does not enjoy talking about his father whom he hates, or so he confides to Brian Kessler, a writer who agrees to take Early along to help share expenses on a trip to California. Parolee Grayce's sudden illegal departure from the state has been prompted by the loss of his job and, even more importantly, the murder of an acquaintance. Along for the ride with Brian and his companion, photographer Carrie Loughlin, is Adele Corners, a naive young waitress whom Early has kept as a near slave to his desires. This odd foursome sees the journey ahead as an adventure of sorts, but quite soon their daydream turns into a nightmare. It becomes obvious that violence has infiltrated every aspect of Early's life, in the way he eats, in his relationship with Adele, in his interaction with others, and, perhaps most tellingly, in his feelings toward himself. His life is out of control so he compensates by attempting to control those around him. Although Early seems lucid at times, he is unpredictable, and his frequent psychotic fits are aggravated by his aggressive nature. Compounding this difficulty is Early's belief that he has visited other dimensions, even though he still believes he can function in this reality. This ability, of going beyond the limits of ordinary people, convinces him he is "special." Although he has a deep need to socialize with others, he continually isolates himself from any deeply emotional interpersonal relationship. Into the path of this sociopathic timebomb wander his unwary traveling companions, Brian and Carrie. Through complacency, inaction and a certain "blind" spot to their danger, the couple abet Early in his power trip, a fact which neither of them seems to comprehend. Instead, they proceed on their journey as if he were innocuous and non-threatening—until it is almost too late. Early goes from one bad deed to another, leading Brian down a path of criminal behavior the author heretofore has only studied for a work in progress. Early, who likes doing things his way, knifes a stranger in a gas station restroom, shoots a gas station attendant, and beats up a man in a bar who has picked a fight with Brian. Adele confides in Carrie, detailing Early's sadistic and abusive control over her. Early's murderous escapades culminate at a house in the desert, where he bludgeons the elderly owner to death with the man's own golf club, then murders Adele. He handcuffs Carrie and Brian, and Carrie offers herself to Early in exchange for Brian's life. He takes her to an abandoned nuclear test site, where he continues tormenting and torturing Carrie, who shoves a piece of glass into Early. His loss of blood does not kill him, but Brian manages to escape and track them down. In a final showdown, Brian shoots the wounded abductor. Early's rage and indifference has stemmed from the abuse and torment he experienced in his youth, which left him cold and in an arrested state of emotional development. His lack of formal education and his psychoses do not indicate a lack of intellect, as he displays every indication of a quick-witted, inventive person. Early, dominated by his past mistakes and a tortured childhood, covets the upscale lifestyle and caring relationship shared by Carrie and Brian, but his method of achieving these ends is warped and out-of-control. Early is shackled to his violent, misanthropic behavior by bonds as durable as the handcuffs he attaches to Brian and Carrie. He recognizes no other course for the future, and he refuses to deal with his troubled past. In his mind it is as if he inhabits a cave with an echo reiterating the same sounds in an incessant pattern as destructive as the nuclear weapons once devised at the test site—and guaranteed to presage an untimely end for him.

ED CONCANNON

Film Source: *The Verdict*
Release Date: 1982
Director: Sidney Lumet
Production Company: Twentieth Century Fox
Color
Running Time: 129 minutes
Performed by: James Mason
Additional Performers: Paul Newman (Frank Galvin), Charlotte Rampling (Laura Fischer).

Physical Description: Ed Concannon, stylishly attired in neat dark suits, is a most distinguished barrister. He is in his sixties, with graying hair, prominent dark eyebrows, and a handsome, memorable face. He speaks with a British accent and has a fine and distinct elocution.

Character Analysis: Ed Concannon is a famous trial lawyer who uses devious means to great advantage in his practice. Pinning their hopes on Concannon's legal maneuvering and expertise, an archdiocese appoints him counsel for two doctors accused of malpractice at their hospital. Winning the case is Concannon's one consideration, so he has no interest in the wellbeing of the girl left in a coma from his clients' poor judgment. Francis Galvin, an alcoholic has-been, who seems decidedly unfit to try the case, is hired by the girl's family, to Concannon's delight. Concannon buys off the most important witness for the prosecution and causes the man to disappear. He then hires beautiful Laura

Fischer to seduce Galvin and spy out his strategy. Galvin discovers Laura's deception in time, and can call for a mistrial, but he decides to pursue the trial to the bitter end, hoping he can defeat the shady Concannon. Galvin finds the admitting nurse who can prove the doctors' guilt, and convinces her to testify against them. Concannon loses the case, failing the powerful clients whom he had defended through prevarication and artifice. An overconfident manipulator, he is defeated when he blunders into a minefield of his own making.

ELLIOT MARSTON

Film Source: *Quigley Down Under*
Release Date: 1990
Director: Simon Wincer
Production Company: Pathe Entertainment
Color
Running Time: 121 minutes
Performed by: Alan Rickman
Additional Performers: Tom Selleck (Matthew Quigley), Laura San Giacomo (Cora).

Physical Description: Elliot Marston is a striking man in his early forties with neatly trimmed hair and moustache. His height and exceptional physique are set off by a traditional black suit, white shirt, and wide-brimmed hat consistent with his place and time. He has a mannerism of standing with arms crossed, as he gazes about, and his sharp eyes miss little. Although most of his companions speak in a coarse frontier fashion, Marston's elocution is nearly perfect.

Character Analysis: Elliot Marston has a very high opinion of himself, and considers himself a "man of refinement," even though he lives on a remote cattle station in the Australian outback. Even his immense wealth, however, cannot reconcile his childhood sorrows. For Marston bears a vengeful grudge against the aborigines who killed his parents, a grudge which has grown into a profound hatred of all the native people of Australia. His hatred is so strong that he has even poisoned flour, leaving it for the aborigines to eat and die a horrible death. If he had his way in fact, he would enslave or kill every aborigine in the country. Marston's hired men also fear him, doing what he demands without question. He must have absolute jurisdiction over his land and every person on it. Never leaving his home, he makes the world come to him. He hires the unwitting American marksman Matthew Quigley to use his amazing skills against the aborigines. Quigley, no fool, asks his host at the elegant dinner Quigley has prepared for him, just what his job entails. His immediate reaction to Marston's revelation is to refuse Marston's demands altogether. Furious, Marston has his unwilling hired gun taken out to the desert to die. Cora, a disturbed young woman whose husband has abandoned her after a tragic event, is befriended by Quigley and sent to die with him. Together the couple manage to survive their wilderness ordeal, and Quigley returns to Marston's station for a showdown. Marston, an admirer of the legendary "Wild" Bill Hickock, fancies himself an expert with a revolver, and challenges Quigley to a duel. He is wrong, however, in believing Quigley is a marksman with the rifle only, and Quigley easily defeats and kills him. Marston is a man of no remorse, and has considered himself "above the law" in his domain. The early loss of his parents has warped his soul, pitting him against more than aborigine neighbors; all about him feel his wrath, and he treats people even less charitably than he might an animal. Marston has never married and, except for his cowboys and servants, he lives a solitary life at his secluded compound. Shut away from humanity by his own disregard for it, he has turned inward, living out his sterile existence in the pursuit of material goods. Marston might have lived a very different life, if he had been able to resolve his grief over his parents' death in a more acceptable manner. Instead, he chose to tie his own hands in a knot of seething rage. Introversion has taken Marston beyond the limit, and has turned him into something like a refined "beast," at total odds with the image he has of himself as a "man of refinement." In the end, however, it his immense ego, more than anything else, that defeats him.

DR. ERIC KIVIAT

Film Source: *Baby...Secret of the Lost Legend*
Release Date: 1985
Director: B. W. L. Norton
Production Company: Touchstone Films
Color
Running Time: 95 minutes
Performed By: Patrick McGoohan
Additional Performers: Sean Young (Susan), William Katt (George).

Physical Description: Dr. Kiviat is fiftyish, a striking individual with a well-tended, graying beard and moustache, and piercing eyes. Slim and of medium build, he is fond of using a walking stick and frequently wears a hat. His conservative attire includes a suit and tie.

Character Analysis: Dr. Kiviat appears from the midst of a crowd, stabs a fellow professor, and appropriates the man's valuable satchel of information. He commits these offenses in order to become the first scientist to unearth a live dinosaur. Dr. Kiviat deviously informs his doctoral student, Susan, that her hypothetical dinosaur bone belongs to a giraffe. Imperturbable for the most part, he slams his fist on a table and yells at an assistant in rage, when he learns the man is searching for his prey in the wrong place. Dr. Kiviat's rage takes a violent bent when he murders the colonel of his band of mercenaries with a poisoned dart. He accuses Susan and her husband, George, of the colonel's death in order to deflect the blame from himself. Susan and George discover a vulnerable baby dinosaur and attempt to protect it when Kiviat forces his wounded helicopter pilot to return for the unique animal. The baby's mother appears, chases down Dr. Kiviat, and kills him in defense of her child. A renowned scholar, Kiviat traded ethics for vanity in his obsessive search for fame. His preoccupation with self-aggrandizement has led him down a sordid path of crime that rewards him with a terrifying death in place of the distinction he yearned to achieve.

ERIC QUALEN

Film Source: *Cliffhanger*
Release Date: 1993
Director: Renny Harlin
Production Company: Tri-Star Productions
Color
Running Time: 113 minutes
Performed by: John Lithgow
Additional Performer: Sylvester Stallone (Gabe Walker).

Physical Description: Eric Qualen's rugged, lantern-shaped face and sharp, intense eyes are his most significant features. He is tall, sturdily built, and strong—for a man who well may be in his fifties. The icy climate in which he finds himself dictates the heavy fur-lined parka and boots he is wearing. When he speaks, in an understated monotone and distinctive accent, he expects the undivided attention of his listener.

Character Analysis: Eric Qualen enjoys both his superior intellect—and the power it allows him to exert over those around him. Qualen, who expects absolute obedience from his underlings, does not suffer noncompliance with patience. He has been most successful conducting multi-million dollar robberies, and he relishes both the comfort of the lifestyle he has purchased with his ill-gotten gains, and the thrill he experiences during one of his escapades. An aggressive, yet sly, man, he serves his own desires at the expense of those around him. A man with "connections," he looks upon everyone with whom he comes in contact as a means to his devious ends, using each one he can in his quest to retain his ill-gotten millions. "Real love is sacrifice," he explains to his lover, tongue firmly in cheek, as he calmly shoots her in order to save his own hide. Qualen goes about his life devoid of sensitivity, as though a glacial "overcoat" has been applied to the essence of his personality. This detachment from love and concern comes naturally to Qualen, and it resembles most graphically bricks laid one atop the other throughout his life until any semblance of warmth and tenderness has been walled up and purposefully forsaken. Obstructing Qualen's retreat is Gabe Walker, a rescue worker still grieving over the death of a woman he could not save from a fall. Unprepared for Gabe's determination, Qualen takes him on—as he does everyone else—and loses all in the process. Qualen is killed while attempting to escape in a stolen helicopter. The money he had "liberated" floats effortlessly to earth, just like the snowflakes which flutter about the icy mountain scene. Although his assistant thinks him mad, Qualen is actually of quite sound, albeit vile and brutal, mind. Just as he believes laws are meant for others, not him, he made the decision long ago that everyone was quite expendable except him. A sense of dread has followed him around like a shadow. As a result, those lucky souls who survive Qualen are more relieved than mournful at his demise.

ERIK: SEE: THE PHANTOM

PROFESSOR FATE

Film Source: *The Great Race*
Release Date: 1965
Director: Blake Edwards
Color
Production Company: Warner Bros.
Running Time: 160 minutes
Performed by: Jack Lemmon
Additional Performers: Tony Curtis (Leslie), Natalie Wood (Maggie DuBois), Peter Falk (Max).

Physical Description: Professor Fate is a stylish blackguard. From his top hat to his shoes, his black attire matches his trimmed and lacquered black moustache and heavy black eyebrows. His wide vocal range, precise enunciation, and tendency to yell, make his voice absorbing, yet grating on the nerves. Fate's expressive features and talent for mimicry prove valuable for chicanery and the eventual safety of himself and his heroic opposition alike.

Character Analysis: Professor Fate, a fraud from the tips of his fingers to the tops of his toes, inhabits a gloomy mansion guarded by vicious dogs and a henchman, Max, who waits on his every need and demand. He usually gets what he wants—and when he doesn't, he throws tantrums, like an *enfant terrible*. As an avocation Fate devises and performs hazardous, generally unsuccessful, stunts—which usually fail to win him the adulation he believes he deserves. He enters into competition with Leslie, a dashing, handsome, young gentleman, as they both seek to win The Great Automobile Race. Fate designs a racing car out-fitted with a mechanism that belches smoke and shoots projectiles; it is as nasty and malevolent as he is, and seems more like a weapon than an automobile. He demands that Leslie tackle the same wildly dangerous feats as he does, but when reporter Maggie DuBois threatens to hit him for his disgraceful behavior, Fate cowers in terror. His cowardice resurfaces during a saloon brawl when he removes himself from harm's way by using the other combatants as a screen. He discovers Maggie, distraught and stranded in the desert, but instead of giving assistance, he laughs at her plight and speeds by her. Fate learns that he is a "dead ringer" for the fatuous prince of a tiny kingdom, and agrees to pose as the prince if, in return, the local authorities will hold Leslie in jail while the Professor is given a head start on the last stretch of the race. He congratulates himself on his "victory" in Paris, but suddenly realizes that Leslie has permitted him to win. Overcome by wrath, Fate insists on a rematch. Fate cannot stand to win unless his victory is on his own terms. His perpetual dissatisfaction with his life and the people in it makes him seem like nothing more than an irritating buffoon. As he continues on his quest to rout Leslie, Fate achieves his crowning ac-complishment—by inadvertently blowing up the Eiffel Tower.

FLANDERS: SEE: PEYTON FLANDERS

FLANNERY: SEE: FRANKIE FLANNERY

FORRESTER: SEE: DARIAN FORRESTER

FRANCISCO SCARAMANGA

Film Source: *The Man with the Golden Gun*
Release Date: 1974
Director: Guy Hamilton
Production Company: United Artists
Color
Running Time: 125 minutes
Performed by: Christopher Lee
Additional Performers: Roger Moore (James Bond), Hervé Villechaize (Nick Nack).

Physical Description: Scaramanga's tall, lanky body, draped in a white, linen suit, slithers snakelike as he walks. His dark, deepset eyes brood ominously. His melodic voice resonates like a stone dropped into a deep pond. Oddly, he is blessed with a third nipple on his chest.

Character Analysis: Scaramanga grew up in a circus family, early be-coming a trick shot and a marksman. During his youth, he shot the trainer who had beaten and killed his favorite elephant, an event which triggered the pleasure Scaramanga now realizes in killing people with his favored weapon of choice, a golden gun loaded with bullets of gold. For him, the act of taking a human life occupies a magical place in his thoughts. None of his obsessions compare, however, with his determination to match skills with legendary British agent, James Bond. Basking on the shore of his island home, where he has erected a likeness of Bond as the principal figure in a "shooting gallery," Scaramanga holds a regal position in the secret paradise he has built on the dead bodies of lucrative assassinations. Scaramanga has now come in possession of a solar gun and a massive solar storage plant. He plans scheduled visits from world dignitaries as bidders on his energy complex. Scaramanga's use of the device for which Bond is searching consolidates his strategy for unlimited riches. The hapless Miss Anders, Scaramanga's mistress, harbors a deep-seated loathing of him, partly because of Scaramanga's practice of making love only before he kills someone. She enlists Bond's aid, and he attends a kickboxing match where she promises to provide him with the invaluable energy device . He finds Miss Anders murdered, however, and is greeted by Scaramanga who brags about his "clean kill." Bond and another agent, Miss Goodnight, overhear the assassin call himself a "great artist" as they sit at Scaramanga's table. Anticipating his personal confrontation with the famed British agent, Scaramanqa believes Bond's death will be his "indisputable masterpiece." Sure of his victory, the assassin permits Bond six bullets to his one for their duel. Outwitted by Bond, Scaramanga dies at the hands of his revered adversary. Following the island's explosion from an accident in the solar plant, Bond and Goodnight are pounced upon by Nick Nack, Scaramanga's loyal servant. For some time Scaramanga had carried on a game of wits and skills with notorious killers, and Nick Nack had hoped one of them might win him his employer's promised fortune by shooting the assassin. Nick Nack, losing everything but his life, is captured by Bond. For Scaramanga, each murder he commits is a celebration. He has accused Bond of taking a secret pleasure in killing, but he is merely echoing his own sense of omnipotence when he appropriates a human life. Experiencing brief moments of fulfillment in the act of killing alone, Scaramanga dies still caught in a lifestyle of emotional destitution.

FRANK BOOTH

Film Source: *Blue Velvet*
Release Date: 1986
Director: David Lynch
Production Company: De Laurentiis Entertainment Group
Color
Running Time: 120 minutes

Performed by: Dennis Hopper
Additional Performers: Kyle MacLachlan (Jeffrey); Isabella Rossellini (Dorothy).

Physical Description: Frank Booth is clad in a pitch-hued leather jacket and dark pants. His hair is combed back, drawing attention to his startling eyes. Slim of physique and not too tall, Frank has the look of a hungry beast. His walk and bearing inspire terror, or, at the very least, subservience in others.

Character Analysis: Frank Booth dwells in a dark abyss of crime and savagery of his own design, while Jeffrey, a naive college student come home to help his family during a crisis, has lived, until now, in the sunshine. Their paths intersect in a small town which is a microcosm of contrasts, and where Jeffrey makes a startling discovery which casts him into Frank's threatening world. Jeffrey meets Dorothy, a lovely, though enigmatic young woman, whose husband and young son are being held prisoner by Frank. Dorothy has become Frank's thrall, and allows him to abuse her in ritualistic and sadistic sexual "dramas" in which she embodies both Frank's torments and desires. To enhance his arousal, Frank inhales a hypnotic gas, takes pills, and drinks excessively. His incessant use of vulgar language, immersion in every form of criminal behavior, and ferocious responses to his associates, have made him a walking obscenity. Jeffrey is horrified to discover that Frank's delight in violence has further manifested itself when he presents a severed ear from Dorothy's kidnapped husband. Jeffrey is fully aware of his hazardous position but still confronts Booth in Dorothy's room. Panic-stricken, yet resolute, Jeffrey summons up the courage to shoot Frank, before he himself is killed by his enraged adversary. Jeffrey has succumbed to temptation for a time, but in the end he rejects Frank's dark and violent world and turns instead toward the light. He valiantly sacrifices himself to save Dorothy, while Frank's death, in contrast, serves as the most logical conclusion to the pain and terror he sought to inflict on others during his lifetime.

FRANKIE FLANNERY

Film Source: *State of Grace*
Release Date: 1990
Director: Phil Joanou
Production Company: Orion Pictures
Color
Running Time: 144 minutes
Performed by: Ed Harris
Additional Performers: Sean Penn (Terry Noonan), Gary Oldman (Jackie Flannery), Robin Wright (Kate Flannery).

Physical Description: Frankie Flannery is starting to bald on top, but he still has hair on the sides and back of his head. He often leaves the top of his shirt unbuttoned, and his suits look disheveled. His hands are strong and capable, and he uses them demonstratively. Flannery has the high flattering forehead of an intellectual, and his facial features are appealing, but his mouth is set like steel—and his eyes are as hard as his mouth.

Character Analysis: Frankie Flannary is a mobster of Irish American descent who has no respect for his own people, not even his own family. He has given up on the joy of life, and is concerned only with himself and his position as mob boss. Even his wife and children are not of any real significance. They are a showcase, just like his beautiful home, far from the city his brother Jackie refuses to leave. Beneath the trappings of family and tradition, Frankie values nothing but his own safety and his continued success. Compassion, if ever he had any, has long since lost its meaning in Frankie's mind. He keeps a pair of hands from a corpse in his freezer to use on murder weapons for his own protection, and when his brother loses his composure and kills some rival mobsters, Frankie agrees that Jackie must die—and does the job himself. Terry Noonan, one of Frankie's old pals, is now an undercover police officer. Terry is fond of Kate, Frankie's sister, but Frankie turns her against his former friend. Terry, realizing it was Frankie who killed Jackie, shoots it out with Frankie's mob, and Frankie loses everything at Terry's hands. Whether under duress or not, Frankie has murdered his own brother, instead of facing consequences for himself, and it is Frankie who must pay the final price for his lack of feeling and compassion for those who are closest to him.

MAMA FRATELLI

Film Source: *The Goonies*
Release Date: 1985
Director: Richard Donner
Production company: Warner Bros.
Color
Running Time: 114 minutes
Performed by: Anne Ramsey
Additional Performer: John Matuszak (Sloth).

Physical Description: Mama Fratelli's stylish dress, gloves, *chapeau*, and creamy pearls are incongruous attire—for a woman with a tattoo of a dragon on her arm. She is over fifty, but her hair is still of a becoming and youthful tint. Her husky voice is her most unforgettable quality, featuring an abruptness which insists on obedience from all within hearing distance. Mama must have had a comely visage at some point in her life, but it has now hardened into a gnarled travesty, marred more by her unseemly deportment than by the natural aging process.

Character Analysis: Mama makes all the decisions in the Fratelli family, and she brooks no objections from her offspring. Following her son's successful jail break, Mama employs her notable driving skills to lead the police on a tortuous chase through city streets and down a beach. She infiltrates an all terrain race in her four-wheel drive vehicle, and loses the authorities by using her quick wits. Mama and her sons join a group of children who are seeking a pirate's hidden treasure and she becomes quite intrigued by the tales of riches she hears from one of them. Displeased by the reticence of the usually talkative child, she threatens to place his hand in a blender unless he tells her more about the treasure for which his small band is searching. Mama's talent for intimidation makes the child divulge every petty offense he has ever committed. During a manic chase through an underground cavern, Mama compels her sons onward toward a buccaneer ship loaded with precious jewels and gold doubloons which the children have discovered. Once on the ship, she forces one small child to walk the plank at swordpoint. Monomaniacal about capturing this prize, she orders her sons to eliminate the children, scolding them as if they are little boys instead of grown men. One of the sons, who is physically and mentally challenged, defies her in order to save the children. Once the children escape, the Fratellis emerge from the watery cavern to find themselves under arrest. Mama Fratelli is defined by her barbed tongue, sullen manner, and felonious behavior. If she has chosen an unprincipled life of crime, her example has had one beneficial consequence. While his brothers have modeled themselves after Mama, Sloth, the son who defies her to help the children, has attained a portion of virtue despite the conditions of his upbringing. From a story by Steven Spielberg.

FREDDY KRUEGER

Film Sources: *A Nightmare on Elm Street*; *A Nightmare on Elm Street 2: Freddy's Revenge*; *A Nightmare on Elm Street 3: Dream Warriors*; *A Nightmare on Elm Street 4: The Dream Master*; *A Nightmare on Elm Street 5: The Dream Child*; *Freddy's Dead: The Final Nightmare*; *Wes Craven's New Nightmare*.
Release Dates: 1984; 1985; 1987; 1988; 1989; 1991; 1994.
Focus: *A Nightmare on Elm Street*; *A Nightmare on Elm Street 3: Dream Warriors*
Directors: Wes Craven; Chuck Russell
Production Company: New Line Cinema
Color
Running Times: 92 minutes, 96 minutes
Performed by: Robert Englund

Additional Performers: Heather Langenkamp (Nancy Thompson), Patricia Arquette (Kristen), Amanda Wyss (Tina), Craig Wasson (Dr. Gordon).

Physical Description: Freddy Krueger's face and body are covered with scarred, puckered skin, the result of the horrible fire which killed him. Freddy is most often attired in a filthy, ragged, sweater, dark pants, and a tattered fedora, which hides his baldness. He has forged for himself a razor-studded glove which can be used as a unique weapon, since each blade can be flexed like a separate digit. Freddy remains unperturbed by the putrid condition of his teeth, leering out at those he assaults. His raspy voice and laugh portend annihilation to his victims, and his slight frame belies his superhuman might. His movements are sudden, yet fluid, resembling those of an eccentric dancer—leaping about the "stage" of his world in haphazard fashion.

Character Analysis: In his *Satires*, Juvenal insisted that "Revenge is the poor delight of little minds."[5] Freddy Kreuger, deceased son of a nurse raped by criminally insane prisoners housed in the psychiatric wing of a hospital, is just such a "small-minded entity." The former janitor was a child murderer in life, and his continued brutality after death can be interpreted as the unendurable manifestation of real and imagined fear that sometimes extends from youth into adulthood. The horror and morbidity of Freddy Krueger echoes many sorrowful and terrifying parallels in history. Through an arcane, supernatural circumstance, his obsessive desire to torture and kill has prevailed. His insatiable vengeance against those who set him on fire is now being visited upon their innocent teenage children, whom he stalks by invading their dreams. Freddy's sick humor contrives nightmares from his victim's most profound fears. In one of the least excusable of these grisly dreams he transforms himself into a mammoth snake, intent on devouring whole the unusually gifted Kristen. Freddy's absolute comprehension of the effects his nightmare visits have on each person is invaluable to him, and he derives satisfaction from his *own* pain, partly from his brashness, yet still more from his worship of agony to the point of death. The undaunted Nancy Thompson, Freddy's most estimable opponent, is an exception in this malignant game, until she, too, succumbs, when Freddy appears as her father. Freddy stabs her, but Nancy musters all her remaining strength—and plunges his razors into his chest. Dr. Gordon, a psychiatrist who accepts Nancy's story that Freddy is real, provides the final stroke by interring the killer's bones (his mother had become a nun before her death, thus setting in motion the efficacy of sacramental rites and relics against her son's evil spirit). Freddy lacked respect for others as an outgrowth of his own lack of self-respect, and he never knew love because he himself had none to give. Had he respected others or known love during his lifetime he might have found peace in his death, but Freddy saw his violent behavior as a special "talent," one that he exercised with care and precision. Since his talent was for destruction alone, the value he could have achieved in life has been swallowed up whole—by the nightmare he created for himself.

GEKKO: SEE: GORDON GEKKO

GEORGE STARK

Film Source: *The Dark Half*
Release Date: 1991
Director: George Romero
Production Company: Orion Pictures
Color
Running Time: 121 minutes
Performed by: Timothy Hutton (who also plays Thad Beaumont).

Physical Description: George Stark grabs the immediate attention of anyone he meets, with slicked-back hair, twinkling eyes, and a charming southern accent. In his thirties, he is tall, lean, and strong. But lately he finds himself deteriorating, his body developing sores and wounds, since he has taken on the identity of "George Stark"—while still remaining connected to his dual counterpart, "Thad Beaumont."

Character Analysis: George Stark (*i.e.*, Thad Beaumont) is at the center of this study (from a novel by veteran horror writer Stephen King), which examines the theoretical duality of personality—a concept embodied in such diverse characters as "Mr. Hyde" and the "Cenobite Leader (*q.v.*)." As a preadolescent, Thad Beaumont underwent an operation which revealed the presence of a twin fetus, still active and functioning within his brain, which the doctors attempted to cut away and remove, apparently with success. Now Thad has become an adult, a college professor, and is attempting to establish himself as a writer. He has little success, however, until he develops an alter ego under the pseudonym "George Stark," whose coarse, "rough-and-tumble" detective novels make Thad a bestselling literary sensation. Thad is contacted by an extortionist who claims to know Thad's "secret" about George Stark, who is, indeed, Thad's "evil twin." Rather than pay the man his "hush money," Thad goes public, burying "George Stark" in a mock funeral during a "photo op" session arranged by his publisher. George won't stay "dead," however. He returns following this bizarre interment, and his wrath is as cold and swift as any depicted in "his" hardboiled books. George, a skillful tormentor, engineers the deaths of those around Thad in the most grisly fashions he can invent, systematically murdering Thad's agent, the photographer from the graveside ceremony, and incriminating Thad, who begins to fear for his family—and himself. George leaves "clues" for Thad, as though he were writing yet another suspense novel. The two meet in a final confrontation in Thad's home, where both entities can now judge just how intertwined their personalties have become. George demonstrates his power by outdoing his "twin" in a forced competition. He ties up Thad's wife, then allows the couple's young twin boys to roam free, placing them in physical danger as a storm brews outside the house, which has become a battleground within. Then, a weird phenomenon occurs, just as it did during the operation on Thad many years before. Millions of sparrows gather and carry George away into eternity, allowing Thad to triumph over his "dark" side. George was at first a creative influence on Thad, but rendered him nearly helpless during their final encounter. Once he had broken free of the bonds of Thad's mind, George became a person not fully realized, and a division in Thad's innermost self. George craved even more liberty to enjoy the "real life" he had been denied thus far, and it no longer mattered how creative his writing was. George sprang into his existence with an appetite for power over Thad and his family and friends. His negation of the human element, both in his detective novels and in his interactions with others, leads him down a path of no return to his final ruin.

GOLDFINGER: SEE: AURIC

GORDON GEKKO

Film Source: *Wall Street*
Release Date: 1987
Director: Oliver Stone
Production Company: Twentieth Century Fox
Color
Running Time: 124 minutcs
Performed by: Michael Douglas
Additional Performers: Charlie Sheen (Bud Fox), Martin Sheen (Carl Fox).

Physical Description: Gordon Gekko is in his mid-forties, with slicked back hair, and the fiery, bright eyes of a "player." His slim physique is complemented by his finely tailored suits, and his voice is a cool baritone. Gekko speaks with the full authority of the powerful position he holds on Wall Street.

Character analysis: Gordon Gekko, beneath his natty lapels, is the cream of corruption. He begins and ends his day in the pursuit of wholesale greed and, in fact, if a part of him ever cared about the morality of what he does, it was so long ago he cannot recall it. Gekko not only cherishes this attitude in himself, hc nurtures it in others with a vengeance. Bud Fox, an impressionable young stock broker-in-training, is just such a person. To seal their business relationship, Gekko sets the younger man up in style, even going so far as to "give" Bud his former lover. Gekko keeps promising Bud more of everything. He will do things for Bud, and Bud must reciprocate. Once Bud gets the "taste," it will never be enough. Bud gives Gekko "insider" information, putting him on to a fantastic deal, but recognizes his error too late. Bud's father, Carl Fox, learns that Gekko intends not merely to buy the airline which employs him, but to liquidate it, putting Carl and his friends out of work. Bud has done some shady things in the past, and he may have wanted to emulate Gekko, but in the end he retains his sense of dignity and self-worth. He acquires evidence against Gekko which will enable him to save his father's company from a shut-down. Gekko's true and remaining goal is "wheeling and dealing," the acquisition of material goods, and the power to be derived from such assets. He lives not to create—but to take, to use, and to abuse. He has no interest in the people he has destroyed. His empire is built on the carcasses of others, their crushed hopes, and their failed dreams. Gekko, a snarling, cursing brute of a man, cannot foresee his own downfall. He wanted the sun, the moon and the stars and finished with nothing.

GRAHAM MARSHALL

Film Source: *A Shock to the System*
Release Date: 1990
Director: Jan Egleson
Production Company: Corsair Pictures
Color
Running Time: 88 minutes
Performed by: Michael Caine
Additional Performers: Elizabeth McGovern (Stella Anderson), Swoosie Kurtz (Leslie Marshall), Peter Riegert (Robert Benham).

Physical Description: Graham Marshall is fiftyish, well-built, and attractive in an understated, offbeat way. His soft-spoken British accent has a touch of the "cockney" about it. He dresses well, though not above his means.

Character Analysis: Some people wish upon the stars, some read their horoscope daily, and others believe in "magic." Business executive Graham Marshall is an ordinary, mild-mannered individual who loves "magic. He believes he has murdered a homeless man in the subway through the use of the "magic" inside him, and, even though it was an accident, the incident transforms Graham into a remarkably serene and efficient murderer. So convinced is he of his "magic" powers in fact, that he takes matters into his own hands and proceeds to change his life as he wishes it to be. Graham is troubled by bills, a nagging wife, and the loss of an expected promotion at the office. He boobytraps the basement of his home, and succeeds in electrocuting his wife, Leslie, while he is away on a business trip. He murders Robert Benham, a business colleague, by trapping him in a boat explosion. He becomes involved with Stella Anderson, a kind young secretary who admires him, drugs her so she is unaware of what is happening, and makes love to her. Stella returns a cigarette lighter, the one piece of evidence that might convict him in Benham's murder, as a gesture of her love and respect. In return Graham sees that she's "promoted" out of town, thus removing her from the scene and out of his life. He engineers a plane crash which removes his competition, and assumes control of the company. Graham, a man for whom deception was out of the question just a short time before, quickly learns methods of trickery and illusive behavior. He has become an insidious "magician" in his mind, extending his expertise into the real world around him for his own pleasure and advancement. If he had not been passed over for the coveted promotion, he reasons, none of this would have happened. It was all a matter of necessity. He was pushed into doing what he did, just as the transient was pushed into the path of the subway car. None of this is true, of course, since Graham made the choice himself to murder those who aggravated him and made his life tedious, and to get rid of those who stood in his way. Graham's "magic" is the treacherous nature which lay hidden beneath the surface of his native decency. It took just a push and he rolled off the edge into a realm of sanguinary deportment. A desperate need for what has been denied him and a driving desire to wield power is the catalyst in Graham Marshall's life. At the end, he smiles contentedly, happy in his corporate tower above the multitude, and no longer the gentle, caring man he used to be.

GRAYCE: SEE: EARLY GRAYCE

GREENHILL: SEE: DAVID GREENHILL

GRIFFIN MILL

Film Source: *The Player*
Release Date: 1992
Director: Robert Altman
Production Company: Avenue Pictures
Color
Running Time: 124 minutes
Performed by: Tim Robbins
Additional Performers: Greta Scacchi (June), Cynthia Stevenson (Bonnie), Vincent D'Onofrio (David).

Physical Description: Griffin Mill's boyish good looks, impressive height, and vibrant baritone voice are all the ingredients he needs to attract attention in the Hollywood *milieu*. In his early thirties, Griffin's slender physique and stylishly groomed hair are accentuated by an expensive, fashionable wardrobe. Of all his assets, however, Griffin's quiet, unassuming manner of speech is his most charming attribute.

Character Analysis: Griffin Mill, a top producer in one of Hollywood's most prestigious studios, has, literally, made a "killing" in the movie industry. Griffin is a "schmoozer" who relishes his power and position, and makes a point of always having the last word. Beneath his charming surface, however, he is an offensive, inconsiderate rascal, devoid of even the least shred of human compassion or depth of spirit. For Griffin is a "feeder," using up and eating alive the subordinates who surround him, including a lovely young scriptreader, his devoted one-time lover, Bonnie. Griffin, in fact, has become a feared and unpopular figure on the studio lot and being neither stupid nor a fool, he becomes convinced that the studio bosses are preparing to usher him out. In the meantime, a far more sinister situation has arisen in the midst of his dilemma. Someone, whom Griffin believes to be disgruntled screenwriter David Kahane, has been sending anonymous letters to Griffin, threatening to further endanger his delicate position at the studio and even his life. Griffin arranges to meet David at a local movie theater and they retire to a bar for a drink. Outside in a nearby parking lot, they begin arguing, a scuffle ensues, and Griffin kills David unintentionally. Remorseful, Griffin becomes acquainted, then involved, with David's beautiful lover, June. Selecting the moment with care, Griffin confesses the accidental homicide to June while making love to her. Although he feels some regret over the incident, particularly as it relates to his own affairs, Griffin does not experience any sincere sympathy or compassion about David's death. June has no idea what a piece of scum her charming new beau really is, and eventually agrees to marry him. A witness comes forward and mistakenly identifies someone other than Griffin in a line-up, and he is "off the hook" for the murder. Griffin's real-life scenario mirrors, ironically, a current film project on which he is working at the studio. The film, which was written as a tragedy, is given an inevitable "happy ending" after being screened for a preview autdience, thus reflecting the way Griffin's "tragedy" resolves itself to his satisfaction in the end. If there is one thing Griffin knows how to do well, it is how to recover from a fumble and take advantage of events and people as opportunities present themselves. Given the right circumstances, he might even chew up his beloved June and spit her out. But Griffin never has to make that choice, at least not within the context of this film. He is posed, like a photograph, not a real person who suffers real consequences. June is a creative, aspiring, young artist who, in Griffin's hands, becomes a mere work of art herself, a fairy-tale princess instead of a real woman, a marriage partner for Griffin, and the expectant mother of their child. Griffin plays out the "role" of his life, as if he were a movie star acting in a film. While his shallowness is not, in and of itself, evil, the results of it can be. Griffin engineers his own life so it will "play well," and succeeds to produce his own "happy ending." He moves into the top position at the studio, and Bonnie, who objects to the latest withering of intellect and value in their mutual film project, is fired. Griffin has no consoling words for his former lover and confidante. His own perfect life is all set to roll before the cameras. In a final note of irony, Griffin hears from the real blackmailer, the person who actually had sent him the threatening letters. Not missing a beat, nor a chance at a high grossing script, Griffin listens as the man, who has guessed the truth, recounts the story of Griffin's foul deed and its aftermath. Griffin carefully promises the man he will take his story under full consideration. A top flight "player," who makes it all happen, Griffin paints his own world, like the pictures on June's canvas, then summons them into reality. As in that deft, immortal satire of Victorian society, Oscar Wilde's *The Picture of Dorian Gray*, Griffin Mill presents one form to the outside world, but, inside, he is a seething wretch, more adapted for the infernal regions than the exalted position in life he occupies.

GRUBER: SEE: HANS GRUBER

HANK QUINLAN

Film Source: *Touch of Evil*
Release Date: 1958
Director: Orson Welles
Production Company: Universal Pictures
B&W
Running Time: 108 minutes
Performed by: Orson Welles
Additional Performer: Charlton Heston (Vargas).

Physical Description: Hank Quinlan is a large, grossly obese man in his fifties. His ugly flattened nose makes his face appear all the broader for it. He is an imposing figure, in his typical, wrinkled "P.I." trenchcoat and hat. Quinlan's most memorable attribute may be his deep, rumbling voice—which can send a shiver of dread into the heart of the casual listener.

Character Analysis: Hank Quinlan, who has served many years as the police chief of a depressed border town between Mexico and the United States, complains that he has nothing more to show for his efforts than a small turkey ranch. His wife was murdered years before, and Quinlan had taken out his grief in drink. He reformed and abstained for twelve years, but "slips" again when current issues get out of hand. A local hero of sorts, he holds dominion over the police force and the towns-people, who dare not question any of his decisions or accusations. Quinlan has no regrets for the many innocent people whom he has helped convict to further his own career, or for the helpless souls he has seen éxecuted in order to keep his own record clean. He is so accustomed to fabricating evidence and lying about it, that he no longer knows the difference between truth and fiction, and does not know when to stop his fabrications for his own good. Quinlan's partner and lifelong supporter cannot believe ill of him, particularly when Quinlan took a bullet for him years before. Most recently Quinlan has set up an innocent man as a bombing suspect and, belatedly, the partner discovers the terrible truth about the ehief's activities. In the meantime, Vargas, a federal agent, and an out-of-towner, enters the scene on a routine narcotics matter. He and his new bride become involved in the local politics, and Quinlan takes advantage of the opportunity to frame Mrs. Vargas for the crime. Quinlan's partner threatens to disclose Quinlan's guilt, and is murdered by Quinlan who is, in turn, felled by another bullet. But no one feels any grief as he lays dying. Lies perpetuated by more lies have seen Quinlan through the best and worst of times, but they will not see him through the scrutiny of Vargas, who is not about to allow Quinlan to destroy his wife. Quinlan should have recognized the power of such devotion, since it had affected his own life so strongly. His perserverance toward crime and the criminals who killed his wife has been twisted into an implacable coldness toward life and the people he has sworn to serve, and has invested Quinlan with a bitter, cheerless spirit. He was at the top of the heap in the microcosmic world he inhabited, yet totally unaware of how much good he might have accomplished—if only he had remained an "honest cop."

DR. HANNIBAL LECTER

Film Sources: *Manhunter*; *The Silence of the Lambs*
Release Dates: 1986; 1991
Focus: *The Silence of the Lambs*
Director: Jonathan Demme
Production Company: Orion Pictures
Color
Running Time: 118 minutes
Performed by: Anthony Hopkins
Additional Performers: Jodie Foster (Clarice M. Starling), Ted Levine (Jamie Gumb).

Physical Description: Dr. Hannibal Lecter's intense pale eyes draw attention, burrowing deeply and inquisitively into everyone he meets. He has a nervous habit of combing back his thinning hair, and he leans forward a bit on the balls of his feet, when he speaks. His deliberately whisper-soft, low-key voice endows him with a magnetic quality. Although slender and slight of build, Dr. Lector, when under pressure, is capable of phenomenal brute force. Altogether, he is a fearsome and formidable individual.

Character Analysis: Dr. Hannibal Lecter, once a brilliant and renowned psychiatrist, now turned notorious serial killer, dwells in a territory of his own device, living out his life incarcerated in a special cell in a maximum security prison, where he has been placed as a result of the numerous, appalling crimes he has committed. Although his doctor considers him "a monster, a pure psychopath," Lecter believes he is "playing God," becoming more powerful each time he kills. Although he is a talented amateur artist, drawing charming pictures which he hangs in his cell, Lector revels in the disgusting, and has a sick and demented sense of humor which embodies both the captivating—and the horrific. He stands behind the safety glass of his cell, shielded from his visitors, but ready at a moment's notice to seize an opportunity to make his way to freedom. Drawn by curiosity to beautiful young FBI agent Clarice Starling, Lector tentatively agrees to help her in the identificaton and capture of "Buffalo Bill," a new serial killer on the rampage. He plays a cat-and-mouse game with Clarice for his own benefit, "setting her up" with false clues, and leading her on with real ones. Buffalo Bill kidnaps the daughter of a state senator who asks Lector's assistance, and agrees to his demands to be moved into a less secure facility. He makes a daring escape by disguising himself as a guard. Clarice puts herself in jeopardy by going after Buffalo Bill without backup. She succeeds iin rescuing the senator's daughter but, in the meantime, Lector has disappeared into the crowd. He places an untraceable phone call to Clarice, promising not to harm her—as long as she does not search for him. Lector has developed a "taste" for cannabalizing the body parts of his victims. For one moment only, he drops his artful degeneracy and reaches out to touch Clarice's hand as she takes a document he has offered for her use. This is a fleeting response, however. We last see him as he follows his former doctor into the crowd, already planning the man's demise. Beneath an outer façade of courtesy and refinement, Lector reeks of the charnel house. He has become a predatory beast whose sadistic butchery of the body and rape of the mind represent the ultimate titillation, bathing his own mind in bloody recollections of his distasteful crimes. Mannered and composed, Dr. Hannibal Lecter resembles a vulture, calmly contemplating the tableau of death before him. The darkest corner is where he makes his home, and he inhabits it in depraved gladness.

HANS GRUBER

Film Source: *Die Hard*
Release Date: 1988
Director: John McTiernan
Production Company: Twentieth Century Fox
Color
Running Time: 132 minutes
Performed by: Alan Rickman
Additional Performers: Bruce Willis (John McClane), Bonnie Bedelia (Holly McClane), Alexander Godunov (Karl), James Shigeta (Mr. Joseph Takagi).

Physical Description: Hans Gruber's charcoal gray trench coat, perfectly tailored suit, and black pullover vest announce the impeccable, regimented individual within, expressing his utmost regard for good taste and style. Gruber's well-tended hair, beard and moustache enhance the unusual curvature of his sneering lips. His voice is deliberate and modulated, and he possesses an uncanny knack for imitating accents. A distinct crease is etched between his eyebrows, above the bridge of his sloping nose. He stares down upon the world around him with jaundiced eyes. Something in the movements of his long, slender form implies the gracefulness of a dancer.

Character Analysis: A small child stands before an angry parent, hearing a sentence so familiar it has become a part of him, "I am going to count to three..." For Hans Gruber this routine scolding has continued into his adulthood, where he has used it more often than even he himself realizes. Gruber and his "associates" interrupt and take hostage a large group of people at a Christmas office party in a high-rise. He interrogates Mr. Takagi, an executive with the firm, looking for the code needed to open the company's safe. Takagi refuses to give out the crucial information, and Gruber repeats his "1-2-3..." mantra entrenched from his youth. Takagi glibly suggests Gruber carry out his threat, but is unprepared when, without hesitation or remorse, Gruber shoots Takagi in the forehead and tells his men to "dispose of that" body. Details fascinate Gruber, who is entranced with a model building he discovers outside the office where Takagi is killed. Along with his predilection for details, Gruber takes wicked delight in wielding his unrestricted authority over others. As he steps off the elevator into the office party, he obviously relishes the sight of the cringing group whom he deems tractable and defenseless. During a conversation with an obnoxious young executive, Gruber tires of the man and shoots him in the head without compunction, just as he has Mr. Takagi. Gruber is confronted by John McCLane, a police officer visiting his wife at the party, who divulges his hidden presence at Takagi's murder. When McClane will not return the detonators he needs for an intended explosion on the roof, Gruber, a dissembler *nonpareil*, enacts a crafty impersonation of an escaped hostage for John, who compliments his opponent on his believable accent. Gruber argues with Karl, his next-in-command, about their plans, and when those plans go awry, Gruber sets off the deadly explosives, even though he knows Karl will be killed. Gruber, beneath his suavity, intellectuality, and virulent behavior, is timid when challenged by a parental figure. Holly Gennaro (who is, unbeknownst to Gruber, Mrs. McClane) insists on the reasonable treatment of the other hostages, and Gruber, in a moment of vulnerability, consents. Gruber is unaware of Holly's true identity, but turns savage when she is identified during a television news interview with her children. Gruber orders all the hostages but Holly to the roof, where he has already scheduled their deaths in a rooftop explosion. He takes Holly into the now-open vault where he and his "associates" toss millions in negotiable bonds into satchels. Holly calls him a "common thief," and he jumps at her, proclaiming himself instead to be an "exceptional thief." He taunts her by reminding her he has now become a kidnapper as well. His implacable faith in his own shrewdness dooms him when he becomes convinced John McClane is unarmed. Gruber drags Holly through an open window where, wounded and dying, he prevents himself from falling by holding on to Holly's wrist. As a final act of retribution, Gruber aims the gun in his free hand at John, smugly certain he will be able to kill both John and Holly before he himself falls to his own death. Gruber glances upward at the last moment and, too late, sees John loosen Holly's watch from his hand—and Gruber descends slowly onto the concrete far below. Gruber has journied from the self-evident heavy discipline of his youth through time spent in a radical political group, learning volumes about severity and manipulation as he went. Gruber's quest for the millions at his fingertips remains subordinate, when compared with his overwhelming eagerness to control those around him, "1-2-3...."

HARKONNEN: SEE: VLADIMIR HARKONNEN

HARRY AND MARV

Film Sources: *Home Alone*; *Home Alone 2: Lost in New York*
Release Dates: 1990; 1992
Director: Chris Columbus
Production Company: Twentieth Century Fox
Color
Running Times: 110 minutes; 120 minutes
Performed by: Joe Pesci and Daniel Stern
Additional Performer: Macaulay Culkin (Kevin).

Physical Description: Harry and Marv are opposites. Harry is short, while Marv is tall. Marv has a beard, moustache, and curly dark hair, but Harry is clean-shaven and has much less hair than his partner. Harry has a high-pitched voice, Marv has a low one. They dress similarly, however, in the heavy, old coats and dark pants suitable to their trade. Harry's favorite added touch is a stocking cap.

Character Analysis: Harry and Marv are an inseparable duo, distinguishable only by their undistinguished actions. They have been labeled "wet bandits" by the police because of Mary's consistent habit of leaving the water on in the homes they rob. Undistinguished or not, they both love their profession, and each one considers himself to be a master thief. Harry and Marv are doomed to meet their match, however, in the unlikely person of Kevin, a youngster who has been left home alone accidentally, when his family goes abroad for Christmas. Kevin, delighted at first with his new-found freedom, is horrified when he realizes Harry and Marv are planning to break in and rob what they believe to be an empty house. His fear quickly fades once he realizes how really stupid they are. Harry and Marv, upon discovering Kevin's presence, are thoroughly convinced they can take on the child and win easily in a game of wits. They threaten Kevin with bodily harm but, after a series of hilarious confrontations, he is rescued by an elderly neighbor and the bemused thieves are hauled off to jail. In the sequel, Harry and Marv have escaped from prison, and in a coincidence which defies credulity, they happen on to Kevin again—in New York City, where he has been diverted by mistake while on a flight with his family. After another series of pranks, adventures, and threats on his life, Kevin is rescued by the kindly old "bird" woman who resides in Central Park. Harry, who is much more ferocious and vengeful in his animosity than Marv, will not be told what to do, think, or say. Marv, who is the more docile (and stupid) of the two, willingly follows Harry's lead. Their true nature surfaces when they rob a toy store on Chrismas Eve, taking money they know is meant for a children's charity. They have no less contempt for Kevin than they did before, and he is just as adept at luring them into a trap as he was the first time out. Although their main goal is the robbery of countless homes, they have shown themselves to be decidedly unsavory, allowing no one to stand in their way, even the helpless child whom they threaten with genuine bodily harm. They are caught once more, and jail is their next stop after their encounter with Kevin. This is the one place they do not want to stay, yet it is the one where they most belong.

HARRY ROAT, JR.

Film Source: *Wait Until Dark*
Release Date: 1967

Director: Terence Young
production company: Warner Seven Arts
Color
Running Time: 108 minutes
Performed by: Alan Arkin
Additional Performers: Audrey Hepburn (Suzy), Richard Crenna (Mike), Jack Weston (Carlino), Samantha Jones (Lisa).

Physical Description: Harry Roat, Jr. is a nondescript man of medium height and build, with short, dark hair and an oval face. He wears gloves, a leather jacket, dark glasses, sometimes a hat—and his shoes squeak inconveniently. He calls his stiletto "Geraldine," an indication of its importance to him. He speaks smoothly, in an icy baritone, and he is physically strong, although his appearance does not indicate it. He is deft at changing his appearance through the art of disguise.

Character Analysis: Harry Roat's cynical perversions have left him with a negative set of values. Detail oriented, Harry permits no one into his life, and it is likely he has no close friendships. When a colleague accidentally brushes against his shoulder, Harry pulls away and shouts at the man angrily. It is not even certain that his name is really "Harry Roat, Jr." Harry's control over his existence begins to unravel when a lucrative shipment of heroin, concealed inside a doll, is handed off in error to an unsuspecting traveler, a photographer on his way home from Europe. Harry, a petty gangster who is responsible for the shipment, contrives an intricate plan for its return. He hires thugs, Mike and Carlino, to help him find and acquire the missing doll, and they gain access to the photographer's apartment while he and his wife are out. Harry touches nothing after he removes his heavy, black gloves except the items he has brought with him, and he puts out his cigarette in a glass jar to disguise the odor, as he hides the evidence of his visit. A corpse is discovered in a closet. It is Lisa, a cohort. Harry has "offed" her, and her torn blouse denotes something more sinister than just a brief struggle between them. Harry threatens to mention the fingerprints the thugs have left everywhere in the apartment and they agree to obtain the doll for Harry—*and* remove Lisa's body. Harry cleans his sunglasses with an article of clothing belonging to Suzy, the photographer's blind wife, inhaling her scent deeply. But passion is not linked with tenderness or affection for the unreasonable, seething Harry. Suzy blunders into their scheme and although she is sightless, she quickly becomes suspicious of the three men and their demands that she produce the doll. She confides in Mike that she believes Harry is as much interested in doing "evil things" as he is in retrieving the heroin. She attempts to divert them to her husband's office where, she assures them, they will find the missing doll. Before leaving, however, Harry cuts her phone cord, planning to return and make a thorough search.

Sickened by Harry's callousnes, Mike and Carlino determine to kill him, but he is too smart for them, and murders them brutally instead. In the meantime Suzy, who is no fool, boobytraps her basement apartment in anticipation of just such a turn of events. She breaks all the lights and closes the shutters, leaving it in total darkness, and giving her the advantage over Harry who can't see in the dark. She knows Harry has returned when she hears his squeaky shoes, a dead giveaway. Harry douses the rug with gasoline and lights a torch. He speaks to Suzy in a pleasant, sardonic tone of voice, asking if she understands what he is doing, and taking tremendous delight in his control over the situation. Terrified, Suzy begs him to stop, but Harry proves her original assessment of him to be correct, and continues to torment her. They fight back and forth and the advantage changes several times, before Suzy, in a last desperate attempt to save herself, throws the remaining gasoline on Harry, and begins lighting matches. To her horror, however, Harry opens her refrigerator door, giving himself needed light, and finally convincing Suzy that she must give up the doll to him. He promises Suzy he will not hurt her, but he pushes her into the bedroom, his intentions clear. She stabs him with a kitchen knife and makes for the door, but Roat has chained it shut. Back in the kitchen, in one of filmdom's most horrifying moments, Harry, whom Suzy has thought to be dead, seizes her ankle. She finally finds the refrigerator plug, and plunges the room back into darkness just in time. Harry, who has everything going for him, expires, losing to a blind woman, who has no defense but her stalwart will. The police arrive with Suzy's husband to save her, but they do not recognize "Harry Roat, Jr." Unloved and unloving, he has severed all ties with others through his ingrained, remorseless behavior. His dehumanization of others is forced back upon him in death, since neither the authorities, nor Suzy and her husband, know anything more about Harry than the brutal acts he has performed. Based on the stage play by Frederick Knott.

HEDLEY LAMARR

Film Source: *Blazing Saddles*
Release Date: 1974
Director: Mel Brooks
Production Company: Warner Bros.
Color
Running Time: 93 minutes
Performed by: Harvey Korman
Additional Performers: Cleavon Little (Bart), Gene Wilder (The Waco Kid), Slim Pickens (Taggart), Madeline Kahn (Lily).

Physical Description: Hedley Lamarr dresses for success—and corrobative evidence to that fact abounds. His ruffled shirts and flashy, finely tailored suits, label him as quite the dandy. He sports distinguished, graying hair, and flashes a crafty smile beneath his waxed moustache. His speech, flowery, and saturated with a profusion of colorful adjectives, recalls that of a blackguard in some Victorian melodrama—and is quite suitable for the successful politician he purports to be. No one values Lamarr's schemes more profoundly, or laughs at his jokes more uproariously than he does.

Character Analysis: Hedley Lamarr's multiple positions in the state government (most amusingly, as state "procurer") all fall short of allowing him to control Rock Ridge, the small western town through which the railroad is destined to run—and where property values will soon double. Lamarr, aided by his henchman, dull railroad foreman Taggart, is willing to use violence against the beleaguered community. Lamarr's avarice and greed are only surpassed by his uncanny efficacy at prevarication. Bart, a Black railroad worker, has been sentenced to hang. Lamarr rescues him from the gallows, and installs him as the new sheriff of Rock Ridge, whose prejudiced townspeople, Lamarr hopes, will devise an untimely end for the unsuspecting Bart. Lamarr seeks to utterly demoralize the people of Rock Ridge through this act, and thus confiscate their land. Lily, Lamarr's dazzling spy, falls in love with Bart, instead of betraying him. Furious, Lamarr ties her up and slaps her around. He further elevates his pettiness to an art form while interviewing outlaws for his private army, when he startles Bart by pointlessly shooting a desperado without hesitation. He is so impressed by his own talent for evil, in fact, that he orders his mercenary recruits to pledge allegiance to him, as they would to the government. Lamarr faces Bart in a gun duel, but claims he has no weapon. Hedley has "cried wolf" once too often, however. He realizes his deception is fatal, when Bart shoots him anyway, unarmed or not. Lamarr's pompousness and snobbery have made him a ridiculous figure, but his casual brutality evokes a ticklish shiver of disquiet among those who have taken him for granted.

HELEN SHARP—SEE: MADELINE ASHTON

HOCHMAN: SEE: KARL HOCHMAN

DOC HOPPER

Film Source: *The Muppet Movie*
Release Date: 1979
Director: James Frawley
Production Company: CBS/Fox Company
Color
Running Time: 94 minutes

Performed By: Charles Durning
Additional Performers: Jim Henson (voice of Kermit The Frog), Frank Oz (voice of Animal)

Physical Description: Doc Hopper hides a distinctive head of gray hair under his white hat. Heavy set, and clad in a suit of white, accentuated by a black, string tie, he artfully disguises his predacity. His charming outer persona is augmented by a classic southern twang.

Character Analysis: Doc Hopper's glib style might fool the general populace, but he encounters some deft opposition in the ordinarily ingenuous Kermit the Frog. Hopper is obsessed with the idea of making Kermit, who can sing and ride a bicycle, the spokesperson for his "frog leg" fast food chain. Unfortunately for Kermit, Hopper's enthusiasm for the project leads him to treat the astounding frog miserably. Kermit is initially intrigued with the offer of $500 per year, but he agonizes over all the frogs Doc Hopper's enterprise has left on crutches. Kermit rejects Doc, not once, but twice, and Hopper determines to chase Kermit down and "exterminate" the hapless frog. Hopper, now angry, enlists the services of a depraved madman, in an unsuccessful attempt to turn Kermit's brain into mush. Hopper's "requests" become ultimatums—and his "ultimatums" degenerate into pure coercion. Kermit finally confronts Hopper with the reality that he is a friendless egotist, but Doc still wants Kermit dead. Doc hires a frog killer in one last effort to bully Kermit, but his violent aims are halted by Kermit's anomalous companion, "Animal." Doc Hopper and his hired guns flee. Each time he is outwitted by Kermit and his friends, Doc's perverse sense of humor twists around and nips him. His self-involvement and obstreperousness only serve to dramatize his absurdity even further, but it is his basic cowardice that becomes the icing on the ill-natured cake of his personality. A man who browbeats and torments vulnerable creatures such as Kermit and his friends cannot be regarded as brave. If Doc Hopper ever had any honor or integrity, he long ago lost them in the "swamp" of his own cruelty and deceit.

MR. HYDE

Film Source: *Dr. Jekyll and Mr. Hyde*
Release Dates: 1920; 1932; 1941
Focus: 1920 film version
Director: John S. Robertson
Production Company: Famous Players-Lasky Corporation
B&W
Running Time: 63 minutes
Performed by: John Barrymore (both Jekyll and Hyde)
Additional Performer: Nita Naldi (Gina).

Physical Description: Dr. Jekyll has produced, through experimentation, an alter ego, "Mr. Hyde." Hyde, who does not resemble the good doctor in the slightest, wears a broad-brimmed hat over tangled, shoulder-length hair and carries a walking stick to assist in his slouching gait. Hyde's leering stare, elongated, gnarled fingers, and distorted form, introduce a most alarming individual.

Character Analysis: Mr. Hyde, since he possesses only the vilest of attributes, is absent of any redeeming features. Dr. Jekyll, who is studying human personality, conducts experiments which have resulted in the doctor's ability to separate, chemically, man's good from his evil nature. Jekyll, albeit with the most laudable of intentions, has inadvertently released the iniquity buried deep inside him, in the persona of "Mr. Hyde." As Hyde, he roughly seizes and kisses a woman on a whim, then knocks down a child in the street, as if he were nothing more than an apple cart. Continuing his disreputable behavior, Hyde becomes intimately involved with Gina, a lovely young dancer, who permits herself to be drawn into Hyde's snare. He keeps her prisoner in a room until he tires of her, then, when she has fallen into a wretched state, Hyde humiliates her and causes her ruination. Jekyl, as Hyde, illustrates to what depths a man can descend without the normal human inhibitions to restrain him. Jekyll unexpectedly transforms into Hyde before his startled prospective father-in-law, then falls upon the unsuspecting man and kills him. Unappeased, Hyde compounds his bestial behavior by beating the expired man's corpse, then laying hands on the doctor's shocked betrothed. Jekyll, conscious that he has been completely subsumed by Hyde, drinks poison, and Hyde meets his death as savagely as he confronted life. Hyde, as his name implies, is the concealed side of human nature, out of view, but ever there, hidden in the shadows of man's psyche. He is the flame that attracts, then scorches the unwitting moth. His virulence, like broken glass strewn across the floor of a darkened room, awaits the unwary. Dr. Jekyll took extraordinary measures to unleash "Mr. Hyde," but such evil natures have been released in the past—often through quite ordinary means. Barrymore's extraordinary performance, changing characters without makeup, remains one of filmdom's most remarkable feats.

IRENE (RITA) TWAIN

Film Source: *Murder by Death*
Release Date: 1976
Director: Robert Moore
Production Company: Columbia Pictures
Color
Running Time: 95 minutes
Performed By: Nancy Walker

Additional Performers: Truman Capote (Lionel Twain), James Coco (Monsieur Perrier).

Physical Description: Irene Twain is diminutive in size, but not in intellect. Although she is endowed with a luxuriant, shoulder-length page-boy, Irene does not have the classic profile of a cover girl, and her raucous laugh and husky contralto voice vie with her deceptive appearance of fragility.

Character Analysis: Irene Twain shows an independence of thought and action not unlike her late father, author Lionel Twain. In fact, if Irene (or the more glamorous-sounding "Rita," as she prefers to be known), were handed the instructions for assembling a complicated piece of equipment, she would probably toss them away, get to work, and finish the project at meteoric speed. Irene has plotted the downfall of her father's colleagues, the world's most celebrated mystery writers, both for monetary gain and, perhaps even more importantly, for her own amusement. To put her plan in motion, Irene has forged her deceased father's signature on invitations to her victims for a weekend of "dinner and a murder" at the Twain mansion. To sweeten the pot, she offers a financial "reward" for the detective who correctly solves the murder. She impersonates her father vocally, and convinces Twain's blind butler that he is still alive. Once he fulfills his role in her masquerade, however, Irene stabs the venerable servant to death. Irene poses as her father at a carefully prepared banquet for her guests, then stages his "murder" at the table for their benefit. Each of them is first stunned, then baffled, when the body disappears from the room. Following an evening complicated with Irene's spurious horrors, the famous writers gather and attempt to provide the standard "drawing-room" dénouement for Twain's murder. Irene, impersonating first the butler, then her father, dismisses Monsieur Perrier with great aplomb, when he correctly accuses her of being Twain's daughter. Irene manages to explain away his theory, however, and the disgruntled writers bolt from Twain's residence in disgrace. Alone at last, as she relishes her sardonic victory, Irene peels off her mask and rejoices in the triumph of her ruse. Her separation from others is a self-inflicted loneliness which defines her as a person. Perrier is correct when he states that Irene's brilliant mind, hidden beneath a plain exterior, has inevitably steered her toward misanthropy. Her acumen, which has led her to humiliate and discredit her late father's colleagues and to murder his lifelong butler, belittles Irene as well. Irene has twisted her grasp at happiness into a grimy farce, the corroded amusement of a despondent mind. Her emotional growth trammeled by the superficiality of those around her, Irene has been left with only one train of thought in mind, that of crushing the dignity of those around her until she feels appeased. From a delightful script by veteran playwright Neil Simon.

IVY

Film Source: *Poison Ivy*
Release Date: 1992
Director: Andy Ruben
Production Company: New Line Productions
Color
Running Time: 91 minutes
Performed by: Drew Barrymore
Additional Performer: Sara Gilbert (Silvie "Coop" Cooper).

Physical Description: Ivy is a beautiful young teenager with blond hair, soft features—and the well-developed figure of an experienced woman. She dresses distinctively in clothes, including a pair of well-worn riding boots, designed to accentuate both her beauty and her individuality. Her sweet, melodious voice has a seductive quality which charms the listener into believing her nature is equally innocent.

Character Analysis: "Evil, however powerful it seemed, could be undone by its own appetite," suggests horror writer Clive Barker in his fable *The Thief of Always*.[4] Beautiful young Ivy has just such an appetite and, just as Barker warns, her hunger foreshadows her eventual ruination. Ivy's designs are less grandiose than those of either the Emperor Ming or Baron Vladimir Harkonnen (*q.v.*), but her appetite is as all-consuming as theirs. She longs for a family, but her means of "acquiring" one are surreptitious. Ivy, who is enrolled in a scholarship program at a private school, meets and makes friends with another lonely student, Silvie "Coop" Cooper. She claims that her mother died addicted to cocaine, and her father has abandoned her. Up until now, Ivy says, she has been living with an aunt for whom she has no profound attachment. Silvie's mother, a beautiful woman in her late thirties, is an invalid with emphysema who remains sequestered in her room most of the time. Silvie's father is a wealthy man who is lost in sorrow over his wife's tenuous condition. Ivy understands, as Silvie does not, that this is a most providential meeting, and one which will have grave consequences in Silvie's young life. Ivy begins to insinuate herself into her "new" family, and makes herself right at home, using everyone she meets. Silvie, who is shy and lonely, admires Ivy's risk-taking bent, and is flattered at her attention. She buys Ivy clothes and convinces her parents to let Ivy move in with them. Once in the house, Ivy formulates a plot to seduce Silvie's father and remove her mother from the picture. Sylvie's father has difficulty resisting the temptation Ivy puts before him, and eventually succumbs to her charms and allows her to take complete control over his life. Silvie ferrets out Ivy's deception, but it is already too late, for her "friend" has thrown Sylvie's mother from the second-storey bedroom window, made love to her father, and has blamed Silvie for a devastating car accident which she herself caused. Ivy even wins over the affection of the family dog by placing special treats in her pocket. Such displays of power mean a lot to Ivy, and are proof to her that she will always have the means to get whatever she wants. Silvie, who has suffered a concussion in the car accident and is still suffering hallucinations, slips out of the hospital and finds her father together with Ivy in a "compromising" position. Ivy poses as Sylvie's mother, and assuages Silvie's fears for a few minutes. The two become embroiled in a bitter struggle and Silvie's father returns from searching for her to find Ivy dead in the street, the victim of the same kind of "accident" as Sylvie's mother. Even her unhappy childhood cannot account for Ivy's heinous, unscrupulous behavior. Ivy is a daredevil who has allowed her troubled past sway over her present life, grasping by the throat the family who took her in and gave her food, clothes, and their respect. Deep inside she is jealous of Silvie, her family, and their wealth, and her aim is the subordination of each of them. Silvie continues to miss her friend long after her death, in spite of Ivy's betrayal, since she sees her as a solitary figure like herself. Their affinity in this, however significant, does not change or excuse Ivy, whose name, coined by Silvie and accepted by "Ivy," is as counterfeit as her friendship and devotion.

JACK LINT

Film Source: *Brazil*
Release Date: 1985
Director: Terry Gilliam
Production Company: Embassy International Pictures
Color
Running Time: 131 minutes
Performed by: Michael Palin
Additional Performer: Jonathan Pryce (Sam Lowry).

Physical Description: Jack Lint, an average-looking man in his thirties, has pleasant features which lend his rather commonplace face an almost amusing quality. He is slender, has short brown hair, somewhat prominent ears, and a pair of flashing eyes. His low tenor voice has a silly, lilting tone.

Character Analysis: From all outward appearances, Jack Lint is a decent, happy family man, and father of triplet girls, who pops up at every social event. Inside, though, he is a competent torturer for the totalitarian government he serves "best." Perhaps it should be "worst"—for Jack has no misgivings about what he does, even if his actions result in someone's death. In fact, Jack believes he is performing a service for his government, and refers to his victims as "customers." It is all quite matter-of-fact to him, not in the least objectionable or disconcerting, and he even allows one of his daughters to join him while he performs his specialty of extracting confessions. Jack is at home in the alternate reality of the film, where the government is inundated with paperwork and bureaucratic administrators. When Jack makes the mistake of interrogating the wrong party, the man suffers a fatal heart attack, and Jack feels no compunction about covering up his "mistake." He is "ruffled," however, when he is told to interrogate a friend, kind, mild Sam Lowry. Jack begins his work wearing a ridiculous mask, but Sam, who has caught Jack in the midst of his dirty work, recognizes him. They exchange words, but Jack is in no mood to listen to Sam's pleas, and Sam makes his escape by leaping mentally into an alternate world of his own. Jack, who does not possess Sam's imagination, keeps on doing his job as usual, since it serves him so well. Jack's narrow focus and disregard for the consequences of the authoritarianism he abets have trapped him in the mire of his world. He is not the jovial, innocuous fellow seen at social occasions. Jack is nothing more than a sinister worker for his government's restriction and control. Jack takes no responsibility for his actions, which allows him to continue without compunction. Still, Jack is no fool—surely the "inner" man comprehends fully the effect his "work" has on the world around him.

JACK NAPIER—SEE—THE JOKER

JACK WILSON

Film Source: *Shane*
Release Date: 1953
Director: George Stevens
Production Company: Paramount
Color
Running Time: 117 minutes
Performed by: Jack Palance
Additional Performer: Alan Ladd (Shane).

Physical Description: Jack Wilson is a lean gunman with the sharp eyes so beneficial to his infamous calling. His head is crowned with the ubiquitous wide-brimmed black hat. He is clad like a working cowboy, in black vest, long-sleeved checked shirt, and pants partially hidden by dark boots. Wilson's stark demeanor and deliberate walk, along with his gravelly voice and coarse laugh, give him a decided advantage over the majority of those he meets in combat.

Character Analysis: Jack Wilson is a hired gun and he makes no secret of the fact, choosing instead to announce it in every gesture. His presence cannot be dismissed, but not many wish to make his acquaintance, since it is obvious his profession is criminal in nature. A wealthy rancher has brought Wilson to town to frighten the local farmers away from their property. Wilson waits for one of the homesteaders outside the local general store and saloon, then he baits him into a gun duel he knows the farmer can't win. The other farmers realize he intends the same fate for them, and must decide whether or not to leave the valley, or stay and fight the rancher and Wilson. Shane is a former gunman who has left behind his violent past. He befriends one of the families involved in the struggle against the rancher's oppression. Aware of Wilson's method, Shane knocks out his friend rather than allow him to be lured into a gunfight with Wilson in town. Sullen, terse, unbending, Wilson sits and watches Shane's entrance into the saloon late at night. Wilson's deliberate manner and fast draw are no match for Shane's expertise. Shane and Wilson, opposing sides of the same coin, have both led turbulent lives. Shane is unselfish enough to sacrifice his peaceful life in order to save his new-found friends. Wilson, who insists on pursuing his lawless occupation to the bitter end, dies in the same vicious manner in which he has lived. Under a shroud of iniquity, Wilson's nonchalant acceptance of who and what he has become causes shivers in the observer. In the end, morbidity has become Wilson's way of life—and death.

JARRETT: SEE: CODY JARRETT

JASON: SEE: DAVID JASON

JESSEP: SEE: COLONEL NATHAN R. JESSEP

JOHN WHORFIN

Film Source: *The Adventures of Buckaroo Banzai Across the Eighth Dimension*
Release Date: 1984
Director: W. D. Richter
Production Company: Sherwood Productions, Inc.
Color
Running Time: 103 minutes
Performed by: John Lithgow
Additional Performers: Peter Weller (Buckaroo Banzai), Ellen Barkin (Penny Pretty).

Physical Description: "John Whorfin" of Planet Ten is one half of the two entities housed within the body of scientist Dr. Emilio Lizardo.

Whorfin's wild hair stands on end, an electrified frizz, and his day-old beard frames rotting teeth. He thrusts his shoulders upward strangely, yet slumps when he walks, like the alien he is. He flaunts a swarm of medals on his gray overcoat worn over a white shirt, tie, suspenders, and pants, and sports a pair of grimy fingerless mitts on his hands. His voice is a composite of Dr. Lizardo's Italian accent and John Whorfin's cacophonous bellowing, and approximates a bassoon played off key. Whorfin/Lizardo's most unforgettable features are his lunatic eyes—which miss nothing.

Character Analysis: "Lord" John Whorfin's self-proclaimed title is repudiated in a holographic recording of one of the members of the group who opposed his ironhanded rule on Planet Ten many years before. Whorfin and his followers, known as the "red lectroids," had been overthrown and assigned to the eighth dimension by the "black lectroids" of his home world. In 1938, Earth scientist Dr. Emilio Lizardo, while conducting an experiment on dimensional transference, had inadvertently contacted the "red lectroids" in their prison in the eighth dimension (an event "documented," according to Banzai, by Orson Welles' infamous *War of the Worlds* radio broadcast). John Whorfin seized his chance for escape by fusing himself with Lizardo (who is driven mad by the subsumation), then returning with him into Lizardo's own dimension. Years later, percipient scientist Buckaroo Banzai, who has been working with Lizardo's former colleague, pierces the eighth dimension once more, thereby opening the doorway for Whorfin's impending return to Planet Ten. Anticipating their vulnerability, the "black lectroids" transmit a message informing Buckaroo Banzai of their plans to wage thermonuclear war on Earth should Whorfin succeed. Meanwhile, an exasperated Whorfin kidnaps and tortures Penny, the woman Banzai loves. He is seeking to extort the "oscillation overthruster" from Buckaroo, as well as the information he needs to escape from Earth. Whorfin loses his patience again and again, killing his own most valuable subordinates with little compunction. He has no regard for humanity, addressing each person he meets with a sneer as "monkey boy." Domineering and officious, Whorfin continually harangues his inferiors as they make ready for their journey home. Banzai chases Whorfin into the skies, destroying the "red lectroid" commander at the final moment before the "black lectroids" are due to set Earth's demise in motion. John Whorfin's adamantine behavior does not reveal his inner terror. By arrogating the title of "Lord," Whorfin seeks to elevate himself on the surface, yet, for all that, he is *not* the daring, self-assured master of all he pretends to be. For him, raw power is the security blanket sought by a child in the night, when fearful things prowl about the darkened room. His bawling speeches are further examples of a trepidation born of private doubt and unanswered wishes. The love and happiness which Banzai finds with Penny have eluded Whorfin. His final "refuge" is in tyrannizing others, which is no refuge at all, as Whorfin is doomed to discover.

JOHNNY ROCCO

Film Source: *Key Largo*
Release Date: 1948
Director: John Huston
Production Company: Warner Bros.
Color
Running Time: 101 minutes
Performed by: Edward G. Robinson
Additional Performers: Humphrey Bogart (Frank), Lauren Bacall (Nora), Lionel Barrymore (Mr. Temple).

Physical Description: Johnny Rocco's arched eyebrows emphasize the piercing gaze of his dark eyes. A short, stocky man of over forty years, he dresses stylishly in smart ties and crisp white shirts with dark pants and belt. His face is not handsome but memorable, distinguished by protuding ears and a mole on his right cheek. He barks orders to all those around him in unrefined baritone "gangsterese."

Character Analysis: Johnny Rocco longs for the happy days of his remembered past as the leader of a sordid criminal empire. Deported and forced into exile, Rocco has landed on the remote island of Key Largo in the Florida Keys, for what he hopes will be a brief, yet lucrative transaction of counterfeit funds with another racketeer. Commandeering an old-fashioned hotel, in the midst of an impending hurricane, he and his men make hostages of the invalid owner, Mr. Temple, his daughter-in-law, Nora, a police officer, and Frank, a drifter and veteran who is visiting the Temples to tell them about the death of his war buddy, Temple's son and Nora's husband. Frank cynically "flatters" Rocco, realizing there is something not quite right about the man, and identifying him as a criminal even before Rocco shows his true stripes. Rocco struts his self-importance as he whispers indecent suggestions into Nora's ear. She spits in Rocco's face, and he brandishes a gun, threatening her and Frank who has intervened. Frank challenges Rocco's violent intentions with the suggestion that he kill all present—or no one. Bristling at Frank, Rocco calls him a "wise guy," then backs down. Rocco has the police officer beaten, but when he regains consciousness, he grabs Rocco's gun and attempts to leave. A battle ensues but, as the officer soon discovers, Rocco has anticipated his actions, and has taken the precaution of unloading the gun in advance. Rocco's lover, an alcoholic "has-been" night-club singer, begs him for a drink, but he refuses. He then suggests that he might reconsider if she will sing one of her old songs. Desperate, she agrees, and warbles a wavering, off-key tune. Rocco, however, refuses her the drink he'd tentatively promised, because her singing is "lousy." Frank, fed up with the insults and viciousness, arises, pours the woman a drink, and gives it to her. Once she has swallowed it and thanked him, Frank is confronted by Rocco, who slaps him several times. In a display of stoic resignation, Frank lets Rocco hit him, then walks away and joins the others, and gains Nora's respect and belief in his decency and courage. As the hurricane approaches, Rocco, shaken by the tempest outside, and in a stunning act of indifference, barricades the hotel to a group of Seminole Indians who have gathered on its porch seeking refuge from the life-threatening storm. Frank is disgusted, and cynically suggests that Rocco shoot at the hurricane and make it stop. But beneath his *braggadocio*, Rocco is essentially a coward with a talent for staying out of harm's way, while casting others in it. Rocco prepares for his flight to safety after receiving the illegal payment for his counterfeit funds. He discovers his navigator has fled, and he commandeers Frank's unwilling services. A final confrontation takes place aboard the craft, and Frank overthrows Rocco's thugs, then shoots Rocco himself. Rocco loses everything he has sought through his insistent and consistent devaluation of human life. Disadvantaged youth may have held some responsibility for Rocco's behavior initially, still he developed his appetite for indulgence on his own. Deported as an undesirable alien, he had longed to reinstate his past influence. He feels no remorse for the deaths of the police officer and the innocent Seminoles, being concerned with his own life alone which, like the counterfeit money, has been no more than venality and sham.

THE JOKER (JACK NAPIER)

Film Source: *Batman*
Release Date: 1989
Director: Tim Burton
Production Company: Warner Bros.
Color
Running Time: 126 minutes
Performed by: Jack Nicholson
Additional Performers: Michael Keaton (Bruce Wayne/Batman), Jack Palance (Carl Grissom), Kim Basinger (Vicky Vale), Jerry Hall (Alicia Hunt).

Physical Description: Jack Napier is distinguished by a wide grin which can not be ignored, nor can Napier's smirk be erased at his discretion. Napier has forfeited his power over his contemptuous grin during a struggle with the mysterious Batman. The impact of a single bullet has severed Napier's facial nerves and has rendered his "smile" indelible. His facial features have been further remodeled permanently when his skin is bleached and his nails and hair are dyed green, the result of an accidental dive into chemical wastes. Napier has made an asset of his physical disfigurement by carefully developing his persona as "The Joker" with a garish, though dapper, wardrobe, including deep violet jackets, varicolored checkered trousers, silk shirts and ties of tangerine and emerald. Last, but not least, is a beloved assortment of headgear—an artist's *chapeau*, a purple beret, and colorful "porkpie" hats. Occasionally The Joker wears a plastic orchid filled with acid, the "better to disfigure you with...."

Character Analysis: Negotiating the sheer precipices of the mind requires unshakable willingness—and a significant desire to change. Poised on a cliff too narrow to accommodate his own self-delusion, Jack Napier has plunged into an abyss of madness he is unmoved and—at last—unable to scale. Napier, the career criminal who murdered the parents of young Bruce Wayne (now Batman), is an aging dandy who constantly checks his suit and tie in a mirror. Alicia Hunt, his lover and also the mistress of his boss, mobster Carl Grissom, compliments him, but he already knows how handsome he is, and his curt response tells her so. Napier considers himself superior to Carl, whom he deems incapable of running the city's crime machine alone, and plots to take his place. But when he is called "psychotic," Napier betrays his own instability with a twitching eye. Grissom, jealous, betrays Napier, who makes a critical error by facing down Batman in the midst of gunfire. Napier is halted with a bullet to the face, and disappears into a vat of toxic chemicals, Washed through the sewer system into the river, Napier, still alive, drags himself ashore, and seeks out the services of a disreputable surgeon. The doctor saves Napier's life, but botches the repair job, and leaves the hapless Napier with an indelibly marked face. Napier who, up to now, has trod the waters of sanity in a lackluster fashion, now hurls all his inhibition aside and takes on the persona he calls "The Joker." Napier has cultivated the concept of The Joker's superiority from his youth, when he realized that the joker in a deck of cards can take the place of the other cards. At the same time, his notions of beauty and passion are transformed into a philosophy of mutilation and torture, each consecutive act of violence becoming, for him, a work of art. The Joker, proficient in chemistry and nerve gas experiments, begins a campaign of terror to gratify his distorted sense of humor. He injects popular cosmetic products with a deadly poison which triggers uncontrollable laughter in the unwary user. Then, once deaths begin occurring, The Joker interrupts a news broadcast with an "advertisement" of the new compound, in which the audience is shown the victims' dead, smiling faces. These caricatures represent The Joker's own distorted vanity but, even more, they mirror his personal yearning for death. In a trick of fate, The Joker, who eagerly examines bystanders' photographs taken at a crime scene, is entranced by beautiful photojournalist (and Batman's friend) Vicky Vale. Now on a downward spiral, The Joker decides it is time to impose his redefined concept of beauty on the waiting world. He disfigures Alicia with acid and provides her with a mask to hide the scars. Then he threatens Vicky and follows her to her apartment where, with a peal of laughter, he terrifies her by smashing Alicia's mask while disclosing his former lover's suicide. The Joker, plays out his wild, unpredictable eccentricity and dreadful perversity during a parade through the city streets. The startled onlookers find themselves choking on his poison gas, but The Joker continues laughing at their plight in an exaltation of morbidity. The Joker, thinking he has bested his old foe, Batman, stomps on the decaying overhang of a cathedral where Vicky and his adversary are trapped, and plummets to his death when it collapses under his weight. The Joker's raucous laughter continues to emanate from the novelty laugh box in his pocket even as his lifeless body lies sprawled on the pavement below. Defined by his vanity and by his unabated use of violence as the one answer to all questons, Jack Napier eclipses his own improbity while in the guise of his "wild" card counterpart. At the end, the final laugh is on him.

Jonathan Brewster

Film Source: *Arsenic and Old Lace*
Release Date: 1944
Director: Frank Capra
Production Company: Warner Bros.
B&W
Running Time: 118 minutes
Performed by: Raymond Massey
Additional Performer: Cary Grant (Mortimer Brewster).

Physical Description: Jonathan Brewster is a lanky, stooped individual who gives the impression of a vulture about to swoop down on its prey. His conspicuous mouth and nose are framed by scars made up of tiny stitches which crisscross his forehead and cheeks. Brewster has been furnished with this distinguishing feature by a surgeon cohort who has botched an operation on him. Brewster's intimidating glare sends shivers up the spines of innocent bystanders who feel an immediate need to "run away."

Character Analysis: Jonathan Brewster is a dangerous man, we discover rather quickly. He has already murdered more than a dozen people, and he does not hesitate to consider Mortimer, his worried, interfering brother, as his next victim. He is an imposing figure who has no difficulty forcing his way into the home of his two elderly aunts. Accustomed to tyrannizing others, he coerces his aunts and Mortimer to permit him to stay until his physician associate can supply Jonathan with a more pleasing face. Thinking his brother plans to turn him over to the authorities, Jonathan ties Mortimer up, then amuses himself by recounting tales of his mistreatment of his brother when they were children. The gloating Jonathan intends a slow, excruciating death for Mortimer. Jonathan's brutal intentions are frustrated, however, by the fortuitous arrival of the police, and the remorseless maniac makes a final furious and reckless acknowledgement of his own guilt.

JUDITH MERRICK

Film Source: *Shattered*
Release Date: 1991
Director: Wolfgang Petersen
Production Company: MGM
Color
Running Time: 103 minutes
Performed by: Greta Scacchi
Additional Performers: Tom Berenger (Dan Merrick), Scott Getlin (Jack Stanton), Bob Hoskins (Gus), Joanne Whalley-Kilmer (Jenny Scott).

Physical Description: Judith Merrick is a most attractive woman. Her beautiful features are framed by radiant dark hair, and she is endowed with a memorable pair of eyes. She speaks softly in a well-modulated soprano voice. In her thirties, her mature charm is paradoxically combined with a youthful verve. With her nearly perfect figure she could be a model for classical Greek sculpture—not to mention classical Greek tragedy.

Character Analysis: An object looked at from a distance in poor lighting may appear far different than when it is scrutinized up close under a bright light. Judith Merrick has made deception into an art form and, for this reason, she bears careful scrutiny under direct sunlight. Even her friend, Jenny Scott, whom she eventually murders, calls her a "pathological liar." A creator of stories, she makes up one so expansive as to put to shame the worst dissemblers of all time. She murders her husband Dan, then persuades her lover, Jack Stanton, to help her hide the body in a derelict ship she finds abandoned in a shipyard near San Francisco. She causes them to crash on a remote mountain road and, according to plan, escapes unscathed, while Jack is severely injured and falls into a deep coma. Jack does not die and slowly regains consciousness. He is suffering from amnesia and, even more conveniently, requires plastic surgery for his damaged face. Judith gives the surgeons photographs of Dan, and they reconstruct Jack's face in her deceased husband's image. This accomplished, she begins feeding Jack misinformation in order to convince him he *is* the real Dan Merrick. In spite of her meticulous and well-conceived plans, Jack becomes increasingly curious as he gradually regains his memory, a problem she cannot resolve through artfulness or prevarication. With the help of an astute P.I. (Bob Hoskins), Jack uncovers the truth, as well as Dan's body—with his face—preserved in toxic chemicals in the bowels of the ship. Judith makes one last fruitless attempt to free herself of Jack's relentless pursuit of the truth, but fails. Making it up as she goes along has been a way of life for Judith, and life itself must do her bidding. Like some character from a Greek tragedy, she has justified her every act with the unspoken excuse, "I had no other choice, so accept it." Lying must have been an early defense mechanism, affording her a shield she has relied on too much, too often, and too long. In the end, her twitchy maneuverings resemble those of a fidgety bird, hopping from branch to shadowy branch, trying to avoid scrutiny in the inevitable light of day.

KANANGA

Film Source: *Live and Let Die*
Release Date: 1973
Director: Guy Hamilton
Production Company: United Artists
Color
Running Time: 121 minutes
Performed by: Yaphet Kotto
Additional Performers: Roger Moore (James Bond), Jane Seymour (Solitaire).

Physical Description: Kananga is an impressive figure of a Black man, tall, with a broad, handsome, face and winning smile. He dresses typically in a business suit. He is gifted at elocution, and his velvet speaking voice captivates his listeners.

Character Analysis: Kananga, the prime minister of San Monique, projects an image of careful moderation. Underneath a façade of tranquility and affection for his people, however, lies the heart of a deceitful man. He concocts an alter ego, "Mr. Big," and lays plans to flood the United States with heroin and corner the market on the heinous drug. A monomaniacal killer in his quest for wealth and power, Kananga relies on Solitaire, a beautiful augur, for whom cards are a means of divination. When her powers are unintentionally removed by an *amour* with agent James Bond, Kananga is enraged. Insulted by his seer's disobedience, he strikes her, proclaiming that he would have removed her powers himself when the time came. Kananga's statement portrays his haughty, self-indulgence with clarity. Kananga exhibits his penchant for fiendishness by decreeing that James Bond will make the perfect repast for hungry alligators. Failing this, he ties Solitaire and Bond together above a tank of sharks, then denotes his warped sense of humor by cutting slashes in Bond's arm to whet the appetites of the predatory animals. Bond frees himself and Solitaire, then grapples with the madman. Bond forces a compressed gas pellet into the dictator's mouth, and Kananga bursts into bits. His avidity and expansive schemes, consequences of his life of crime, are, in the end, blown away just as he is.

KARL HOCHMAN

Film Source: *Ghost in the Machine*
Release Date: 1994
Director: Rachel Talalay
Production Company: Twentieth Century Fox
Color
Running Time: 98 minutes
Performed by: Ted Marcoux
Additional Performers: Karen Allen (Terry Monroe), Will Horneff (Josh Monroe), Chris Mulkey (Bram Walker).

Physical Description: Karl Hochman, a man in his early or mid-twenties, is invested with an abundance of good looks. His eyes are clear, his curly hair is appealing, and his physique is muscular. His wide nose does not detract from his handsome face. What he lacks in height he makes up for in carriage. He wears striped, button-down shirts and casual pants. His voice ranges from low tenor to baritone, offset by a rasping undertone and an unsettling laugh.

Character Analysis: An expressionistic painting done in reds and blacks hangs on one wall of Karl Hochman's apartment. From the torrent of its swirling frenzy surfaces the depravity and upheaval of Karl's mind. The mystery of why Karl behaves as he does remains unsolved, with just a hint of supposition about his hatred of "caring systems." Known as the "Address Book Killer," he murders families in their homes, taking with him their photo albums and pictures when he leaves the scene. His preferred method of killing is the use of a set of butcher knives. As he leaves the home of his most recent victims, Karl stretches and waves good-bye. He is "artistic" in his methods, arranging one family he kills in a group on their living room couch. He does not stop at killing people, but drowns the Monroe's dog in their pool so the pet will not be able to protect them. Karl has a genius for computers and a talent for fixing machines. A trusted employee in the computer store where he works, he keeps to himself, attracting neither attention nor suspicion. After three years of serial murders and extreme brutality he still retains his status of anonymity. In the store he meets young Josh, who has come in with his mother, Terry Monroe. When Josh, curious about what Karl is repairing, almost touches a live wire, Karl grabs his arm and holds it, warning him about a possible shock. Visibly unnerved by Karl's manner and his grip, Josh moves away. Catching sight of Terry, Karl gives her a shy smile, followed by a look of understated desire. This disturbs Terry, who averts her eyes. Quiet and reserved, unless rattled, Karl emits a silent alarm to Terry. Athough his glance suggests timidity, he has already begun formulating sanguinary dramas in his mind. His opportunity for new slaughters arises after Terry forgets her address book in the store, leaving Karl in an euphoric mood as he fondles and inhales the scent of the book. In the same moment he contemplates mutilating her, he is obviously smitten with Terry. On the road to her home Karl drives recklessly in a thunderstorm, laughing as his car flips over, then takes him on a breakneck ride through a cemetery. While undergoing testing at a local hospital, a power surge caused by the storm launches his consciousness into the computer network the facility utilizes. Still obsessed, his first act is to search for Terry. His full awareness of the vulnerability of everyone within his reach galvanizes Karl further, dissolving the last tiniest remnant of his self-control. He begins sending Terry piles of lingerie, accompanied by, as she puts it, "nasty little notes." Once he erases her bank balance, he thumbs through her address book, entered in a computer by the manager during a previous demonstration at the store, and begins systematically killing, in alphabetical order, those listed in it. He "microwaves" her former employer in his own kitchen, engulfs in flames a man Terry is dating, then electrocutes Josh's babysitter. At an arcade Josh encounters Karl in the computer as he plays a virtual reality game with a friend. Having already contacted the befuddled Josh on his home computer, Karl makes a grotesque face as he asks the boy again to join him in the computer world, and throws Josh off a parapet into virtual space. The murders he has commited and the attempts to draw Terry and Josh into his world, stimulate Karl's passion for carving up whole families even further, leaving an extended trail of destruction which threatens to grow worse. By designating his program "Family Values," he focuses his antipathy and jealousy of a joyful home and hearth into a furious onslaught on Terry and her family and friends. In his mind, nothing deserves preservation less than those loved and cared about by others. Extrapolating from his remarks, it can be surmised that Karl is a misogynist, since he torments Terry and spouts aspersions at her. More than anything, as computer hacker Bram Walker tells Terry, Karl is "mean." He likes being cruel, and murder, for him, is a stimulant comparable to intoxication from alcohol or narcotics. After Bram infects the database with a computer virus, Karl joins Terry, Josh, and the hacker in a control room near a huge magnet. His ferocious attacks on each of them, almost choking both Terry and

Josh, are ended when Terry shoots a hole in the glass around the room and the magnet wrenches Karl's atoms into "oblivion." Genius derives many outlets and travels various avenues, yet Karl's genius centers on the performance of virulent evil. A loner, he experiences life through the deaths of others. Death itself has a charm for him like nothing else. Holding sway over life and death intensified in his mind after his consciousness entered the computer world, a place far less limited by physical laws than his old one. In this world he could have gone on indefinitely, wreaking carnage anywhere the network allowed. His secret life of multiple killing became more personal after Terry and Josh became his targets. Perceiving them as a ready-made family, he tore everything from them until he had them in his virtual grasp. What he lost was not the chance for new hope or a new life, but the chance, in his mind, for an unrestricted succession of one murder after another.

KATHARINE PARKER

Film Source: *Working Girl*
Release Date: 1988
Director: Mike Nichols
Production Company: Twentieth Century Fox
Color
Running Time: 115 minutes
Performed by: Sigourney Weaver
Additional Performers: Melanie Griffith (Tess McGill), Harrison Ford (Jack Trainor), Philip Bosco (Mr. Trask)

Physical Description: Katharine Parker is flawless. She expresses majesty in her bearing and posture. In her *haute couture* suits and gowns, she could pose for the cover of a top fashion magazine. She wears her make-up in the same understated, elegant manner as her attire. Rippling, shoulder-length hair crowns her head. She uses reading glasses. Effortless in manner, and well-groomed in style, her speech and grasp of languages confirms a background in the finest schools.

Character Analysis: Self-delusion breeds its own form of desensitization. Over time any idea or feeling, no matter how base, can be inhered as ethical, if a person sanctions it. Katharine Parker has spent her life asserting her will over other people. Anxious for success, she has progressed from a wealthy, pampered background into an executive suite. Duplicity serves as the essence of her personality. Responding to her latest secretary as mere hired help, Katharine manipulates the creative, ingenuous Tess McGill through a series of heartfelt discussions on trust. She convinces Tess she is interested in her future, promising her an opportunity for entry into an administrative program. While her words make Tess feel like a colleague, Katharine's thoughts are less than egalitarian. Through study and comparison Tess has unearthed a novel way for a major industry to diversify. Persuaded of her new boss's sincerity, Tess leaves her concept with Katharine. In an instant Katharine recognizes the talent in her secretary—one she herself does not share with Tess. Deftly, Katharine purloins Tess's idea, then deceives her, at the same time reminding her of their mutual need for "trust." Conscious of her department's poor record, Katharine basks in the opportunity provided her by Tess. At a business party Tess becomes her lackey, waiting on the guests while Katharine gives orders. Her perception of Tess as a servant conforms with Katharine's self-appraisal as the team "quarterback." After Katharine feigns interest in an obnoxious party guest, she warns Tess not to make enemies. Unaffected by her own advice, Katharine institutes personal disaster through her hypocritical dealings with Tess. As she readies for a skiing holiday, she chats with Tess about her plans for marriage. In her discussion of her imminent betrothal Katharine associates matrimony with incorporation. Every relationship is a business venture to her. When she breaks her leg skiing, Katharine leaves Tess "in charge." Her physical mishap compounds when Tess discovers Katharine has stolen her idea. Angry and determined, Tess jeopardizes her future by posing as an executive while Katharine is away. Since she finds herself vacationing in the hospital instead of on the slopes, Katharine spends her convalescence having parties and flirting with doctors. On her return Katharine announces herself, tosses her luggage to Tess, and calls Jack Trainor, the business executive she has selected for marriage. Uninformed about the relationship Tess has developed with Jack during her absence, Katharine inveigles a meeting with him. Wearing her most seductive lingerie, Katharine tells Jack, "Let's merge." Katharine pouts when Jack makes a gracious excuse and leaves to join Tess for a decisive business conference. After carrying suitcases for Katharine, bathing her, retrieving her medication, Tess forgets her notebook in her boss's room. Having lied minutes before about the reason her secretary's idea appeared as her own on a computer disc, Katharine pries into her notebook. Once she knows Tess has been working on her idea with Jack, Katharine dresses, then arrives at the conference unannounced. Marching into the room, she almost hits a man with one of her crutches. Accusing Tess of thievery and deceit, Katharine watches as her humiliated secretary apologizes to the group and quietly leaves the meeting. Jack Trainor acknowledges Katharine's brazenness with a reproachful glance. Jack, who has fallen in love with Tess, has already begun questioning his feelings for the demanding, spoiled Katharine. Now, in this moment of shock, he appreciates the differences between the two women. Katharine, believing herself justified in her verbal flaying of Tess, settles into her executive chair as though all the work had been her own. The next day Katharine finds Tess outside an elevator gathering up her papers, as she prepares to leave the building and her job, and jeers at her about her supposed larceny. Jack helps Tess, and asks her why she has not contacted him. Unlike Katharine, who thinks of herself as flawless, Tess is convinced her own actions have discredited her with Jack. Tess, supported by Jack, then challenges Katherine to tell Mr. Trask, the magnate around whom the business proposal revolves, just how she came about the idea for the merger. Katharine implores Jack to help her, but he refuses. Tess wins admiration from Trask, who hires her on the spot as an executive trainee—while firing Katharine for her own disreputable behavior. Dissembling may have served Katharine in the past, but without the respect of her colleagues or the talent for innovation, she exits in quiet rage for a final visit to her private office.

KHAN

Film Source: *Star Trek II: The Wrath of Khan*
Release Date: 1982
Director: Nicholas Meyer
Production company: Paramount Pictures
Color
Running Time: 113 minutes
Performed by: Ricardo Montalban
Additional Performers: William Shatner (Captain James Kirk), Leonard Nimoy (Mr. Spock), Paul Winfield (Captain Terrell), Walter Koenig (Commander Chekov).

Physical Description: Khan, as a result of genetic programming, possesses indefatigable strength and vitality. His long hair, a mass of wild gray, matches the bare, sinewy chest flaunted by his primitive, homemade outfit. He wears a black glove on his right hand. While no longer a young man, Khan seems fit, trim, and robust. His chiseled features are ruggedly handsome. He could be charming if he desired—but he doesn't.

Character Analysis: Khan is a man obsessed. His life objective has been and remains the destruction of Admiral James T. Kirk of the starship Enterprise. Khan blames all his misfortunes, including the tragic death of his wife, on Kirk. He is a despot from the past, whose body lay in suspended animation for two hundred years. A survivor, Khan has known unlimited power in his lifetime. He has kept his group of followers alive on their planet of exile under the most inclement of conditions. He subdues, with utmost delight, Captain Terrell and Commander Chekov of the starship *Reliant* by placing tiny, dangerous creatures in their ears. Intensely single-minded, he searches for Kirk throughout the galaxy. He ruthlessly tortures the unarmed space lab team on Regula I, and captures an awesome device known as Genesis for his own selfish ends. Khan attacks the Enterprise, but is startled when Kirk outmaneuvers him. His final revenge against Kirk is barred by Mr. Spock, the valiant, half-human, half-Vulcan who sacrifices his own life to protect the starship, its crew, and his friend James Kirk. Khan's turbulent savagery causes the needless deaths of himself and his own people, as well as those of his enemies. Spock's selfless valor assures him a place in the halls of history and in the hearts of his comrades. Khan's grandeur has passed him by, and history will accord him with only the memory of his fury, vengeance, and destruction.

THE KILLER: SEE: SCORPIO

KIVIAT: SEE: DR. ERIC KIVIAT

KLEBB: SEE: ROSA KLEBB

PRINCE KOURA

Film Source: *The Golden Voyage of Sinbad*
Release Date: 1974
Director: Gordon Hessler
Production Company: Columbia Pictures
Color
Running Time: 104 minutes
Performed by: Tom Baker
Additional Performer: John Phillip Law (Sinbad).

Physical Description: Prince Koura, robed majestically in black, crowns his impressive height with a turban. His appearance is made even more flamboyant by the many rings he wears on his expressive fingers, and the ornate embroidery on his cape. His neatly-groomed beard and moustache are accented by a huge, derisive grin and mocking eyes. Koura's deliberate speech persuades his listener that he selects each word with care.

Character Analysis: The legendary Captain Sinbad calls Prince Koura "...a great black bat of a man," most assuredly an insult to the bats he conjures up! Koura thinks of nothing but the power at his fingertips, when he summons up demons to do his will with drops of his own blood. Even the fact that he places his health in jeopardy each time he calls up the malevolent beings, is not reason enough to desist. And not even the cautionary reproof of his devoted underling can persuade him. Amassing power and riches is Koura's overriding passion. Koura and his servant are captured and confronted by Sinbad and his men, and the Prince evokes a statue of the mythological goddess Kali by using a vial of his own blood. He commands her to attack, armed with swords in each of her six hands, and Kali obeys but is slain by Sinbad. The Prince then sends a monstrous centaur to do battle with Sinbad. Sinbad kills the creature and Koura dons a magical cloak that renders him invisible. At last, boasting that he can slay Sinbad and his friends any time he wishes, the Prince does his own fighting. Koura is taken by surprise and bested by Sinbad. In a gesture of humility, Sinbad places a fabulous diadem on the head of the legitimate ruler of the land Koura had sought for himself. Sinbad's selfless act restores the face of the ruler, whom Koura had viciously disfigured with fire years earlier. Such altruism is unknown to Koura, who willingly risked his blood to gain power. His conceit has dictated his actions, even as his insensibility toward others has guaranteed his defeat. He is, truly, a "bat out of hell."

KRUEGER: SEE: FREDDY KRUEGER

KRIS BOLIN

Film Source: *The Temp*
Release Date: 1993
Director: Tom Holland
Production Company: Paramount Pictures
Color
Running Time: 99 minutes
Performed by: Lara Flynn Boyle
Additional Performers: Timothy Hutton (Peter Derns); Faye Dunaway (Charlene Towne).

Physical Description: Kris Bolin's striking features, velvet tones, and svelte figure add up to a highly visible young employee. Whether her hair is caught up or flowing down, its richness increases her beauty. She has a penchant for wearing short, tight skirts as part of her business wardrobe. Her twinkling eyes attract more attention. Efficient, talented, charming, she will let no one stand between her and success.

Character Analysis: Kris Bolin is going to the top the shortest way possible—and she doesn't care how she gets there. She's on a track faster than any secretary could envision. Disguising herself as an efficient, sweet-natured temporary employee for executive Peter Derns, she throws herself into a frenzy of underhanded deeds cunningly designed to ensure her rapid advancement in "Mrs. Appleby's Famous Cookie Company." First she gets rid of Peter's assistant, for whom she is filling in, by booby-trapping the copier so that his hand is nearly torn to shreds. Next she slips in a brilliant cookie recipe on a tour of the baking section, and catches the eye of company president, Charlene Towne. A carefully placed (though deceitful) remark about having attended Stanford garners even more respect for newcomer Kris from Charlene. Whether she is sabotaging a batch of cookies being tested in a grocery store campaign, or faking the murder of a company vice president to look like a suicide, nothing is too great an obstacle for Kris. Peter suspects Kris of wrongdoing almost from the beginning, but his history of paranoia holds him back. As people in the company begin dropping like flies, Kris quickly moves up the corporate ladder. At last she murders Charlene, and Peter is forced to acknowledge that his misgivings about Kris are not delusional. Peter is made company president and, knowing Kris will soon make an attempt on his life, he reports his suspicions to the police then fires her. Frustration has led Kris into her life of crime. Although she has the natural talent to succeed, she lacks the necessary degree. Her most prodigious gift is the ability to deceive people. She has seduced, discredited, maimed and even killed those who stood in her way. Once Peter is on to her game, Kris loses, but we can assume she will not mend her ways. Not even the threat of a jail sentence will correct this temp's "shorthand."

KRISTATOS: SEE: ARI KRISTATOS

KYLE, SELENA: SEE: CATWOMAN

LAMARR: SEE: HEDLEY LAMARR

LARGO: SEE: MAXIMILIAN

LASSPARRI: SEE: RUDALFO LASSPARRI

LEARY: SEE: MITCH LEARY

LECTER: SEE: DR. HANNIBAL LECTER

LEX LUTHOR

Film Source: *Superman—The Movie*; *Superman II*; *Superman III*; *Superman IV: The Quest for Peace*
Release Dates: 1978; 1980; 1983; 1987
Focus: *Superman—The Movie*
Director: Richard Donner
Production Company: Warner Bros.
Color
Running Times: 143 minutes
Performed by: Gene Hackman
Additional Performers: Christopher Reeve (Clark Kent/Superman), Valerie Perrine (Miss Tessmacher), Ned Beatty (Otis).

Physical Description: Lex Luthor is a thick-set man whose girth is offset by his height. His baldness—psychologically—is his one distinctive feature, since it motivates his use of various toupées. He has a fondness for ascots and showy attire. His smile, sharklike, is an ostentatious array of teeth. Often when he speaks in his hoarse baritone, he gestures in regal fashion with manicured fingers.

Character Analysis: Lex Luthor, during his initial encounter with Superman, insults the intelligence of his amazing, new opponent when he insists that a doctrine of violence and crime exists which eliminates any likelihood of reform. Luther expresses this vaunting pomposity in his every word and action. It is Luthor's own judgment, in fact, that *he*, not Superman, is a universal genius and a man of culture. His inept henchman, Otis, endures a continuous bombardment of sarcasm and mental and physical abuse from Luthor, as does Miss Tessmacher, his secretary and *paramour*. Almost nothing suits him better than giving people commands. He shouts orders to Otis and Miss Tessmacher like a drill instructor at boot camp. When a police officer ferrets out his lair, Luthor obstructs the man's access by pushing him onto subway tracks in front of a train at full speed. Luthor is a calculating swindler who purchases valueless desert land and resolves to convert it into an expensive seaside resort with the use of a purloined guided missile. He is absorbed by his future prosperity rather than the myriad deaths the missile will surely cause. Luthor equates killing people with the clearing of debris from his acquisitive pathway. He esteems humanity of so little worth that he remains unmoved by the destruction a second missile will cause when it reaches a town on the east coast of the United States. Following his capture by Superman, Lex Luthor introduces himself to the prison warden by removing his wig as if it were a hat. As certain of his own intelligence and ability as he is of the absence of it in in others, he eschews the notion of his defeat. Luthor's low opinion of other people has a direct bearing on his behavior. Owning expanses of precious land corresponds with his avariciousness, while controlling people reflects his valuation of himself as the ultimate authority in all matters. See also: GENERAL ZOD.

LINT: SEE: JACK LINT

LITTLE BILL DAGGOT

Film Source: *Unforgiven*
Release Date: 1992
Director: Clint Eastwood
Production Company: Warner Bros.
Color
Running Time: 130 minutes

Performed by: Gene Hackman
Additional Performers: Clint Eastwood (William Munny), Morgan Freeman (Ned Logan), Richard Harris (English Bob).

Physical Description: "Little Bill" Daggot, although balding, does have some curly grayish hair ringing his head. An imposing man of more than six feet in height, and riveting eyes, he appears sturdy and extremely sure of himself in the rough-and-tumble world of the Old West. Although he is no longer a young man, Daggot's weather-beaten exterior does not disguise his rugged good looks. His garb is comfortable and practical wear for the western town he inhabits, but his reading glasses seem incongruous in the rough *milieu* in which he holds sway.

Character Analysis: Sheriff Daggot, known as "Little Bill" to those around him, runs a small Wyoming town circa 1880. Daggot thinks twice before whipping two ranch hands from a large spread who have cut up a prostitute's face. The powerful rancher's feelings count for more than those of the prostitute and her companions, who are virtual prisoners in the house of ill repute they inhabit. Daggot does not demand a fair restitution for the girl's disfigured face. Instead he suggests that the men bring in two ponies with which to "pay off" the prostitute. His solution is a reasonable one, to his thinking, since it guarantees no trouble from the rancher, and the girl should be thankful for what she gets. The women of the house are disgusted by this turn of events, and they quickly pool their savings in order to hire William Munny, a former gunslinger from outside, to come and settle their differences with the ranch hands. Will Munny arrives carrying a gun, and since the sign outside town prohibits firearms, Doggett disarms Will, then pistol whips him to "teach him who's boss." Nevertheless, Will, paid by the women to call out the ranch hands and kill them, does so. Will's friend Ned Logan, who has come along to help, is accused of the killing and, in a despicable act of vengeance, Doggett beats Ned to death. He props the badly bruised body up in a coffin in the center of town, where Will will be sure to see it. Will challenges Little Bill to a gun duel and, in a final blazing confrontation, he draws down on the sheriff and kills him. Both men have had a checkered past, but Will, at least, has some feelings of concern about his colleagues and the women who have hired him. Little Bill used the town and its denizens as his own personal kingdom to run as he pleased. He saw no reason to justify himself or his decisions. He preserved the "peace" by crushing anyone who stood in his way. Will returns home to continue raising his two young children after the gun fight, but Sheriff Daggot, in his bid for control, has lost everything, including his life. He monopolized his town, demanding complete obedience of everyone, as a way of keeping law and order, but the stringent, pitiless manner he used to carry out his aims was untenable. Living by the gun assured that he would die by it as well. Hackman won a Best Supporting Actor Oscar for this role.

LO PAN: SEE: DAVID LO PAN

LONNEGAN: SEE: DOYLE LONNEGAN

LUTHER, CHARLES: SEE: DR. CHARLES LUTHER

LUTHOR, LEX: SEE: LEX LUTHOR

MAAX

Film Source: *The Beastmaster*
Release Date: 1982
Director: Don Coscarelli
Production company: MGM
Color
Running Time: 120 minutes
Performed By: Rip Torn
Additional Performers: Marc Singer (Dar).

Physical Description: Maax's riveting eyes complement his beak-like nose. His tight grin opens on a mouth brimming with decayed teeth. While most of his hair is an unruly mass of gray, two long braids fall along either side of his face, clasped at the ends by diminutive skulls. He wears a dark shirt and trousers under a rusty cloak fastened with a buckle of gold filigree. His boots appear worn from riding and trudging dusty paths.

Character Analysis: When conviction degenerates into fanaticism, waste is its most often yield. The quest for power can turn conviction into fanatical behavior if it becomes the individual's principal goal. Maax, whose ambition is the basis of his fanaticism, imposes his control over others through fear, and waste is the result. Barbaric hordes threaten invasion at any moment, but Maax assures his own protection by surrounding himself with magicians and temple guards. Maax justifies his acts of violence against those he claims to serve with a self-declared position of infallibility. The most unconscionable tenet of Maax's dogma by far, however, is the sacrifice of innocent children and young women to the deity known as Ar. When faced with a prediction that he will die by the hand of his king's unborn son (who will be named Dar), Maax dispatches one of his minions to slaughter the baby, but the plot fails. In later years Maax is opposed by Dar, and his willful response parallels the belief Maax has in his own infallability.

Maax is immovable about permitting another to dispute his theocracy because he has never questioed the validity of his own behavior. Dar challenges Maax at the very altar where so many villagers have lost their babies and Maax falls to his death in the fiery sacrificial furnace. Relentless in his absolutism, Maax trampled upon anyone he wished, until he too is unseated and killed—due more to his own *hubris* than because of a prophecy fulfilled.

MADELINE ASHTON AND HELEN SHARP

Film Source: *Death Becomes Her*
Release Date: 1992
Director: Robert Zemeckis
Production Company: Universal Studios
Color
Running Time: 103 minutes
Performed by: Meryl Streep and Goldie Hawn
Additional Performers: Bruce Willis (Dr. Ernest Menville); Isabella Rossellini (Lisle).

Physical Description: Madeline and Helen are both lovely women who change from "beautiful" to "brittle" (in every sense of the word) through the use of a magical potion guaranteed to keep them young and gorgeous. Since the elixir also makes them immortal, they must live on after their "deaths," becoming more and more decrepit and battered as time goes by. Helen Sharp had gained too much weight before her alteration into a svelte, youthful person. Madeline Ashton had overused plastic surgery in her pursuit of youth. Sudden "death" forces decay on each of them, until they turn into wretched, crumbling husks of their former selves.

Character Analysis: Good friends, jealous enemies, and the most foolish women imaginable, Madeline Ashton and Helen Sharp are alike in every way. They both value themselves above anyone else; and they both covet the same man, Dr. Ernest Menville, a noted plastic surgeon. Like the famed fables of Aesop that warn against vice and folly, the intertwined paths of stage and screen legend Madeline Ashton and brilliant author Helen Sharp take a ludicrous, outrageous turn. Obsessed by their outward appearances each is drawn into a nightmarish abyss from which there is no escape. Clever, wicked Lisle offers the women, at a high cost, eternal life, youth and beauty in the form of a secret potion. The women get what they thought they wanted, but the price can not be measured in money alone. Madeline Ashton, although she is warned to be careful, argues with Ernest, whom she stole years before from Helen. She accidentally tumbles downstairs to her "death," but revives, her neck twisted and broken. Ernest repairs her body as best he can, then finds himself in the midst of a brawl as Helen seeks revenge on Madeline because of their longstanding discord. As usual, thinking of themselves alone, they coerce Ernest into abetting them. At first, he agrees, but balks when Lisle offers him the potion as well. Narrowly escaping with his life, Ernest leaves Madeline and Helen, a much stronger man than the "wimp" they give him credit for being. Attending his funeral service many years later, they laugh and make fun of the fine eulogy he is given. But by this time they are worthless—mere faded, rotting reminders of their former lovely entities. Neither has learned anything of value in all the time they have been given, and neither cares. Stuck with each other for an eternity, they are indeed, as the diminutives they have given each other indicate, "Mad" and "Hel."

MAITLAND: SEE: VICTOR MAITLAND

MANTEE: SEE: DUKE MANTEE

MARSHALL: SEE: GRAHAM MARSHALL

MARSTON: SEE: ELLIOT MARSTON

MARV: SEE: HARRY AND MARV

MARY ANN SIMPSON: SEE: MATTY WALKER

MASTERS: SEE: RICK MASTERS

MATTHIAS

Film Source: *The Omega Man*
Release Date: 1971
Director: Boris Sagal
Production Company: Warner Bros.
Color
Running Time: 98 minutes
Performed by: Anthony Zerbe
Additional Performers: Charlton Heston (Robert Neville).

Physical Description: Jonathan Matthias, in his thirties, was once a well-groomed television newscaster with glasses and shoulder-length hair. He contracted a malignant disease in the aftermath of worldwide bacterial warfare and, along with many others, he has developed albinism and open sores. His eyes, like those in the tertiary stage of the illness, are unbearably light sensitive. Compensatory to this negative factor is an ability to see in darkness. In place of his former suit and tie, Matthias now wears a black robe. His best feature, a smooth baritone voice, is chillingly hypnotic.

Character Analysis: Opportunity provides the impetus on which influential decisions are often made, and the calculating individual who discerns opportunity with precision can elevate himself to a station of autocracy. Jonathan Matthias may have felt some responsibility in his role as a journalist at a time of global war and the ensuing devastation of plague which followed, but his motive for organizing the remnant of diseased victims in the Los Angeles area is hardly altruistic. Initially he has united these people on the premise of having saved their lives by burning the dead plague victims. Upon completion of this rite, Matthias has placed himself in a position of indisputable authority. He further has instituted a theocratic doctrine, regarded as inviolable by his followers, which advocates the incineration of all books containing scientific or technological knowledge that he denounces as part of the "old way." In fact, he presses for the eradication of all science which, in his opinion, had brought about their suffering. He now seeks the death of scientist Robert Neville, whom he sees as a threat both to his ideas and to the power he holds. Matthias admits his opposition to Neville's idea that a cure for the disease can be found, but he refuses to accept the notion, fearing the loss of the sweeping command he presently holds over his terminally ill adherents. Matthias' hatred of Neville is carefully transferred to his followers with all the proficiency of a tyrant, and any interference is squelched without hesitation. A teenager, hoping to make Matthias aware of the serum that Neville has discovered, is dismissed as a conspirator and murdered. Lisa, the youth's sister, falls under the spell of Matthias after succumbing to the tertiary stage of the illness, and it is she who leads Matthias into Neville's home. For his part, Neville had killed many of the plague victims, not only out of fear for his own life, but because he felt there was nothing he could do as a physician to help them. Once he discovers others who are not in the later stages of the illness, Neville devotes himself to a cure. He recognizes his violence is nonproductive, and seeks to assist those left whom he can reach. When Matthias invades the scientist's home with his followers, he expunges Neville's "world" by smashing his televisions and destroying his medical lab. Matthias claims Neville's life with a spear that the scientist fears may be aimed at Lisa. Neville's last act sets him, with all his own violent tendencies, apart from Matthias. He gives a bottle of serum made from his blood to a former medical student, who is leaving for the mountains with a small group of children still unaffected by the later stages of the disease. Matthias' declaration that Neville is from a dead past far better summarizes his own future and that of his "Family." Matthias attempts to destroy books containing what he judges is "dangerous knowledge," but he forgets that, as precious as they are, books are not the sole source of ideas. Matthias may control his followers' thoughts, but he cannot dominate the thoughts of those whose lives are spared by Neville's antitoxin. Neville's memory may fade, but Matthias' own grandiose delusions obscure from him the possibility of a world he will never experience or help construct. Based on Richard Matheson's *I Am Legend*.

MATTY TYLER: SEE: MATTY WALKER

MATTY WALKER (MARY ANN SIMPSON)

Film Source: *Body Heat*
Release Date: 1981
Director: Lawrence Kasdan
Production Company: The Ladd Company
Color
Running Time: 113 minutes
Performed by: Kathleen Turner
Additional Performers: William Hurt (Ned Racine), Richard Crenna (Edmund).

Physical Description: Matty Walker's alluring, sultry, siren's voice blends well with her voluptuous form and insinutes itself memorably into the imaginations of her listeners. Billowing blond hair falls about her captivating face. Conscious of her appearance, Matty dresses in a fashion that guarantees her rapt attention from her admirers. A "come-hither" look emanates from her sensuous, vulpine eyes.

Character Analysis: Beneath Matty Walker's sweltering expressions of passion lurks another blaze. Born Mary Ann Simpson, she had longed for a future of luxury and travel. Appropriating the name and identity of a high school friend, Matty Tyler, Mary Ann has earned herself an affluent husband, Edmund Walker. Her husband's business ventures are unscrupulous, but that is immaterial to Mary Ann/Matty, who has been receiving extortion demands from the real Matty. Desperate, she frames an ingenious means of escape from her blackmailer, and from her sordid life with Edmund. Matty tempts ne'er-do-well lawyer Ned Racine into a tempestuous affair. His judgment obscured by passion, Ned agrees to assist her in her plan to murder Edmund. He believes her when she promises they will eventually share her deceased husband's wealth in a tropical paradise far away. When Matty cheats Edmund's rightful heirs out of their inheritance, Ned becomes first distrustful, then horrified, when Matty incriminates him for her husband's murder. In a final confrontation, she traps Ned on her property, where she has planned his death. Ned is wary, however, and Matty is forced to alter her plans. As Ned watches in the distance, Matty runs toward the boat house, which explodes into flames. Ned peruses Matty's high school yearbook and finds pictures of the real Matty Tyler and her "friend," Mary Ann Simpson. Ned makes the final connection, and now understands that Mary Ann has disposed of her blackmailer in the boat house fire. On a beach far away, "Matty" lounges on the sand beside a new lover. Her lovely face depicts none of the joy and satisfaction she should be feeling. Instead, she is reminded of the man for whom her passion blazed so deeply—the man whom she has destroyed. Ned, imprisoned for Matty's murder as she had planned, sits in his cell, oblivious of his former lover's melancholy. It has been said a person should not wish for something too much, because it just might happen. In the case of Matty Walker, it did.

MAX CADY

Film Source: *Cape Fear*
Release Date: 1961, 1991
Focus: 1961 film version
Director: J. Lee Thompson
Production Company: A Melville-Talbot Production
B&W
Running Time: 106 minutes
Performed by: Robert Mitchum
Additional Performer: Gregory Peck (Sam Bowden).

Physical Description: Max Cady is a barrel-chested rowdy ex-con whose face is twisted in a perpetual sneer of jaded scorn. His rugged good looks, charming southern accent and trademark Panama hat and cigar are attractive to women, but rouse suspicions in the men he meets. Cady possesses unusual strength, and has no compunction about using it. Anyone crossing his path should proceed cautiously.

Character Analysis: Max Cady's single-minded focus on retaliation confirms Francis Bacon's assertion that: "a man that studieth revenge keeps his own wounds green, which otherwise would heal and do well."[3] Cady, newly released from prison, plans the destruction of Sam Bowden, the lawyer who prosecuted him. Bowden understands what is going on, but Cady taunts him, deviously staying within the law—and out of jail. Bowden offers to buy off his nemesis, but Cady, who misguidedly believes Bowden caused the breakup of his marriage, refuses to leave Sam and his family alone. Instead, Cady escalates his threats, and finally flaunts his baseness by his dispassionate murder of the police officer who is trying to protect Bowden. Terrified, Bowden hides his family in a deserted bayou, where they are trapped and further threatened by the madman. Cady's determination, however, cannot overcome Bowden's protective regard for his family. When he attempts the rape of Bowden's adolescent daughter, Cady finds himself over-thrown by the tenacity and courage of the lawyer he blamed for his own errors. The revenge Cady longs for obtains him nothing but waste. Based on a novel by John D. MacDonald.

MAXIMILIAN LARGO

Film Source: *Never Say Never Aqain*
Release Date: 1983
Director: Irvin Kershner
Production Company: Warner Bros.
Color
Running Time: 134 minutes
Performed By: Klaus Maria Brandauer
Additional Performers: Sean Connery (James Bond), Kim Basinger (Domino).

Physical Description: Maximilian Largo's eyes, overshadowed by arched eyebrows, become narrow slits when he smiles. His chin has a slight, attractive cleft in it. He wears glasses on occasion. Along with a receding hairline, he has tiny, rather eye-catching moles scattered about his face. Largo's sturdy build and energetic gait indicate a high level of activity.

Character Analysis: Errant billionaire Maximilian Largo uses de-structive methods to achieve power, control others and amass an im-measurable fortune. He hides his self-exalting, predatory intent beneath his cover as a noted philanthropist and benefactor of children. Largo is endowed with prodigious intelligence and a wide range of skills, which include piloting a helicopter and scuba diving, but he applies these var-ied talents toward deleterious ends. He has a fondness for *objets d'art*, which extends to Domino, his lover, whom he treats as a possession in-stead of a woman. Largo meets agent James Bond at a ball given in honor of his favorite charity, and the two men are instantly at odds for Domino's affections. Largo takes Bond's measure as an opponent by challenging him to a computerized wargame based on world supremacy. During this game Bond receives electrical shocks when losing, but con-tinues to play in spite of Largo's warnings. Eventually, Bond masters the game, and it is Largo who finds himself undergoing the shocks. Oblivious to pain, Largo jerks his hands from the controls with *bravura* at the last second, grins, then mockingly blows on his fingertips. Showing no interest in the money he has won, Bond piques Largo even further when he requests a tango with Domino. Largo has misled Domino about her brother, Jack, whom a brutal seductress has dis-patched. Bond persuades Domino of her brother's murder, then con-structs a scene between himself and Largo's *inamorata* that insures a response from the obsessively jealous Maximilian. While an enraged Largo smashes mirrors with an axe, Bond uses his time productively against his foe. In high dudgeon, Largo attempts to "sell" Domino to desert nomads and forces Bond to listen to tango music as further "punishment." In the end, Largo reveals the location of a stolen nuclear warhead to Bond, but having once threatened Domino with a slit throat if she left him, Largo finds himself the victim of arrogance when his lover retaliates by killing him with a spear gun from his scuba gear. By placing himself and his desires so far ahead of the concerns of others, Largo has unwittingly guaranteed his own eradication by the one who cared about him most. Remake of *Thunderball* (1965).

McDAGGETT: SEE: PAUL McDAGGETT

MERRICK: SEE: JUDITH MERRICK

MARQUISE DE MERTREUIL

Film Sources: *Les Liaisons Dangereuses*; *Dangerous Liaisons*; *Valmont*
Release Dates: 1959; 1988; 1989
Focus: 1988 film version
Director: Stephen Frears
Production Company: Warner Bros.
Color
Running Time: 120 minutes
Performed by: Glenn Close
Additional Performers: John Malkovich (Valmont), Michelle Pfeiffer (Mme. de Tourvel).

Physical Description: The Marquise de Mertreuil, with robin's egg blue eyes, and high cheek bones, is a woman of great natural beauty. She wears her light blond hair pulled back from her face in a style that accents her arched eyebrows. Her expensive jewelry and elegant gowns put her at the height of eighteenth century fashion. Augmenting her physical charm is her voluptuous and melodic voice. A mature woman, she has sustained her attractiveness, the essence of which arises, in every way, from her graceful, steady bearing.

Character Analysis: The Marquise de Mertreuil has gained power, fame, and the respect of her peers through manipulation, fear, and deceit. Her wealth and domination of those around her have allowed her to maintain an enviable station in life. Regardless of her success, however, the Marquise has not given a decent thought to anyone in years. Her mind is an overgrown tangle of burgeoning weeds and muddy swamps, and life for the Marquise is a series of one sorry intrigue after the other. She takes her greatest pleasure in the debauching of innocents. She avenges herself on her enemies by "twisting ropes about their necks," an activity which has become her everyday fare. At one time she had loved the notorious Vicomte de Valmont. Although their affair had ended in mistrust and discord, they have remained close allies in the pursuit of lascivious, ruinous games played with the lives of others. The Marquise prides herself on her icy demeanor, which stems in part from her inability to sustain love. Now her present lover has betrayed her, and she sets about to revenge herself on him. She schemes with Valmont, who will be placed as a guest in the house where her former lover's bride-elect, is staying. There he will seduce the innocent young girl—and make a fool of her deceitful lover. Valmont exacts a price for his role in this plot, a night of pleasure with the Marquise, and she assents. Yet she never intends for it to happen. Although she yawns as if bored, the Marquise is shocked when Valmont confides that he has fallen hopelessly in love with Mme. de Tourvel, another guest in the house, who is a truly decent and lovely person. The Marquise is jealous and pitiless, forcing him to quit the other woman if he is to obtain her favors. In the end, after Valmont has seduced the young woman, and has left the tormented Mme. de Tourvel—has indeed done all she asked—the Marquise still refuses him, instigating a "war" between them. Their impasse results in Valmont's death in a duel and the Marquise's downfall in society. She has remorse for none but herself, however, and her tears are not for Valmont, but shed in grief over her own loss. She considers everyone around her to be beneath her in wit, charm, and beauty, and treachery has become both an art form and a weapon for her amusement and gain. In a time and place where men hold the reins of power she uses her wealth and quick mind against them all. No man, not even the dashing, seductive Valmont, may take precedence over her own self-importance. Snubbed by her peers, the Marquise forcefully removes her make-up, as brutal toward herself as she has been toward others. Her outward behavior is seen at last as the forgery it is, but she still remains unrepentant. Deprived of her mask of virtue, the Marquise is left to the consuming flames of her own resentment. Oscar-winning screenplay by Christopher Hampton.

MICHAEL MYERS

Film Sources: *Halloween*; *Halloween II*; *Halloween III: Season of the Witch*; *Halloween IV: The Return of Michael Myers*; *Halloween V: Revenge of Michael Myers*; *Halloween VI: The Curse of Michael Myers*
Release Dates: 1978; 1981; 1982; 1988; 1989; 1995
Focus: 1978 film version
Director: John Carpenter
Production Company: Falcon International Productions
Color

Running Time: 92 minutes
Performed by: Tony Moran
Additional Performers: Donald Pleasance (Dr. Sam Loomis), Jamie Lee Curtis (Laurie).

Physical Description: Michael Myers is a young man in his twenties, of brawny build and large stature. He does not speak. His face is hidden behind a Halloween mask (of *Star Trek*'s Captain Kirk), and his exact facial features remain a mystery.

Character Analysis: Michael Myers murdered his sister with a butcher knife in 1963, according to the legend surrounding him. He was remanded to a minimum security prison because of his age, but he has not spoken a word in fifteen years. He has been diagnosed as a catatonic schizophrenic, but Dr. Sam Loomis, a psychiatrist studying the case, disputes this conclusion. Michael is no less than evil incarnate, in the good doctor's estimation. Michael being no fool, considers the astute Dr. Loomis to be his one actual threat. On Halloween, Michael writes "Sister" in blood on his door, and escapes the institute in a car—even though he has never driven before. Shocked and angered at his colleagues' indifference to his theory about Michael, Dr. Loomis warns the police, and sets out after him, knowing Michael will return to Haddonfield, and his long since abandoned home. Michael has acquired a "Captain Kirk" Halloween mask, which has less to do with Halloween itself than with his strong desire to conceal his true inner self from others. It pleases him that those around him, from his family to the doctors at the institution (with the exception of Loomis), have all been easily deceived by him. It is not the heroism, loyalty or sensitivity of "Captain Kirk" that most attracts Michael, but, instead, it is Kirk's resilience, determination, and near invincibility he admires. Michael also seeks this character's potency, which he believes will be fulfilled through killing, rather than creating. Murder is a form of self-expression, his own paradoxical, appalling view of procreation through destruction. Revenge slanted toward young women who remind him of his sister, as well as with anyone who stands in his path, interweaves itself into the fabric of his mind. He perceives himself as unconquerable so he cares not if his opponent is helpless or capable. Laurie, a high school student, has been in jeopardy since Michael's reappearance in town. She discovers her murdered friend and the young woman's boyfriend, also dead and hanging in a closet. Laurie, who is babysitting, races back to her charges, where she is stabbed by Michael. A fight ensues, and Laurie stabs and unmasks Myers. Dr. Loomis comes on the scene and shoots Michael several times, causing him to fall over a banister to the ground below where he disappears. Still calling Michael "pure evil," Dr. Loomis suspects he has not died. In this Dr.

Loomis has discerned a significant aspect of Michael Myers, who sees himself not only as indomitable, but immortal as well.

MILADY

Film Sources: *The Three Musketeers*; *The Four Musketeers*
Release Dates: 1974; 1975
Director: Richard Lester
Production Company: Twentieth Century Fox
Color
Running Times: 105 minutes, 108 minutes
Performed by: Faye Dunaway
Additional Performers: Michael York (D'Artagnan), Raquel Welch (Constance), Oliver Reed (Athos), Christopher Lee (Rochefort).

Physical Description: The radiant beauty known only as "Milady," dressed in exquisite gowns, glitters almost as much as her jewels. Her courtly speech has a blunt edge to it. On one hidden shoulder she bears the brand of a criminal. Her suggestive eyes, rippling blond hair, and tempting smile compose a picture both lovely and forbidding.

Character Analysis: Milady disguises her feral nature, with carefully balanced servings of modesty and restraint, from all but those whom she cannot mislead. Her predilection for extravagance is suggested by her opulent gowns and jewels. She demands the best, grasping at every scrap of wealth and power her treachery can obtain. Milady strides through the courts of eighteenth century French royalty, persuaded that her criminal past is guarded by her own elusiveness. She is in error, however, since Athos, her former husband, and now a musketeer, knows her for what she is. Milady is sent to reclaim two diamond studs from the Duke of Buckingham, as evidence of his possible liaison with the Queen of France. She loses no time in seducing the Duke and retrieving the stones. She hands the diamonds to the assassin Rochefort, explaining that the hardness of her heart and the jewels are similar, an established part of her persona, as is her obsession with riches and influence. Milady is detained and imprisoned by the Duke. She cozens her reverent jailor, Felton, who is disciplined and exemplary in conduct, by steadily reading aloud from the Bible. Felton is seduced by her false earnestness, and he helps her escape. Convinced of Milady's innocence and her accusations against the Duke, he makes an attempt on the nobleman's life and fails. Felton's ruin holds no significance for her, however, while the downfall of a prominent adversary is requisite, and a source of joy to her. She entices young D'Artagnan, a novice musketeer, into her bed, but discovers he is not the simpleton she assumed him to be. Milady threatens D'Artagnan's life and he takes flight. Counter to her former husband's warning, Milady ferrets out the secret location of the servant, Constance, for whom she has acquired an order of execution. Dressed as a nun, Milady enters the convent where the artless maid, the true *amour* of D'Artagnan, has been hiding. Transforming an instrument of prayer into a weapon, Milady contemns religion and the value of life as she strangles Constance with a rosary. His warning about Constance unheeded, Athos arranges for an executioner to behead Milady. D'Artagnan, in his grief for Constance, ignores her pleas for mercy. Milady, the center of her own narrow universe, sees herself as the superior of everyone about her. Insensitivity and the pleasures of wealth and advantage have enticed Milady more potently than she has enticed any of the lovers over whose ruin she has gloated. Her willful denial of Athos's judgment against her echoes her impudent roaring of self-congratulation for her multiple acts of evil, which have been performed with neither conscience nor restraint. From the classic tale by Alexandre Dumas.

MILL: SEE: GRIFFIN MILL

THE EMPEROR MING

Film Source: *Flash Gordon*
Release Date: 1980
Director: Mike Hodges
Production Company: Universal Pictures
Color
Running Time: 111 minutes
Performed by: Max von Sydow
Additional Performers: Sam Jones (Flash Gordon), Melody Anderson (Dale Arden), Topol (Dr. Zarkov), Ornella Muti (Princess Aura).

Physical Description: Emperor Ming of Mongo has eyes capable of broad expression, which draw and grasp the attention of others in a conflagration of impassioned pyrotechnics. Ming's lean form and great height are accented by his gaunt face, bald head, and arching, jet eyebrows. His rigid mouth is embellished with a curving moustache and straggling beard in the Oriental style. His majestic vermilion robe, blazoned with a gilded mantle, crests in elliptical fashion behind his head. At times he is seen in an ebony skull cap and black robes decorated with a sunburst of crimson. He occasionally wears a sword, but is never without his bejeweled ring, whose magic he alone understands.

Character Analysis: The Emperor Ming traces the halls of his palace toward the chamber that holds his latest desire, Dale Arden from the planet Earth. His movements, as he flexes his elongated fingers, define his nature—grasping, arbitrary, and bored. While some boredom may initiate creative thought and action, Ming has applied negative solutions

119

to the rigors of his personal *ennui*. Ming, discontented with his sovereignty over the planet Mongo and its attendant satellites, reaches into other parts of the universe in his yearning for control over all that exists. He has attained the status of a deity in his world, but the result has corrupted his life into one of extreme debauchery and untamed violence. Profligate in his early days, Ming's restlessness has swallowed him up in a whirlpool of adamantine truculence. His excitement and gratification remain the same—whether he is shattering the castle of his subjects, the Hawkmen, or murdering the prince of the Moon of Ardentia. Ming offers Flash Gordon dominion over the nearly destroyed Earth, but Flash is one opponent who does not respond well to bribery. Preferring to see himself as a person rather than an almighty ruler of the universe, Flash refuses to partake of Ming's society or its rewards. His offer refused, Ming leaves Gordon on the Moon of the Hawkmen as it is being blasted. Ming decrees he will marry Dale Arden, whom he considers a superior individual. Dale, while awaiting her enforced wedding, explains her own particular code of honor to Ming's daughter, the bewildered Princess Aura, whose father has made less than earnest promises to Dale. Aura tells Dale that her father is planning to execute Dr. Zarkov of Earth and Aura's betrothed, Prince Barin, in contradiction of his assurances to the opposite, but Dale remains unswerving—her pledge is her bond. Ming scoffs at Dale Arden's tears as evidence of human inadequacy, and forces Aura to undergoe torture, with a detached *hauteur*. Flash sends his new allies, the Hawkmen, out of danger, then guides one of Ming's own war rockets into The Emperor's armed palace. Skewered by the projectile nose of the rocket, Ming growls his continued, but less effectual, assertion that he cannot be bested by an inferior being such as Flash Gordon. Mongo's bestial sovereign, enabled by his magic ring, vanishes. The Earth he had played with like a toy is rescued from annihilation by the selfless, but intrepid, Flash Gordon and Dr. Zarkov, the brilliant scientist who first understood the danger Ming presented to Earth. Flash has become the catalyst for Ming's defeat, but it is The Emperor himself who is most responsible for his own downfall. Ming's subjects have placated him because they fear him, not from feelings of love or respect for him. Their uprising is inevitable. Ming, by acceding to the unrestrained indulgence of his own passions, has shaped himself into the fullest possible threat to his imperial reign. Inspired by the popular '30s serial.

MITCH LEARY

Film Source: *In the Line of Fire*
Release Date: 1993
Director: Wolfgang Petersen
Production Company: Columbia Pictures
Color

Running Time: 127 minutes
Performed by: John Malkovich
Additional Performer: Clint Eastwood (Frank Horrigan).

Physical Description: Mitch Leary's constants, without make-up, are his height, his deep-set eyes, his thin lips, his balding pate, and his protuding ears. Like a chameleon, he changes himself into older, younger, heavier, or slimmer men at will. He alters his clothing to fit the rest of his look. Leary's disguises are an essential aspect of his being which allow him to play a man of varying parts for various needs. He cannot, however, disguise his distinctive, whining voice.

Character Analysis: Mitch Leary's mind is a maze of terrifying chambers which Secret Service agent Frank Horrigan enters at his peril. Mitch enjoys "mind games," and he has carefully studied Frank's role as a Secret Service agent who was present at President John F. Kennedy's assassination. Mitch is a former C.I.A. agent, trained as an assassin, who has been "de-classified" and whose fingerprints have been kept out of public files. He has been unable to adjust to civilian life and, after fifteen years, he believes he has a "rendezvous with death," and plans to go out in style. Cold, hard, but in control, he murders Frank's rookie partner, then nearly murders Frank. His masterful disguises make it difficult for Frank to track him, although an acquaintence he once threatened is able to identify him for the agents. He opens a bank account under a false name from which he makes a large contribution to the President's campaign fund. He thus secures a coveted invitation to a fundraiser at which the President will appear and, in preparation for this event, Mitch constructs an ingenious disassembled plastic gun which the metal detectors will not pick up. In what will turn out to be his one big tactical error, Mitch murders the bank officer and her friend to cover his tracks. Mitch continues to bait Frank with phone calls, questioning whether or not the agent has "the guts" to take a bullet for the President. Frank overreacts and is taken off the case. He belatedly learns about the phony bank account, and decides Mitch has gained admittance to the campaign function. He rushes the meeting room just in time to "take one for the President." In their final confrontation Frank is taken hostage by Mitch on an elevator in the highrise. They scuffle and Mitch falls to his death many floors below. Mitch, who prided himself on being such a careful judge of character, has completely "mis-read" Frank—who certainly does have "the guts" to take a bullet. Mitch long enjoyed his opponent's reactions to his staged scenarios. Gifted and cosmopolitan, he is unafraid of death, when he finds he no longer has any life to consider. Mitch's thoughts are wrapped in sheets of twisted vengeance against the government he once served. A relentless pursuer, his anger has given him purpose. He is obsessed with assassinations and those who are involved with them, as the photographs tacked up in his vacant room prove. Instead of becoming one of the unforgettable assassins of history, however, Mitch becomes just another crime statistic, and doomed to well-deserved obscurity.

DR. MOREAU

Film Source: *Island of Lost Souls*; *The Island of Dr. Moreau*
Release Dates: 1933; 1977
Focus: 1933 film version
Director: Erle C. Kenton
Production Company: Paramount Pictures
B&W
Running Time: 70 minutes
Performed by: Charles Laughton
Additional Performers: Richard Arlen (Mr. Parker), Kathleen Burke (Lota), Stanley Fields (Montgomery), Bela Lugosi (Sayer of the Law), Leila Hyams (Ruth).

Physical Description: Dr. Moreau, out of respect for the climate of the South Sea Island he inhabits, attires himself in a three-piece white suit, a wide-brimmed hat to match, and a black tie for contrast. Moreau is an expert in the use of both gun and whip, and carries each with him at all times. He gives his black moustache and goatee careful attention. While he has a British dialect, a hint of his Australian boyhood remains in his speech. Moreau's heavy frame is braced by sturdy legs accustomed to extended walks. From his own comments he must be past forty. A haughty, gruff laugh and impish grin are preferable to the darkening terror of his more serious facial expressions.

Character Analysis: Dr. Moreau enjoys luxury of uncommon proportions. With the help of his assistant Montgomery, a disgraced medical student, he has set himself up as omnipresent potentate over creatures he has fashioned through lengthy experimentation. Dr. Moreau fled England—and a scandal over his experiments on animals—and for the last twenty years has made his home on one of the tiniest and most remote of the South Sea Islands. Moreau has continued his experiments on animals to verify his theory that all animal life has inclined itself toward humanoid development. Throughout his years on the island, Moreau has succeeded in manufacturing bipedal creatures capable of speech. Had gentleness and consideration been a part of Moreau's scientific method, and perceiving their capacity for speech and learning, he might well have developed a modicum of of kindness toward them. Instead, Moreau snaps his whip and his creatures disperse in terror of their master's despotic brutality. He remains unmoved by the excruciating pain his procedures cause, and works doggedly toward his goal, intoxicated by his unnatural achievements. Parker, a shipwreck survivor, faces Moreau with his disgust over the doctor's experiments, and Moreau smirks condescendingly at him, concluding that his "guest" has no understanding of science. Moreau has installed a fail-safe system in each of the creatures for his own and Montgomery's security. Manipulating them through a "Sayer of the Law," the doctor reduces these experimental tools to cringing slaves who deem Moreau godlike and invulnerable. His "laws" order their abstinence from meat, that they walk upright, and remind them constantly of their deepest horror—The House of Pain (where the experiments take place). The Sayer of the Law has been instructed by Moreau to make the creatures think of themselves as men, but Moreau himself considers them as anthropoid vassals. Montgomery, who has assisted the doctor for years, is clearly full of self-reproach regarding his affiliation with Moreau, and considers himself nothing more than an ignominious wretch. Parker becomes fond of Lota, the doctor's only female "experiment," and condemns the doctor for what he has done to her. Lota's animal-like claws regenerate, and Moreau concedes defeat—then reconsiders when he realizes that Lota has become the first of his creatures to weep real tears (although he has treated her as if she had no feeling). Montgomery undermines his superior's plan for further experimental torture on Lota by causing a malfunction in the laboratory apparatus. Parker's fiancée, Ruth, arrives on the island with a ship's captain, providing Moreau with a new idea. Still entranced by the conceit of mating one of his creatures with a human, he permits one of the males access to Ruth's bedroom. Making sure Ruth is safe from harm, Montgomery, who now distrusts Moreau, questions him closely about the incident, but Moreau equivocates and confesses nothing. In a final moment of anger, brought about by years of festering guilt and disgust, Montgomery renounces the doctor and his experiments. Reminded by Moreau of the charges awaiting him if he leaves the island, Montgomery states that he prefers a jail sentence to the doctor's company. Desperate, Moreau has the ship's captain murdered by one of his creatures, which shocks and infuriates the other mutants, since all form of killing is against Moreau's "law." The captain's death exposes Moreau's fallibility to his creatures and they come after him while Montgomery guides Parker and Ruth through the jungle. Lota dies in Parker's arms, following an assault by a male creature, and he mourns her death as a being who contained a humanity Moreau did not comprehend. The Sayer of the Law condemns Moreau, and accuses the doctor of having produced "things" rather than men. Moreau, cracking his whip, runs from his enraged creatures who drag him into the House of Pain, scene of their torment, where the doctor undergoes similar tortures at their hands. Moreau's compound is set ablaze by the creatures and burns to the ground. As Montgomery rows them away from shore, he admonishes Ruth and Parker not to look back. Montgomery looks ahead to the world he once fled as a refuge from the abhorrent prison he leaves behind. Moreau's dreams of fame and triumph perish with him, but the degradation of his victimized creatures endures in the memories of the three people who witnessed the conclusion of his experiments. Moreau believed in his own rightousness from the moment he began his work, and expected success as his due. His true desire became the adoration he received from his creatures, but he found himself defenseless when he lost their respect. In spite of all his intelligence, Moreau could not comprehend that his creatures' fear-laden homage would surely lead to contempt. Had he placed more value on compassion, a quality that defines both humaneness and "humanness," Moreau might not have become the victim of his own shame. From the classic tale by H. G. Wells.

MOTT: SEE: PEYTON FLANDERS

MYERS: SEE: MICHAEL MYERS

NAPIER, JACK: SEE: THE JOKER

COLONEL NATHAN R. JESSEP

Film source: *A Few Good Men*
Release Date: 1992
Director: Rob Reiner
Production Company: Columbia Pictures
Color
Running Time: 138 minutes
Performed by: Jack Nicholson
Additional Performers: Tom Cruise (Lt. David Kaffee), Michael De-Lorenzo (Pfc. William T. Santiago), Demi Moore (Lt. Commander Jo Anne Galloway), J. T. Walsh (Col. Markunson).

Physical Description: Colonel Jessep, dressed in his military best, is a strong figure of a man. His receding hairline and flashing eyes add to his looks rathcr than detract. He must be over fifty, but still looks fit. Although raspy, his voice has much charm. Jessep's most outstanding characteristic is his supreme confidence in his ability to lead his men.

Character Analysis: Col. Nathan R. Jessep's overriding concern is his position as commander of his troops, a responsibility he regards with deep respect and care. His post at Guantanamo Bay, on the Cuban border, is one of the most demanding and insecure in the free world. Private William T. Santiago, stationed on Guatanamo, is perceived as a "slacker" by his fellow Marines, and a "Code Red" is called on him—with Jessup's discreet acquiescence. The improper—and illegal—"hazing" procedure is meant as a disciplinary action only, but it backfires, causing Santiago's death. Two young enlisted men are arrested and charged with inadvertently killing Santiago, and a court martial is convened to deterine their guilt or innocence in the matter. Colonel Markunson, Jessup's subordinate, had been opposed to the Code Red, but had carried it out under Jessep's orders. Jessep, who believed he could "train" Santiago into the kind of Marine he should be, had refused to transfer the young man out of his command. Markunson's loyalty to Jessep is so great that he eventually commits suicide, rather than testify against him at the trial. No one dares question the Colonel or his method of command, and no one dares to tell him how to run his company. He is an extremist and a zealot in the service of his country. Subscribing to a military code of the strictest type, he sees his position as a Marine as the most significant any person can hold. The nobility of this concept sours in the hands of Jessep, whose respect for humanity and life has been lost in his pursuit of an ideal. He pointedly insults legal counsel Lt. Commander Jo Anne Galloway in front of her fellow officers, and he has no qualms about stating his opinions forcefully. A most non-evasive person, Jessup relates his feelings and reasons for his actions in the firmest possible manner before the court when he takes the stand. Jessep, who had been tapped for a top position on the National Security Council, lets nothing interfere with his responses to defense counsel Lt. Daniel Kaffee. Even when he is forced to admit his role in Santiago's death during cross examination by Kaffee, Jessup still sees no reason for his subsequent arrest by the military authorities. No one can alter the image he has built of himself and his command. He has expected blind devotion from his troops, but he has received it at the needless cost of the life of one of his men during peacetime. To him, his foremost duty is to protect and defend his country and its people, but his ideals have been twisted into aberrations of all that he once held true and dear. Strength, courage, and an abiding belief in his nation's security, have formed the positive side of Colonel Jessep and, in the past, he has served his country well. He refused to transfer an unhappy private out of his command because, to him, that would have been an admission of a weakness and failure which he could not abide. But Colonel Jessep's "code of conduct," no matter how gallant its goals, has led him instead into a type of close-minded behavior which is infinitely more reprehensible than any he had noted in the tragic Private Santiago.

DR. NO

Film Source: *Dr. No*
Release Date: 1963
Director: Terence Young
Production Company: United Artists

Color
Running Time: 111 minutes
Performed by: Joseph Wiseman
Additional Performers: Sean Connery (James Bond).

Physical Description: Dr. No's dark eyes, honed into acuity, gaze out over a sharp nose and thread-like lips. His jet hair is combed straight back, accentuating his high forehead. He is a lean man of average height, but his appearance is deceptive. His hands have been replaced, in the aftermath of a nuclear accident, with black steel prostheses, which contrast effectively with his oyster-white suit. He speaks in distinct, fluid syllables, reminiscent of a gurgling brook. His gait and movements are sure, commanding respect from others.

Character Analysis: Dr. No is an engineer who has designed an underwater viewport with unusual magnifying properties. His remote island retreat is but an outward indication of the inner distance he thrusts between himself and the remainder of the world. Unwanted and unloved as a child, Dr. No has become a cold, impassive adult who plans to punish the entire world for disregarding him. His attitude has been exacerbated by the amputation of both his hands, which raises a further barrier between him and the other humans with whom he comes in contact. Domination over them remains his single-minded goal. Dr. No has arranged a "dinner party" for Bond, who has become his prisoner, where he condemns the principal nations of the world for rejecting his services. Bond comments on the vulnerability of the island, and the doctor casually tells him this base is a temporary, expendable one, where he will contemplate his own restructuring and management of the world. The doctor's ambition centers on subjugation, and he uses fear as his operative insurance against disloyalty, as a woman in his employ attests when she conveys her terror of the scientist to Bond. Bond is not interested in a job in the doctor's nefarious organization, and Dr. No pronounces him a "stupid policeman." A colleague disobeys Dr. No's orders and is ordered to kill James Bond with a deadly tarantula. Dr. No's intended application of nuclear power for sabotage and extortion nullifies any potential good which he might have made of his work. Dr. No pummels Bond with his metal hands during a confrontation in his control room, and the platform they are on lowers into the contaminated water. Bond escapes, but the doctor cannot grip the metal support with his artificial fingers. Irradiation ends Dr. No's life, just as his earlier experiments with radioactivity destroyed his hands. Had Dr. No made better use of the sorrow and ostracism in his life, he might have benefitted millions of people. This choice existed for Dr. No, but he resisted it in order to pursue power and vengeance instead. In the end, Dr. No's self-glorifying achievements detonate at once with him and his island. Film based on Ian Fleming's character started it all.

O'BRIEN

Film Source: *1984*
Release Dates: 1955; 1984
Focus: 1984 film version
Director: Michael Radford
Production company: a Virgin Films/Umbrella-Rosenblum Films
Color
Running Time: 123 minutes
Performed by: Richard Burton
Additional Performers: John Hurt (Winston Smith), Suzanna Hamilton (Julia).

Physical Description: O'Brien, frail and in his sixties, resembles a human tombstone, with his plain clothing and unwavering frown. His cropped hair is tinged with gray. Metal-rimmed reading spectacles soften the inflexible glare of his eyes. Speaking in a methodical, low, whisper, and in spite of his grandfatherly appearance, O'Brien clutches his listener in terror, with each somber word.

Character Analysis: Psychologist Erich Fromm, in his remarks on aggression and sadism has said: "The person who has complete control over another living being makes this being his thing, his property, while he becomes the other being's god." Language, both verbal and written, is a vital ingredient in humanity's development and, by its effective use, its capacity for influence is boundless. O'Brien is a high-ranking official in a future reality who facilitates his land's stark tyranny by corrupting the thinking process of its inhabitants through the manipulation of language. He deems the abridgement and regimentation of communication to be the bedrock of his government's perpetuity. To this end "history" is modified daily into whatever "truth" conforms with the desires of those presently in power. O'Brien's responsibility is the eradication of personal freedom for anyone who resists his party's implacable oppression. Workers outside the party live in squalor, are uneducated, and are fed a constant diet of obscenity and propaganda concerning a fictitious leader, "Big Brother," and a counterfeit war whose opposing sides alter as party rulers specify. O'Brien's stratagems in defense of his party illustrate authoritarianism at its pinnacle. He "befriends" a minor bureaucratic employee, Winston Smith, complimenting him on his knack for tweaking journalistic propaganda, and bestowing upon him the gift of a freshly modified dictionary. Winston discovers the proscribed work of a silenced seditionist hidden between the pages of this sparse lexicon. He reads the book and begins keeping a diary, violating his party's interdiction against such acts. To add fuel to the fire, he meets, and falls in love with, Julia, a hopeful revolutionary, another act which is totally forbidden. Winston and Julia are apprehended by the police, and forced to undergo repulsive torture at O'Brien's calculated discretion. O'Brien sets forth his order's ambitions during Winston's torture, ironically disclosing his own collusion with the author of the forbidden book. He discovers Winston's diary, cynically noting his prisoner's naive confidence in the invulnerability of his freedom of thought. O'Brien uses implements of torture to physically break Winston and, at the same time, he attacks Winston's reasoning process by confusing him with selections from the diary, and by imprinting upon Winston's mind his own version of the sum of two plus two. Once Winston has been subjugated fully, O'Brien completes the process of undermining his internal liberty by confronting Winston with his most profound horror—rats. O'Brien mentions Julia's swift betrayal of Winston in passing, indicating that her torments must have been every bit as hideous as her lover's. O'Brien, by his own admission, believes in lying to his victims, debasing them miserably, and instilling unrelenting terror in them, in order to achieve his ends. By bringing about the loss of will and the emotional degradation of those like Winston and Julia, O'Brien has eradicated all traces of integrity and creative thought from his society. The party has bombarded the language of its adherents with unceasing new dictionary editions. O'Brien, in a similar manner, compresses his repellent view of the future for Winston: "...imagine a boot stamping on a human face—forever...." In O'Brien's reality atomic wars had devastated the planet, leaving behind anarchy, sickness, and hunger. He has ventured into a trembling, inconsolable world, alert to its every nuance of rage and lament. His eyes, so gifted at studying others, have explored the impoverishment and despondency around him, calling forth his deepest desire for power. O'Brien organized his plans for the future of his society long before he threatened Winston Smith with the cageful of rats, in whose bestial image O'Brien himself can be seen.

OSWALD COBBLEPOT: SEE: THE PENGUIN

OVERDOG

Film Source: *Spacehunter: Adventures in the Forbidden Zone*
Release Date: 1983
Director: Lamont Johnson
Production Company: Columbia Pictures
Color
Running Time: 90 minutes
Performed by: Michael Ironside
Additional Performers: Peter Strauss (Wolff), Molly Ringwald (Nikki).

Physical Description: Overdog is fitted with giant metal talons in place of hands which he manipulates no differently than ones of flesh. His body, human and machine, is a "junk pile" composed of knotted interlacings of wires and pumps; a hydraulic lift provides greater mobility for his aging form. A scrap metal plate covers the right side of his bald head. His eyes glint from their cavernous sockets like two points of light. Milky skin stretches over a cadaverous face distinguished by steel teeth and purple lips. When he speaks or laughs he hisses in a gritty, bass voice. Compact missiles under each of his huge arms protect him from attack.

Character Analysis: Dr. McNab, a physician specializing in plague abatement, was originally one of a medical team sent to provide assistance to the plague-ridden colony, Terra II. Quarreling with his colleagues after their arrival, McNab selected the appellation of "Overdog," and took charge of Terra II, plunging it into vitiation and chaos. Abetted by his assistant, "The Chemist," he has been conducting experiments on the planet's diseased inhabitants. Three women from Earth crash on Terra II, and a "spacehunter," Wolff, sets out after them for the reward offered. Wolff meets Nikki, a young girl who offers to lead him in his search. During their journey they are forced to defend themselves against the mutated, deformed victims of Overdog's experimental lunacy. They find their way to the stronghold where Overdog's slaves are kept to amuse him by running through a tortuous maze containing rotating saws, acid pits, and a spike-encrusted car. Nikki is forced through the maze but survives. Impressed, Overdog replenishes his energy by draining Nikki of hers, breaking his prior pledge to release her. Wolff comes to her rescue by electrocuting Overdog with a loose cable. Overdog exchanged his honorable code of medical ethics for an oppressive rule. Domination and malignity became addictions for him, proportionate with his expansive vanity. The formidable dilemma of the planet itself, intensified by his intense egoism, may have hurled Overdog into his relentless misanthropy. He turned his back on the original purpose of his journey to Terra II, and contaminated the colony further. His perfidious treatment of the colonists became nothing more than a sadistic entertainment for him. Wolff unselfishly risked his life to save Nikki, but Overdog repudiated such altruism by attempting to use her as an energy source for his own aging body. Until his death Overdog has reveled in the world he torments. In a grotesque parallel of the maze he created, Overdog contorted himself into a living horror.

PARKER: SEE: KATHARINE PARKER

PAUL MCDAGGETT

Film Source: *Robocop 3*
Release Date: 1993
Director: Fred Dekker
Production Company: Orion
Color
Running Time: 105 minutes
Performed by: John Castle
Additional Performers: Robert John Burke (Robocop/Alex Murphy), Nancy Allen (Ann Lewis).

Physical Description: Paul McDaggett, a distinguished looking man in his fifties, possesses a most ingratiating smile and noticeable dimples. Aside from his well-honed physique, he has a pair of memorable eyes and a finely trimmed crop of gray hair. His British accent is enhanced by his polished diction. A military commander, he wears a khaki uniform.

Character Analysis: For some the journey on the path of depravity is a haphazard road of uncertainty and regret, but for Incident Commander Paul McDaggett it is a march unbroken by contrition or scruples. McDaggett, fresh from a near-future war in the Amazon, has transferred with his loyal men to Detroit, Michigan to oversee the relocation of people who stand in the way of a renovation project. The chairman of Omni Consumer Products is unconcerned about his tactics, and has given him extreme latitude in handling the eviction of tenants of Old Detroit. McDaggett's use of barbarous coercion is the logical result of his wartime philosophy. He confronts a rebellious woman in the streets, knocks her down with his gun, then commands one of his men to "Shoot her if you have to...." This said, he tells one of his officers how happy he is with the "progress" of the operation. Beneath his icy, aloof, exterior his devious mind swelters in much the same way as the rain forest he has just vacated. He makes deals for his own advancement and financial gain, a path which leads him into an uneasy alliance with the head of the Japanese corporation which is backing the floundering Omni Consumer Products. He allows no one to inquire into his "methods"—not even those who employ his services, and he dictates to everyone, including the intimidated chairman who hired him in the first place. Robocop, a cybernetic police officer, is the only obstruction to his schemes. This is, after all, only a robot, and McDaggett despises robots. His loathing is directed also at Robocop's alter ego, Alex Murphy, a man who has devoted his life to the protection of those who are being victimized or harmed. McDaggett commands Murphy and his partner and friend, Officer Ann Lewis, to "get out of his way" from the steps of a church which is sheltering some of the homeless rebels for whom McDaggett has been searching. Ann defies him, something no one else has ever dared to do, and McDaggett shoots and kills her in front of Murphy, further evidence of his Arctic soul. He captures a scientist who may lead him to Robocop, and views the woman's rage on closed circuit television. "No one's listening to you, sweetheart," he whispers, grinning broadly. For him it will be "fun" to destroy Robocop. McDermott prefers being "in charge." He exercises his power over others, and the act of giving orders, not taking them, has become the center of his existence. McDaggett's confidence in himself, and the remarkable valor he displayed during the war, have decayed, transforming him into nothing more than a callous egotist and an authoritarian despot. An experienced liar, he convinces the press that Robocop is responisible for the murder of Ann Lewis. In a solemn voice he deplores this act of violence, fully cognizant of his own involvement in it. Once, in his past, he must have stood before two doors, one a passage into the history books as a dedicated soldier who inspired the respect of his troops, and the other a dark, gaping chamber permeated with viciousness and filth. Having proceeded through the latter door he became steeped in those traits he might once, in his youth, have found distasteful. Typifying the "filth" within him is his hiring of bloodthirsty criminals to succeed the police officers who refuse to assist him in his rampage. He leads his men into skirmishes unafraid. He faces Robocop, and points a gun at the head of the chairman of Omni Consumer Products, all acts suggesting a person who considers himself to be invulnerable. The Japanese magnate sends in androids who fell Robocop. McDaggett places his foot on Alex's metal frame and points his gun at the escaped scientist and the child with her. Threatening their deaths, he cautions his foe not to display any "flashy bravery." Undimininshed cynicism has eroded any trace of decency in McDaggett's personality. Left behind, his legs burned as Robocop ignites his experimental jet pack and rescues the scientist and the child, McDaggett strains to cancel the impending explosion. War and the making of it, rather than the longing for peace as the eventual outgrowth of the sorrows and torments caused by warfare, have conquered McDaggett's outlook. His death ends a career marred by the misuse of power and the unquenchable striving for more.

THE PENGUIN (OSWALD COBBLEPOT)

Film Source: *Batman Returns*
Release Date: 1992
Director: Tim Burton
Production Company: Warner Bros.
Color
Running Time: 126 minutes

Performed by: Danny DeVito
Additional Performer: Michael Keaton (Batman/Bruce Wayne), Christopher Walken (Max Shreck).

Physical Description: Oswald Cobblepot is a most unusual individual—from the tip of his super-elongated nose to the soles of his wide, flat feet—and his short, stout frame gives his walk a distinctive pitching gait. He has beady eyes, a broad mouth, and purple-and-black lips. He must hold everything carefully, since he has but three claw-like fingers on each hand. Oswald's hair is long, balding on top, and stringy on the back of his head. He is pale from living underground for much of his life. Everyone reacts negatively to the stench of the smelly fish he eats. Oswald is first seen in a long black coat that drags on the ground, and dark pants, but a public relations man soon attires him in finery. His honking voice and laughter resemble the bird whose name he has appropriated: The Penguin.

Character Analysis: Oswald Cobblepot's gruesome exterior hides a far worse interior. Abandoned as a toddler, and raised among the penguins, Oswald has returned to Gotham City, ostensibly to search for his long-lost parents. His real aim, however, is a bloody vengeance against all first-born male children in the city. He is the leader of a gang of circus people linked with criminal activities, but no one suspects his dealings except wealthy philanthropist Bruce Wayne. Wayne's alter ego, crime fighter Batman, foils many of The Penguin's plots behind the scenes, so Cobblepot boobytraps the famous Batmobile and sends the masked defender of justice off on a dangerous "joy ride" through the city. Cobblepot finds favor with the citizenry of Gotham who, blinded by his tale of an unhappy childhood, take him in and care for him with real compassion. Ultra-powerful business tycoon and political boss, nefarious Max Shreck, decides to replace Gotham's Mayor with the easily-manipulated Cobblepot—thus giving Oswald even more opportunities to take out his revenge on his host city. From the outset, Cobblepot has sought retribution for what his parents did to him. Now, in his rage, he decides he will kill all 100,000 inhabitants of Gotham City! Just as Cobblepot begins to speak before an admiring throng, Bruce Wayne takes over the loudspeaker, and plays a recording of Oswald venting his true intentions for the people of Gotham. Now, rejected by all but his faithful penguin friends, he wanders off to die, and is buried in a watery grave beneath the city he reviled. See also: CAT-WOMAN.

MR. PERRY

Film Source: *Dead Poets Society*
Release Date: 1989

Director: Peter Weir
Production Company: Touchstone Pictures
Color
Running Time: 128 minutes
Performed by: Kurtwood Smith
Additional Performers: Robert Sean Leonard (Neill Perry), Robin Williams (Mr. Keating).

Physical Description: Mr. Perry is a tall, slender man in his late forties, balding, and graying at the temples. He has a wide mouth, thin lips, and prominent ears. His high baritone voice possesses a commanding quality which is difficult to ignore. His eyes hold the attention of those around him, just as his voice does. He dresses in the conservative business suits and hats typical during the late 1950s.

Character Analysis: Mr. Perry could be described accurately, if sadly, as a "vise" which has taken human form in a manner both unthinkable and dreadful. Perry's wife and son Neill, two loving, devoted individuals, are a part of his life, but Perry, as unyielding as a rock wall, permits neither of them to make their own decisions. "Choice," in fact, is not a popular word in Perry's vocabulary, nor is he willing to extend the freedom of it to Neill. Perry has "sacrificed" by sending Neill to a preparatory school of note, thereby ensuring his entrance into the best medical school in the country. Perry chastens Neill for an imagined affront, then forces him to drop his work on the school annual which, in Perry's opinion, is interfering with his son's academic achievement. The advantages of the future, Perry believes, far outweigh anything he requires of Neill at present. Neill, although obedient to his father, has discovered in himself a gift for poetry and acting, and Neill's literature professor, Mr. Keating introduces the lad to these marvelous new experiences. Keating encourages Neill, feeling that an individual's dreams are meant to be pursued. But acting is not in Perry's grand plan for his son, who must conform to his father's wishes. Neill is treated by his father as an object to be chiseled into some perfect mold, rather than a sensitive young man who is maturing into an adult with his own creative personality. Neill's mother, who might have protected him, is also cowed by Perry's domination. Creative alternatives, in Perry's mind, are nothing more than useless distractions which undermine the perfect course of action he has planned that will benefit his son for the remainder of his life. Parents who love their children guide and direct them, yet parental love may also be expressed by providing the child with tools for independent decision-making, self-confidence, and self-expression. Neill finally makes some decisions on his own, but secretly, and without his father's required consent. He joins other students who gather, with Keating's encouragement, for private poetry readings in a cave near the school. This experience encourages him in his interest in performing on stage, and he realizes this dream when he is cast as a lead in the school play, Shakespeare's *Midsummer Night's Dream*. Keating advises Neill to attempt to explain his love of acting and his desire to do the play to his father, but Neill, cognizant of his father's likely response, refrains from this sound counsel. Neill is confident that his father will agree with his decision—once he observes him on stage, but the performance results in an angry Perry dragging Neill in disgrace from the theatre, while Keating, sympathetic and concerned, attempts to intervene. Perry has already determined his son's future, however—he will be removed from Keating's "subversive" influence and placed in a military academy where he will behave himself as he has all his life. Neill can no longer abide such treatment. He knows none of his requests will be granted, and he has no defense against his father's ultimatums. Perry expects absolute acquiescence from Neill, as though his son were still a child of five or six. Neill sees only one solution to his father's uncompromising absolutism—suicide. Neill abjures his position as the extension of his father's will, and leaves behind a shocked and tormented couple when Perry and his wife find their son dead. Perry's treatment of Neill was not, in itself, sinister or malevolent, yet it was extreme, and it is this selfsame extremism which leads Perry to call for Keating's removal from his dead son's prep school. Perry sees Keating as the true destroyer of his son's life, and reaches out with the tenacity of an octopus to force the school's administration to require most of Keating's students to sign an accusatory document which enables them to censure the educator. Perry does not blame himself for his son's demise. His distraught wife, traumatized by her son's untimely death, might see things differently, yet she still cannot defy her husband. Keating had inspired his students by opening new horizons for them and by raising their sights. In so doing he may have triggered the tragedy, inadvertently, by encouraging Neill in ambitions which his father found foolhardy and useless. Neill saw no relief from his father's sovereignty and omnipotence. He refuses further capitulation, however, an action Perry does not expect from his "dutiful son." Keating, dismissed and his reputation in ruins, leaves his classroom for the last time. Some of the students stand up in sympathy with their former teacher and Keating, grieved by Neill's death, thanks them and makes his leave. Perry's grief after Neill's death is genuine and remains unaltered. It has resulted from Perry's stifling, autocratic, and possessive "love" of his son as an object, which has denied him, ironically, a positive, lifelong relationship with a son who loved him genuinely in return.

PETER THORNDYKE

Film Source: *The Love Bug*
Release Date: 1969

Director: Robert Stevenson
Production Company: Walt Disney
Color
Running time: 108 minutes
Performed by: David Tomlinson
Additional Performers: Dean Jones (Jim Douglas), Buddy Hackett (Tennessee), Michele Lee (Carole).

Physical Description: Peter Thorndyke is a ruggedly handsome Englishman in his forties. His "dress for success" wardrobe tallies well with the top echelon of prosperous *entrepreneurs*. His shaggy eyebrows seem incongruous with his otherwise fastidiously groomed moustache and hair. His baritone voice can ascend into a falsetto twitter, whenever he is upset.

Character Analysis: Peter Thorndyke is a wealthy automobile *entreprenour* whose perceptions concerning the distinctions of class and social rank monopolize his thoughts nearly as much as winning races does. Thorndyke meets race car driver Jim Douglas and sees him not only as a prospective customer, but as a fellow sportsman as well. When he realizes he is mistaken, and Jim is *not* a person of means as he had first thought, Thorndyke plucks the drink from Jim's hand and bids him a brusque farewell. Before Jim can leave Throndyke's fancy showroom, however, an event portentous for both men takes place. Jim is mystified and the already ruffled Thorndyke loses his composure when a car the dealer wants to "dump" enters the showroom more like a sentient being than a machine. Neither of them believes the car is in any way "alive," yet Jim eventually is forced to trade his incredulity for understanding when he becomes the car's owner. Thorndyke is annoyed when he learns the car wins races, and plots its destruction, thereby alienating Carole, his most favored employee, and "driving" her over to the other side. Thorndyke regrets his sale to Jim, who begins winning all his races. At last Thorndyke's meager patience gives way as he snarls: "That little car is driving me biffy!" Jim worries about the car, nicknamed "Herbie," falling into Thorndyke's hands if he loses the next race. Thorndyke, preparing for the race as though he were waging a battle, wagers everything he owns on regaining "Herbie." When his underhanded methods backfire, causing him to lose the race, Thorndyke finds himself working for the businessman with whom he had placed his bet. While Jim's gratitude and concern for "Herbie" and his friends endow him with a fresh and positive outlook on life, Thorndyke makes no such inner strides. He remains as petty and inconsiderate of others as before, despite his reversal of fortune. His experience with "Herbie" further circumscribes his horizons, rather than broadening them.

135

PEYTON FLANDERS (MRS. MOTT)

Film Source: *The Hand That Rocks the Cradle*
Release Date: 1992
Director: Curtis Hanson
Production Company: Hollywood Pictures
Color
Running Time: 110 minutcs
Performed by: Rebecca De Mornay
Additional Performers: Annabella Sciorra (Mrs. Bartel), Matt McCoy (Mr. Bartel), John de Lancie (Dr. Mott).

Physical Description: Peyton Flanders's beautiful face and fabulous figure are merely a fraction of her physical attributes. She has lovely long, blonde hair, she speaks in dulcet tones, and her manner is understated and winning. Her glowing, knowing eyes may be her most potent feature.

Character Analysis: Dr. Mott, fearing an impending arrest on charges of molesting his female patients, commits suicide. His wife, who is pregnant at the time, loses her baby following news of her husband's death and her own impending financial ruin, and slips over into dementia. She changes her name to "Peyton Flanders," and goes on a vengeful quest to find Mrs. Bartel, one of the patients who had brought charges against her husband. She secures a position in the Bartel household as a nanny to their two children, a little girl—and a newborn son. Peyton surreptitiously begins taking over, making herself indispensable, and inserting herself into the lives of the Bartels, who remain unaware of her deception. She secretly nurses the baby, having kept her own milk flowing, and plots to seduce Mr. Bartel. Peyton engineers a bizarre accident which kills one of Mrs. Bartel's friends and triggers a near-fatal asthma attack in Mrs. Bartel. Mrs. Bartel is made of sturdy stuff, however, and Peyton's attempt fails. Mr. Bartel rejects Peyton's seductive advances and even the little girl recognizes her for the fiend she has become, wriggling out of her grip once she does. During a final confrontation with Mrs. Bartel in the attic, Peyton falls from the window and is impaled on the picket fence below. She had dreamed of a rosy future in the arms of Mr. Bartel, with his children at her side. Had she found the same courage and inner strength which saved Mrs. Bartel, she might have begun her new life in a positive way. Peyton's misery led her to sinister plotting and needless cruelty. The future she secured through her machinations was no future at all. For all her efforts, Peyton ends up impaled on her own miserable failings.

THE PHANTOM (ERIK)

Film Source: *[The] Phantom of the Opera*
Release Dates: 1925, 1943, 1962, 1989
Focus: 1925 film version (silent)
Director: Rupert Julian
Production Company: Universal Pictures
B&W
Running Time: 86 minutes
Performed by: Lon Chaney
Additional Performers: Mary Philbin (Christine), Norman Kerry (Raoul).

Physical Description: Erik shrouds his ravaged countenance, more skull than flesh, beneath an elegant opera mask. His brooding eyes are nothing more than hollowed sockets, encircled by pitch-dark rings. Knobby spurs protrude from his taut, ashen cheeks, flared nostrils emphasize a corneous nose, and crooked teeth are housed between shriveled lips, investing his misshapen visage with eeriness. Graceful hands and fingers seem incongruous with his disfigurement. He normally wears black pants and vest, a white shirt accented by a black, silk cravat and, over all, a long, ebony cloak. Occasionally he dons a pair of gloves. Erik attends a masked ball at the opera house he inhabits, costuming himself as Poe's terrifying "Red Death," swathed in a vermilion cape, a plumed hat and, appropriately, a skeleton mask over his own destroyed face. Erik gains the attention of the throng of revelers as he pounds his staff on the floor beneath him.

Character Analysis: The Phantom, once known as "Erik," is a mysterious, ghostly figure suspected of being an escaped criminal. Unseen by most, he roams the bowels of the Paris Opera House, leaving warning notes which frighten the managers and performers, and which underscore Erik's claim of authority over everyone. He has comandeered a favorite box where he is allowed to view the opera in seclusion. He becomes enamored of Christine, a talented young soprano, whose vocal skills he begins nurturing while concealed behind her dressing room mirror. Christine, intrigued by the Phantom's exceptional voice, his adulation of her, and his secretive manner, obeys his instructions and demands. The Phantom intimidates the opera's *diva* until she falls ill, which will allow his beloved student to take over the leading role and fulfill his ambitions for her. Erik, convinced that his pupil returns his love, finally beckons her into the halls behind her dressing room, where she encounters her "master" in the flesh for the first time. Christine recognizes him as The Phantom and faints at the sight of his masked face. She awakens in Erik's furnished chambers beneath the opera house where he shows her a coffin, explaining that it reminds him of his impending death which will deliver him from the torment of his affliction. Obsessed, he has decorated a room especially for her, full of clothes, shoes, and a wedding gown and veil. Erik has left a cautionary note for her which admonishes her not to look beneath his mask. Erik, seated at his organ, begins a virtuoso performance of his own composition. All meaning in the piece is lost for both of them, however, when Christine rashly unmasks him as he plays. In this moment revulsion becomes the focus. Vowing to be faithful, Christine leaves an enraged, tormented Phantom for the opera above his living quarters. At the yearly masked ball Erik, costumed as the Red Death, strides through the crowds of gamboling masqueraders, reproving their actions and reminding them of the slain who are entombed in the catacombs beneath their feet. As he speaks he notices Christine and Raoul, her lover, on the landing. Infuriated, he follows them onto the opera house roof, where he overhears their plans for marriage and escape. Christine's betrayal jars the Phantom, who abducts her during a performance. He has no interest in her explanations. Satisfied of his claim on her, he tells Christine she must be his at last. Having already strangled a prop man who found his hiding place, Erik drowns Raoul's brother. Raoul and a policeman follow Erik to an ancient torture chamber outside his apartment where he releases first a sweltering heat, then flood waters upon the two struggling men. His preoccupation with Christine steadily impairs Erik's waning reason, until he contemplates nothing except her accession to his demands. Christine pledges to become his wife in order to save Raoul, and Erik rescues the two men from drowning. Christine soothes her lover, and Erik's savage jealousy assails him once more. Clutching her arm, he drags her above ground into the coach meant for her escape with Raoul. Mindful of the opera house crowd behind him, Erik races through the streets. The coach overturns, and Erik leaves Christine to flee. The crowd surrounds him near the river. Jeering at them, Erik menaces them with an upheld fist, then unfolds his empty hand in mockery. The angry mob seizes The Phantom, and flings him into the river. Christine is led away by Raoul, and Erik dies, tormented by the loneliness he has endured during a lifetime of imprisonment and madness, and convinced he deserved some recompense for all he had lost through his disfigurement and confinement, Erik declared himself Christine's "master" as his right. He hungered for passion, tenderness, and love, but Raoul stood in the way, a goad Erik could not tolerate. Unflinching, Erik imposed his will on everyone about him. He added insult to injury by mocking the crowd who pursued him. His last defiant gesture, flung in the faces of those who had rejected him, was a blatant admission of his own lack of self-acceptance—rather than an indication of his misanthropy toward the crowd. Erik hid his twisted madness from himself much better than any mask could ever conceal his disfigured face from the rest of the world.

PRISON DIRECTOR POE

Film Source: *Fortress*
Release Date: 1993
Director: Stuart Gordon
Production Company: Dimension Films
Color
Running Time: 95 minutes
Performed by: Kurtwood Smith
Additional Performers: Christopher Lambert (John Brennick), Loryn Locklin (Karen Brennick).

Physical Description: Director Poe is either an "enhanced" human, or an advanced cyborg. He is tall, balding, and "fortyish" in appearance. His biting baritone voice, although abrasive at times, is polished in tone. His suits and high-collared shirts are stylish for the near future world he inhabits. Special orifices in his abdominal area accommodate tubes for his monthly intake of food and fluid. He neither sleeps nor dreams, but he does possess unusual strength.

Character Analysis: Prison Director Poe was removed from his mother at birth and raised (or created) away from his parents in a futuristic United States where a corporation, known as "Men-Tel," has nearly as much power as the government itself. Poe is cold and aloof as a result of his lack of contact with any nurturing individuals, and the single-minded pursuit of his life, as ordered by "Men-Tel," has been to run the monstrous underground multi-level penitentiary known as "The Fortress." He has accomplished this task in an efficient, though oppressive, style. Within the sterile environment of his living quarters he enjoys every convenience and luxury he craves. He "intakes" food at scheduled intervals, however, rather than actually eating it, and he has never traveled beyond the walls of the prison. Poe longs, therefore, for what he has never experienced. Here, in a future when people are reduced to the status of merchandise through the laser branding of barcodes on their arms, Poe lives in his isolated tower, longing for the family and humanity denied him through his "enhancement" and careful training. Torture, on the other hand, has become quite routine for Poe, and he administers it whenever and in whatever degree he deems necessary—or as recommended to him by the master computer. At this point in time, only one child per couple is allowable in the United States, no matter what the circumstances. John and Karen Brennick had lost their first baby at birth. Daring to consider a second pregnancy, they made an escape attempt into Mexico, but they are quickly arrested and convicted. John is brought before Poe who tortures him with a small metal device known as an "intestinator." When activated, this device acts as a mechanism of hideous pain, resulting in severe cramping or even death. Poe subjects John to this extreme conditioning which leaves him catatonic. The Director then probes John's mind while he dreams, and witnesses the prisoner's sexual recollection of Karen. A "light" switches on in some hidden recess of Poe's mind, inciting him into the unexplored areas long forbidden him by "Men-Tel." After a lifetime of adhering to the routine and dictates of his office, Poe now finds himself yielding to temptation. He coerces Karen into sharing his living quarters as his "companion." Although a cyborg, or techno-human, who cannot "make love," so to speak, he *does* crave intimacy, although later, as Karen discusses the highly advanced master computer with him, Poe threatens her "and her unborn child" with unimaginable pain if she ever betrays him. Poe's admonition speaks volumes about his unfeeling, truculent nature. The person he desires to be is so much at odds with the person he really is, that he fools himself into believing Karen actually wants him. He compels her to agree to marry him in order to set John free—and further to prevent her unborn baby from being "enhanced." Poe's concerns about Karen's loyalty are well-founded, however, since Karen, a former computer technician, feels nothing but disgust for Poe—no matter how he might try to please her. She convinces Poe of her "love" with her submissive behavior, then sets in motion an elaborate escape plot. Poe uncovers her deception and sends Karen off to have her baby delivered and her killed. Playing at love like a game of checkers, he neither understands nor realizes what it is to care for another more than himself. Proud of his "enhanced" status, he sees himself as far superior to ordinary humans. Not understanding the nature of love, he remains mired in wanting a person as an object for his pleasure and amusement. He offers Karen her husband's freedom and her baby's safety, not out of love and devotion, but from a willfulness originating in a lifetime of controlling others. Once Karen stood against him, and he saw his power waning, he had no trouble imposing a death sentence on her. Karen and John, who love each other unconditionally, in a way Poe could never understand, win their freedom and that of their child when the master computer destroys Poe, since he is the only target on which it can set its sights. Poe, nearly obliterated by the computer, lies on the floor, a mass of tubes and wires. He appears to be more machine than human in his final agony. His effort to transcend the *inhumanity* of "Men-Tel" and the horrific prison it had created for him was not enough to prevent his succumbing to the thrill his superiority and domination had created for him.

MR. POTTER

Film Source: *It's a Wonderful Life*
Release Date: 1946
Director: Frank Capra

Production Company: Republic Pictures
B&W
Running Time: 129 minutes
Performed by: Lionel Barrymore
Additional Performers: James Stewart (George Bailey), Donna Reed (Mary Bailey), Thomas Mitchell (Uncle Billy), Todd Karns (Harry Bailey).

Physical Description: Mr. Potter's thick eyebrows draw the casual observer's attention to the piercing squint of his eyes. His rounded cheeks are offset by a stubby nose and pursed, narrow lips. Feathery strings of white hair rest on the collar of his jacket. His standard business attire of dark suit, white shirt and tie, enhances his husky frame. He might gain sympathy, confined as he is to a wheelchair, with hands folded serenely in his lap, but his coarse surly growl of a voice is offputting.

Character Analysis: Henry Potter has lived his life alone in the small town of Bedford Falls. His only companions have been servants and other employees. While money and power are not evil of themselves, the desire for one or both can cultivate an evil nature, one which its owner frequently refuses to acknowledge. George Bailey, son of the founder of the town's respectable Building and Loan Association, is invited into Potter's office for a chat. Potter has used endless stratagems to destroy his sole competition. Now he offers George a fabulous job working for him rather than the institution his family has maintained through perseverance. George shakes hands with Potter, excited about this prodigious opportunity, then hesitates. Recalling the insincerity of the man, George reconsiders and refuses to take the offered position. Potter is infuriated, and seeks retribution. George has no idea of the depth of Potter's trickery. George's absent-minded Uncle Billy mistakenly wraps an envelope full of money for deposit from the Building and Loan in a newspaper he hands Potter. Potter is overjoyed when he discovers the envelope's contents, but makes no mention of the money he has found to George, who is frantically searching for the "missing" money. Potter is filled with pleasure as he verbally attacks his competitor, threatening the downfall of the Building and Loan—and a possible jail sentence for George. George, who loses all hope and contemplates suicide, is befriended by an angel who grants George his request—never to have been born. The angel shows George the town without him. Bedford Falls has become "Pottersville," a sordid microcosm of debauchery and privation. George's mother is an embittered widow, his uncle is in a mental hospital, and his brother, whom he had saved from drowning, is now dead. No person in the town has remained untouched. Potter, who now owns everything, has enslaved the town's entire population. Potter had told George that "...ideals without common sense can ruin this town." In this ominous representation

George realizes that it is Mr. Potter who, if unopposed, would become the source of the town's ruination. Potter, hollow, irascible, and grasping, regards the town as his own possession. George, his real world restored to him, faces his troubles happily, grateful for a life which now seems more prosperous for what he can contribute to it, than what he can gain from it. Potter gloats over George's approaching calamity, but George's wife, Mary, calls on their friends and associates for help. George is greeted by hands extended to him in the same unselfish manner as he has extended his own to others. People from the community are willing to give their money to the man who has protected them from Potter's machinations. George's best friend wires a blank check and, braving a blizzard to help in any way he can, George's brother Harry, thrills his recently dejected sibling with his unexpected arrival. George hugs his family and thanks his friends, while Mr. Potter rejoices over his thievery to no purpose. No one will display such concern for Potter, should the need arise. He has closed each door of friendship, love, and warmth on every person in Bedford Falls. Potter's money will be all he leaves behind after his death. His inhospitality and avarice will never be missed in Bedford Falls.

PRINCE PROSPERO

Film Source: *Masque of the Red Death*
Release Date: 1964
Director: Roger Corman
Production Company: American International Pictures
Color
Running Time: 88 minutes
Performed by: Vincent Price
Additional Performer: Jane Asher (Francesca).

Physical Description: Medieval Italian Prince Prospero is a handsome man, middle-aged, tall, with a slim physique, dark hair, and riveting eyes. He has maintained his strength and speaks in an eloquent baritone. Schooled in falconry and the use of the bow, he is a model of his aristocratic upbringing. Along with his chain of office, he dresses in the ornate costumes of his day.

Character Analysis: Prince Prospero may love death, yet he fears his demise at the same time. In his fabulous castle his debauched guests amuse themselves as the "Red Death" ravages the countryside beyond his stronghold. Prospero is the descendant of an inquisitor, an avowed disciple of "The Evil One" who stands against the church and God. His studies of dark rites and arcane ideas have led him into a world of ruthless saturnalian pleasures. Others have embarked upon a similar path of iniquity under his tutelage, and they are doomed to be destroyed at Prospero's whim for the appeasement of his demonic master. He is a cynic who ridicules all things decent. He spies on Francesca, a young woman from a nearby plague-stricken village, and he decides he must lead her too from the "light" into the "darkness." He takes her, her father, and her betrothed prisoner—then has everything and everyone else in the village burned. Francesca not only fears for the lives of her family, she must defend herself against Prospero's fiendish "instruction." Unable to turn Francesca, Prospero has her father and beloved brought into his banquet hall to play a deadly game—which her father sacrifices his own life to end. Her lover is exiled into the plague-infested kingdom outside the safety of the palace gates, a sure death sentence. Prospero then forces Francesca to attend a masquerade in the palace where, clothed in black, he has several more villagers put to death while he ignores their pleas for mercy. Ironically, even as he abjures the religious fanaticism of his ancestors, he himself persists in his own unchecked worship of evil. To his horror, "Death" personified comes for Prospero in the midst of the ball, and admonishes the terrified prince not to fear his touch, since his "soul has been dead a long time." Prospero is powerless to prevent his own demise, in spite of his exalted station in life—a reality he cannot accept. As his revels are ended, the plague also subsides. The virtuous Francesca and her beloved are both saved, preserved from the "Red Death" and released from Prospero's hold. Prospero, who cherished "sin," followed the course he desired, and perished in his pursuit of wickedness.

QUALEN: SEE: ERIC QUALEN

QUINLAN: SEE: HANK QUINLAN

NURSE RATCHED

Film Source: *One Flew Over the Cuckoo's Nest*
Release Date: 1975
Director: Milos Forman
Production Company: Fantasy Films
Color
Running Time: 129 minutes
Performed by: Louise Fletcher
Additional Performers: Jack Nicholson (R. P. McMurphy), Will Sampson (Chief), Brad Dourif (Billy Bibbit).

Physical Description: Nurse Ratched is a slender woman in her mid-thirties, of medium height, who appears strong and capable in her starched white uniform and prim nurse's cap. She wears little or no makeup, and her otherwise lovely eyes are cold, offering no relief from her stern features. She speaks in a civilized, well-modulated tone,

143

keeping her voice low—unless circumstances cause her to respond more harshly to her charges.

Character Analysis: Nurse Ratched could embroider the words: "conformity, obedience, routine," in bold capital letters across her uniform. This is the standard by which she measures all others. Her domain is the isolation ward for the insane where she works, a tiny island where she rules with impunity. Her authority is supreme at the insitution, where others defer to her judgment. She is aware of her position, and does not hesitate to use it to her advantage. Her profession has been a source of power for her from the beginning of her career in nursing. Most of the patients on her ward remain there by choice, and she has inculcated in them an unhealthy dependency on her and fear of the outside world. An example of her "healthy" routine is her habit of playing "relaxing" music so loudly that it disturbs rather than calms most of the men on the ward, her excuse being that the music should be loud enough to be heard by even the deafest of patients. Into Ratched's sinister web wanders R. P. McMurphy. McMurphy is an independent soul whose slick talk has delivered him from prison into Ratched's clutches, and she immediately recognizes him as a challenge to her authority to be confronted and defeated. McMurphy who is less suited than the others to this type of confinement, quickly "learns the ropes," and begins to challenge Ratched and incite the other patients to revolt. He becomes a special protector and mentor to Chief, a catatonic schizophrenic, and Billy Bibbit, a young man whom Nurse Ratched totally dominates as a Mother figure. Ratched's treatment results in the young man's suicide and McMurphy, angered by the injustice of it all, goes on a rampage. More for revenge than for need, Ratched coldly authorizes a lobotomy for McMurphy, knowing full well that he is not a legitimate candidate for this procedure. In the 1960's such drastic solutions for incorrigibles were more common; still Ratched has abused her authority abominably, and with a vengeful nature which she somehow continues to disguise from her superiors. Chief discovers what Ratched has had done to his friend McMurphy and uses his inner desire for liberty and unusual physical strength to smash his way out of his catatonia. He kills McMurphy then spurs himself on to escape from the tormented world which the nurse has created for her victims. Ratched is like a concrete "ice cube." The world has no color for her, and she has painted her world in a single hue of gray, with all her stern words, her unloving regulations, and her uncaring procedures. All dignity and independence have been suppressed from her charges, and she has stolen their hopes and dreams from them without mercy. Her autocracy, disguised as benevolence, does not prevent Chief's escape, which is more from Ratched than from the institution itself. She will not be able to remove *this* thorny defeat from her side quite as easily as she silenced the unfortunate McMurphy. Film based on the novel by Ken Kesey won five Oscars. See also: NURSE DIESEL.

DR. REINHARDT

Film Source: *The Black Hole*
Release Date: 1979
Director: Gary Nelson
Production Company: Walt Disney
Color
Running Time: 97 minutes
Performed by: Maximilian Schell
Additional performers: Robert Forster (Dan), Yvette Mimieux (Kate), Anthony Perkins (Dr. Durant).

Physical Description: Dr. Hans Reinhardt is a mesmerizing figure of prepossessing qualities. His sculptured countenance and eyes of pene-trating fire draw attention to his handsome features. His robust physique belies his years, giving him the appearance of youthful vigor. Elongated fingers invest his broad gestures with magnetic appeal. Whether attired in a knee-length white lab coat, beige shirt, and black pants, or dress uniform of carmine, Reinhardt holds his audience en-thralled. His mellifluent, kettledrum voice commands acquiescence from even those who disagree with the scientist's ideas.

Character Analysis: Dr. Hans Reinhardt has enjoyed twenty years of incontestable authority aboard the massive exploratory vessel, *Cygnus*, which he commands. Reinhardt and his crew have been on a mission to discover habitable planets. The famous scientist, who is recalled as being full of genius and ambition, with a "flair for theatrics," is still in fine form when he introduces himself to the crew of the much smaller craft which has just encountered his vast ship. Kate, a scientist en-dowed with empathic abilities, is seeking information about her father, one of Reinhardt's crew members. Reinhardt speaks of his tragic death as an accident which occurred as they ventured too close to the edge of a "Black Hole." In reality, however, Reinhardt had thought only of his own interest in the scientific project. Defying a direct order to return to Earth, he sublimated the wills of his crew utilizing a grotesque machine capable of enslaving the men, and developing an army of robots which serves for his own protection and comfort. Reinhardt fears only the gi-ant Maximilian, a powerful metallic creation who rules beneath his master. Maximilian disobeys Reinhardt's order and kills one of the vis-iting scientists. The doctor entreats the appalled Kate to stay with him and protect him from his own creation, but Kate resists his demand. Angered by her defiance, Reinhardt sends her to his laboratory for "conditioning." Kate is rescued by a friend, but her own captain leaves with his ship, abruptly abandoning his crew members to Reinhardt's devices. Maximilian begins to take over *Cygnus*, which heads towards the Black Hole as the others escape in Reinhardt's probe ship. Reinhardt, crushed by falling debris, cries out for help. But his pleas fall unheeded on the men he has programmed to be his slaves. As the probe escapes to safety, Reinhardt is absorbed into Maximilian, and is posted as a sentry in the world of the Black Hole. Reinhardt believed that the Black Hole contained infinite knowledge and the key to immortality. He had longed to become the one individual in history to explore such a phenomenon. Now Reinhardt will evermore be recalled as the victim of his own creation. Inclined toward theatrical displays, and obsessed with his control of others, Reinhardt's final role as "watchman" over a grim realm is a suitable one. Perched on a crag, he guards a hellish domain. Preoccupied with his own intellect and achievements, Reinhardt willingly sacrificed his crew and his principles for his ultimate journey. Reinhardt's deliberate pursuit of the Black Hole has left him isolated on his cliff, with an eternity to reflect upon the silent robots and automatons he created. They heard every word he spoke—but in the end, being less than human, they could not or would not respond to his desperate cries for help.

REVOK: SEE: DARRYL REVOK

RICK MASTERS

Film Source: *To Live and Die in L.A.*
Release Date: 1985
Director: William Friedkin
Production Company: New Century Productions Ltd./Slim Inc.
Color
Running Time: 114 minutes
Performed by: Willem Dafoe
Additional Performer: William L. Petersen (Richie).

Physical Description: Rick Masters is thirtyish, lean and fit, with dark hair, light eyes, and a square jaw. He adds a touch of mystery with his black attire. His deep voice has a singular quality. He cannot be called "handsome," but Masters makes a strikingly effective impression upon those he meets by virtue of his unusual facial structure and confident air.

Character Analysis: Rick Masters, once convicted for armed robbery, is an artist who has bastardized his artistic ability by producing counterfeit money. He walks in on his lover with his associate whom he shoots, more because he suspects the man of siphoning off extra money for himself than out of jealousy. Richie, a police officer, finds the body and concocts an elaborate plan to apprehend Masters. Richie is killed and Rick, who is shot, flees. Rick had expressed his inner self through his art, but the contrast between who he is inside and what he does publicly signifies his ambivalent, irresolute nature, and culminates in the purging of the artistic portion of himself. Cornered, he sets fire to his paintings and destroys them, then dies in the fire, thus repudiating his own creativity through the self-destructive urges within him. Ecstacy lights up his face as he dies, consumed by the fire he himself has set. He inhabits one body occupied by two opposing minds. Entrenched in lawlessness, one part of him pursues the lucrative venture of counterfeiting perfect bills, while the other part of him burns the art he has created, never quite believing it is perfect enough. It never can be, given his own self-doubt that he himself is good enough to create it.

ROAT: SEE: HARRY ROAT, JR.

ROCCO: SEE: JOHNNY ROCCO

ROSA KLEBB

Film Source: *From Russia with Love*
Release Date: 1963
Director: Terence Young
Production Company: United Artists
Color
Running Time: 118 minutes
Performed by: Lotte Lenya
Additional Performers: Sean Connery (James Bond), Daniela Bianchi (Tatiana Romanova).

Physical Description: Rosa Klebb, a short, stocky woman in her fifties, has reddish hair pulled behind her ears and, on occasion, wears thick glasses. She is habitually stern in her correctly tailored clothes. Although she is a smoker, she has remained able-bodied, testing the fitness of a male fellow agent with her brass knuckles.

Character Analysis: Rosa Klebb is a former agent of the KGB who has joined up with the vile organization known as SPECTRE. She has been assigned the task of procuring a crucial device, which is also being sought by British secret agent James Bond. Klebb schemes to set Bond up with Tatiana Romanova, a lovely and talented Russian agent whom Rosa desires for herself. Klebb films Tatiana and Bond during a sexual encounter, an openly indecent act committed ostensibly to obtain information. Instructed by her employer to dispatch Bond, Klebb lunges at him with the poisoned knife concealed in her shoe, but is shot by Tatiana instead. Her nimble wits have advanced her power, but Klebb has used her talents exclusively for acts of iniquity and destruction. Her inconsiderate domination of Tatiana leads the younger woman to betray Klebb, whose life is ended as she lived it, in the most violent way possible.

ROTWANG

Film Source: *Metropolis*
Release Date: 1926
Director: Fritz Lang
production Company: UFA
B&W
Running Time: 115 minutes
Performed by: Rudolf Klein-Rogge
Additional Performers: Alfred Abel (Jon Fredersen), Brigitte Helm (Maria), Gustav Frölich (Freder).

Physical Description: Rotwang is an aged scientist with an untamed shock of white hair and a burning gaze. His artificial right hand, the result of an accident he experienced while experimenting in the field of robotics, is kept concealed in a jet black rubber glove. Beneath Rotwang's belted black laboratory coat he wears a white shirt under a dark vest. His pockets, wide and deep, match the profundity of the inventor's mind well.

Character Analysis: Rotwang, a peerless scientist, has single-mindedly toiled over many years to create a perfect lifelike automaton. He kidnaps Maria, the spiritual leader of the workers of Metropolis, whose ideas on civil disobedience have angered Jon Fredersen, a leading citizen of the city. Taking Maria prisoner, the scientist informs her of his intention to model his android in her image. Rotwang is visited by Fredersen and lifts his artificial hand high above his head as he fervently proclaims his "sacrifice" for his work to be a reasonable one. He announces to Fredersen the end of a need for human workers because of his robotic invention, and agrees to Fredersen's demand for the aggressive utilization of his Maria "look-alike" without question, his one consideration being universal acceptance of his robot as a human being. At a public event, Rotwang and Fredersen exult when the robot is accepted as a human, but it is the scientist who rejoices most at his accomplishment. Alone in his house with the "real" Maria, Rotwang, monomaniacal in his dream, ponders the triumphal confirmation of his experiments. He remains unfeeling about the real live human being he has dragged into his laboratory and kept captive there. Marching from his house like a somnambulist, the inventor learns his "false" Maria is burning at the stake. Disregarding the sorrow his robot has brought to the workers and their families, and knowing how angry they will be once they learn of his treachery in sending a robot into their midst for the purpose of sabotage, Rotwang does not admit his own duplicity when he recounts the essence of Fredersen's stratagem to them. The "real" Maria escapes, and Rotwang chases her down and abducts her again. Fredersen's son, Freder, who truly loves Maria and believes in her teachings, follows the scientist and his captive into a cathedral where, after a frenzied struggle, Freder rescues Maria. As Rotwang falls to his death from a scaffolding, Jon Fredersen, watching in horror from below, repents his injudicious maneuvering and recants. Rotwang, in his quest for greatness and achievement, has shed his humanity at the cost of his life. He has separated himself from the rest of the world, and this severing of all human ties clutches at him, hedging him in, so that he sees only the narrow design of his own personal universe, which languishes and perishes without the human touch. Classic SF.

ROY: SEE: AARON/ROY STAMPLER

MRS. RUBY DEAGLE

Film Source: *Gremlins*
Release Date: 1984
Director: Joe Dante
Production Company: Warner Bros.
Color
Running Time: 106 minutes
Performed by: Polly Holliday
Additional Performer: Zach Galligan (Billy Peltzer).

Physical Description: Mrs. Deagle's black hat, covered with soft feathers, seems incongruous above her frowning brow. She is a graying matron of slender build who parades through the streets of Kingston Falls, dressed in ostentatious, though antiquated, clothing. Beneath her auburn wig and a slathering of cosmetics, the creases in her face seem to have been etched by her almost indelible glower, rather than the more benign furrows left there by time.

Character Analysis: Mrs. Deagle expects to be first in Kingston Falls where she lives, or anywhere else, for that matter. She snaps at people on the street, forces her way to the front of lines, and generally exhibits no courtesy to anyone unfortunate enough to pose a hindrance to her. Her lack of respect for others has been fashioned from the lifetime she spent with a gangster husband—who has left her the wealthiest widow in town. Mrs. Deagle exhibits her view of the world when approached by a woman with two small children in tow. The woman and her husband have not as yet been paid at their new jobs, and the children being ill, she is requesting an extension on their mortgage payment. Mrs.

Deagle insults the woman, reminding her that her only interest is in the money due her. Mrs. Deagle proceeds into her bank where she shoves the head of her destroyed "snowman" ornment into bank teller Billy Peltzer's face. His dog has exhibited "unruly behavior" toward the snowman. Billy offers to pay for the broken ornament but is dimissed by Mrs. Deagle, who demands Billy turn the animal over to her for extermination. Impatience and anger epitomize Mrs. Deagle, but she does have a soft place in her granite heart for her throng of cats, who represent her single link with positive emotion and decency. Her home is accidentally invaded by the malicious imps unleashed through Billy Peltzer's pet, Gizmo. Her lack of conscience enables these little horrors to propel her straight from her chair lift to her death. Money and power do not necessarily go hand in hand with inclemency, but Mrs. Deagle was swayed by them until her entire world became centered on what she had and what she could take from others. If she had displayed less hostility toward the people in her community, she might have won their respect and love. The residents of Kingston Falls were merely conveniences to Mrs. Deagle, who looked upon them as walking currency, not people with feelings and needs. Mrs. Deagle's rancorous, antisocial personality makes her death a relief to her town—instead of being first in their minds and hearts, she is the last person they'll mourn.

RUDOLFO LASSPARRI

Film Source: *A Night at the Opera*
Release Date: 1935
Director: Sam Wood
Production Company: MGM
Color
Running Time: 84 minutes
Performed by: Walter King
Additional Performers: Marx Brothers, Allan Jones (Ricardo Barone), Kitty Carlisle (Rosa).

Physical Description: Rudolfo Lassparri's suits, the finest money can buy, complement his physique. He often wears a homburg in public. A thin moustache, dark hair, and good looks are accentuated by a rakish smile. Hints of scorn undermine his already discordant operatic tenor.

Character Analysis: Herman Gottlieb. owner of the New York Opera has declared Rudolfo Lassparri to be its most eminent tenor and, as a result, Lassparri's pride remains his most noteworthy feature. Lassparri uses the excuse of laryngitis when he refuses to sing for his admirers on the dock while awaiting his departure on a ship bound for New York. With a flippant wave of his hand he turns from the crowd and declares openly that money alone will induce him to sing. Meanwhile, Ricardo Barone, a lesser known member of the company, is asked for a number and responds with grace and style. The talented Rosa, the comely soprano Lassparri has been wooing with little success, accurately perceives Lassparri's intentions toward her as dishonorable. During a banquet on shipboard Lassparri praises himself as a singer, while Rosa listens unmoved. Conceit leads Lassparri to believe that by ensuring the female lead for Rosa she will surrender to him, but his jealousy of Barone will eventually lead Lassparri to seek to have Rosa fired. He acts with an artificial gentility which often clashes with his true violent nature. He shows his dresser every courtesy in order to impress someone one moment, then whips him out of anger the next, an act of heavy-handed abuse which repels Rosa. She rebuffs Lassparri and he handles his frustration like a three-year-old having a tantrum, stamping his foot and clenching his fists, as if he might actually punish her physically for her actions. Several of Rosa's friends, all of whom consider Lassparri to be a pompous ignoramous, demolish the opening night of Verdi's *Il Trovatore* in order to kidnap Lassparri and prevent him from performing. Rosa then suggests to Herman Gottlieb that he replace Lassparri with Barone—who so delights those in attendance that the irascible Lassparri is booed off the stage when he returns. Fame does not inspire conceit or lack of integrity any more than it precludes them. Lassparri became what he is long before he became a star with the opera. He insists on the world rotating about him, and has no patience whatever with any other viewpoint. In fact, Lassparri's self-importance is his most conspicuous attribute, and he refuses to look upon his operatic failure as an instructive experience. Learning and change may represent lifelong activities for others, but they hold no interest for Lassparri, who exits stage left, grudging and acrimonious, petulance intact. Hilarious Marx Brothers classic.

SADOR

Film Source: *Battle Beyond the Stars*
Release Date: 1980
Director: Jimmy T. Murakami
Production Company: New World/Roger Corman
color
Running Time: 104 minutes
Performed by: John Saxon
Additional Performers: Richard Thomas (Shad).

Physical Description: Sador, hair cropped short, is much advanced in years, although his youthful looks conceal it. Parts of his body have been replaced with the limbs and organs of those he has conquered and, when first met, Sador's right arm is in a sling, awaiting a replacement from some unwitting, compatible donor. His face, as a whole, is attractive, although a bluish diamond-shaped discoloration, possibly a birthmark, or a symbol of his class and rank, runs from just above Sador's left eyebrow to the middle of his left cheek. Sador is of medium height and sturdy frame. He wears his gaudy uniform with the assurance of command. His low tenor voice has great personal charm, which is somewhat offset by his stark and ungracious delivery.

Character Analysis: Sador has lived his extended life in the pursuit of twin goals: the conquest of alien worlds—and his own immortality. Nothing can prepare a planet targeted by Sador for the brutal force both threatened—and used by him. For years Sador has brought many worlds under his dominion, while obliterating still others with his "stellar converter." Sador's first act, as he enters the orbit of the peaceful, non-violent world of Akir, is to destroy a weather station, then demand complete capitulation of the planet within seven days. He is pleased when informed of his compatibility with the indiginous population of Akir, since he is presently in need of a replacement donor for his decaying right arm. Subordinates left behind to guard Sador's intended colony speak of a fellow crewman whose left foot their commander now wears. No one can remain tranquil or secure under Sador, since his prolonged existence is dependent on the intentional deaths of others. He has placed himself above any legal system in the universe, and rejects all codes of ethics. Chained to his unquenchable, futile pursuit for omnipotence, however, Sador is more a prisoner to his theoretically unconquerable ship, than a captain of it. The one joy in his life is his tyranny over others. He speaks of how much "pleasure" it gave him to destroy an entire world during a battle with one of its survivors. His emissary is killed by a planet resisting his mastery, and Sador turns it into a star. Finally, a single fighting ship piloted by Shad, a young inhabitant of the destroyed world of Akir who is supported by a miniscule collection of mercenaries, defeats Sador and renders him a fool, instead of the titan he envisions himself. His ship lost and his gangrenous arm now amputated, Sador wails like a baby that he must "live forever." Ironically, Sador, who has reigned as tormentor of the galaxy, ends his existence at the hands of those whose planet had the highest regard for all life forms. Sador had no time or respect for any form of life, therefore his death calls forth no grief from any of them. Beginning his voyages as a tyrant over many worlds, he concludes his journey as no more than a shabby, one-armed, bawling driveler.

SCARAMANGA: SEE: FRANCISCO SCARAMANGA

SCORPIO (THE KILLER)

Film Source: *Dirty Harry*

Release Date: 1971
Director: Don Siegel
Production Company: The Malpaso Company
Color
Running Time: 102 minutes
Performed by: Andy Robinson
Additional Performers: Clint Eastwood (Harry Callahan).

Physical Description: "Scorpio" is a young man whose eyes glower like twin incenerators deep in the cavern of his face. Of medium height and weight, Scorpio's deceptively weak frame is set off by the rumpled clothing and unkempt hair he habitually sports. His exaggerated mouth and thick lips are exacerbated by the churlish delivery and vulgarity of his speech.

Character Analysis: The sole representative characteristic of the killer who identifies himself as "Scorpio" is viciousness, a trait which has proliferated in him since his youth. A nervous, lonely child inside, he makes up the rules by which he plays as he goes along, manipulating and blaming others to vent his anger. He attempts to extort $200,000 from the city of San Francisco with his threats of mayhem, but beyond the money, his true motive is to satisfy his captivation with the twin acts of violence—torture and murder. Scorpio uses his talent as a sharpshooter to kill a woman swimming in her rooftop pool high atop a building. A scrawled note to the police remarks on how he might enjoy killing a Black individual, or even a priest, and he selects his next victim, a young Black man, while waiting on a roof across from a church. Scorpio's harsh impersonal touch finds expression when he encloses a tooth pulled from the mouth of a fourteen-year-old girl in the ransom note he sends to the police. Harry Callahan, an inspector with the San Francisco Police Department, is a man casehardened by the ungovernable violence he has struggled against for years. He senses Scorpio's underlying irrationality, and he fast loses patience with his superiors' acquiescence to the crazed killer's demands. Callahan delivers the ransom, then endures a ferocious beating at the hands of Scorpio, who tells Callahan in a crazed giggle that the young girl will die anyway. Scorpio threatens Callahan's life and wounds his partner, but Harry rallies and thrusts a knife into the surprized killer's leg. Sickened by Scorpio's ruthless vow to let the kidnapped girl die, Callahan chases Scorpio onto a nearby football field and corners him. Horrified, Scorpio screams for his rights, while Callahan uses the extreme measure of pressing on the man's injured leg until Scorpio gives up and divulges where he has hidden the girl, but escapes. Callahan follows Scorpio everywhere, hoping to abort the killer's next move, but the killer, enraged and intimidated by the inspector's actions, lashes out in a perverse manner. Scorpio hires a man to "beat him up" for a fee, then accuses Callahan of brutalizing him. Callahan, furious over the allegation, denies any guilt when questioned by his superior. Not satisfied, Scorpio once more issues a ransom note. This time he has seized a school bus, and is holding the children and their driver hostage. Callahan overtakes the killer on an overpass, and leaps on top of the bus to flush Scorpio out. Scorpio protects himself by holding his gun on a child, certain that Harry would not dare fire on him. He is dumbfounded when Callahan shoots him anyway. As the killer falls into the sea, Callahan, fully aware of the orders he has disobeyed, throws his badge in after him. Callahan bends and breaks the rules to save a child, but Scorpio accepts no rules at all. He has lived a short, nasty, life, and his chosen alias fits him well; scorpions are vicious crawling killers—not to be trusted. Scorpio developed his bestial mentality while still a child, when his rankling against authority, his misogyny and bigotry, were all thoroughly entrenched in his inherent ego. Scorpio's response to his own emotional vacancy took the form of explosive criminality—and he became a man who inhabited the fringes of society, crawling, ever crawling, toward oblivion. Classic Eastwood.

SELENA KYLE: SEE: CATWOMAN

SHARP, HELEN: SEE: MADELINE ASHTON & HELEN SHARP

SIKES: SEE: BILL SIKES

SIMPSON, MARY ANN: SEE: MATTY WALKER

STAMPLER: SEE: AARON/ROY STAMPLER

STARK: SEE: GEORGE STARK

DR. TERMINUS

Film Source: *Pete's Dragon*
Release Date: 1977
Director: Don Chaffey
Production company: Walt Disney
Color
Running Time: 128 minutes
Performed by: Jim Dale
Additional Performer: Sean Marshall (Pete).

Physical Description: Dr. Terminus draws everyone's attention, dressed in his ostentatious garments, like some tall, motley placard. His black waistcoat and bright orange vest are topped by grey-and-white pinstriped pants, a grey cape, and a ruffled collar trimmed in black satin. He wears orange garters around his white shirt sleeves, and white gloves. His costume is complemented by a fancy black top hat, encircled with an orange headband. Dr. Terminus has glittering eyes and a long face, punctuated with a moustache and beard. His great booming voice and huge grin are excellent attributes for his role as a medicine show charlatan.

Character Analysis: Dr. Terminus's occupation is defrauding people, and his entrance into—and exit from—the towns he visits is quite spectacular. His flashy medicine show vehicle provides more than a means of escape for Terminus and his associate, however. It also houses his array of spurious remedies. He careens into the seaport of Passamaquaddy, smashes a fence, then tears down the staircase leading up to the mayor's office. The town's residents scream insults at him as soon as he begins hawking his useless wares and, while he sings and dances, he engages in repartée with two dissatisfied customers. He offers no apologies for the misfortune he has caused, as he compliments a woman who holds a less than enthusiastic view of his "weight loss" formula, and an angry man's hair has turned from gray to pink, the result of another one of the doctor's bogus elixirs. The man is not impressed when Terminus assures him that "the color is so becoming." The pursuit of money commands the doctor's life, and he postpones his departure from town when he learns of Elliot, a real live dragon, and friend of Pete, an orphaned child. He ruminates on the extraordinary wealth he might gain from potions made from the creature. He is so overcome by his dream of riches, that he allows Pete to be captured by his former "family," a disreputable group who used Terminus as a slave before he escaped them. Elliot is trapped under a giant net, and Terminus aims a harpoon at the creature. Elliot escapes, however, taking Pete with him, and leaving Dr. Terminus hanging upside down from a pole in the middle of town. Dr. Terminus is a good-for-nothing charlatan who finds himself topsy-turvy, suddenly undone by a boy and his unusual companion, who out-fool the fool.

THORKEL: SEE: ALEXANDER THORKEL

THORNDYKE: SEE: PETER THORNDYKE

TOMMY UDO

Film Source: *Kiss of Death*
Release Dates: 1947, 1995
Focus: 1947 film version
Director: Henry Hathaway
Production Company: Twentieth Century Fox

B&W
Running Time: 99 minutes
Performed by: Richard Widmark
Additional Performer: Victor Mature (Nick Bianco).

Physical Description: Tommy Udo is a presentable man in his late twenties, of medium height, and slight of build. He wears dark pants and shirts, set off by light ties, and occasionally he dons a hat and overcoat. Tommy's bizarre, offensive, and high-pitched giggle is his most noticeable and unforgettable quality, putting everyone's nerves on edge—even as it holds the attention of those he meets or knows well.

Character Analysis: In baseball, an untrained person who exhibits exceptional talent is dubbed a "natural," and Tommy Udo is a "natural" at violence. Tommy grew up too fast, too cold, and too hard. He responds to the idea of "love" with an earsplitting snicker. "Love is for squirts," he spits out curtly, in gruff, angry tones. He treats the woman he is with, as he does anyone who is decent, kind, or gentle, as an object of contempt, or a piece of furniture to be kicked about as he sees fit. At a boxing match, Tommy shouts at his favorite contender to "rip the other eye" of his opponent who is taking a beating. Given the task of finding—and silencing—a "squealer," he confronts the man's elderly mother who is confined to a wheelchair. Since he considers sympathy to be a trait for "squirts," he has no qualms about shoving her down a flight of stairs (a classic scene), as his unrestrained giggle rises above her screams. He thinks this dastardly deed out in advance, enjoying even the thought of his malicious act, wiping his hand across his mouth in anticipation, as he often does at times of tension or excitement. At an earlier time in his life he has been friends with Nick Bianco, an ex-con, and together they have taken in the sleazy nightclubs and brothels. Nick, a widower with two children, falls in love and marries, and sets about to change his life. He finds a job, leaving his criminal past behind him. Nick's past comes back to haunt him when he is asked to testify against his former buddy. Fearing reprisals from Tommy, he lives in terror when the killer is unexpectedly acquitted. Nick sends his wife and daughters away to safety, then confronts Tommy, demanding to be left alone. Udo threatens Nick, telling him about his plans to "have lots of fun" with him and his family. Tommy orders a special dinner for Nick, his "pal," but the owner of the restaurant refuses since it is near closing time. Tommy slaps him and leaves, but he waits outside in ambush for Nick, who has called the police. Nick confronts Tommy and they fight. Nick is shot, but lives, and Tommy is taken into custody. He will find himself in a disquieting predicament—once Nick and other witnesses testify on this charge and the crimes he divulged to Nick during friendlier times. Unlike Nick, Tommy resisted change and the redeeming value of love. He wallowed in his cruel behavior instead, convinced he was beyond the reach of the law—until the law proved him wrong. Tommy Udo is a "natural" all right—a natural born killer who will be asked to pay the price.

TONY AARON

Film Source: *Under Suspicion*
Release Date: 1992
Director: Simon Moore
Production Company: Columbia Pictures
Color
Running Time: 99 minutes
Performed by: Liam Neeson
Additional Performers: Laura San Giacomo (Angeline); Kenneth Cranham (Frank); Maggie O'Neill (Hazel); Alphonsia Emmanuel (Selina); Michael Almaz (Stasio).

Physical Description: Tony Aaron is in his mid-thirties, above average in height, ruggedly handsome, with expressive eyes and a boyish mop of hair. He speaks his cockney dialect in a low and charming baritone. Although his finances don't always allow him to dress as well as he might like, his commanding build plays well off any attire he chooses, and he embodies many of the charming qualities most wished for in a man of his type.

Character Analysis: Tony Aaron longs for wealth; his eyes are on a star, out of reach and gleaming brightly. He has made many errors in judgment over his lifetime, but has seemingly learned nothing from them. He has an affair with Hazel, supposedly a rich man's wife, and thinks he has his future set. His poor timing gets both her husband and one of Tony's fellow police officers killed, thus destroying his reputation. Tony marries Hazel, only to discover her deceased husband's many debts. He sinks further and further into a mire of deceit, having married a woman he lusted after but does not love. Their relationship further deteriorates when Tony begins using Hazel in his dangerously illicit business; she poses for a fee, as a "lover" of husbands who must prove their adultery to obtain a divorce under English law in the 1950s. As part of the arrangement, Tony bursts in upon the pair and photographs them in a compromising position. A new client, the famous artist Stasio, will provide the means for Tony's escape from tedium. In a calculated maneuver Tony schemes with Selina, Stasio's wife, to murder both Hazel and Stasio as they await his agreed upon entrance into their hotel bedroom. Hazel's death frees Tony, and Stasio's death provides Selina with revenge on her husband's beautiful young model and lover, Angeline. An added benefit will be their sharing of the artist's fortune in paintings. By plan, Tony stashes evidence which will

157

clear him and implicate Angeline, even though he has fallen in love with her. He knows he will be arrested and tried for both murders. He is convicted and sentenced, trusting that his long-time friend, Frank, a police officer, will find the planted evidence soon enough to save him from the hangman's noose. Stasio's severed thumb tip is produced by a frantic Frank just as Tony is being led off for execution; Angeline is subsequently arrested and convicted. Certain that she will receive a life sentence instead of execution, Tony visits Angeline once more in prison. To satisfy her curiosity about his guilt, he whispers the answer into her ear. His new life in the United States will be the culmination of his childhood dreams. With two violent and senseless murders and the imprisonment of the guiltless woman he loved behind him, he visits Selina in a magnificent hotel. During their conversation Selina reminds Tony he now has everything he ever wished for. But Tony's eyes are still set on another far away star he yearns to touch and will be forever denied. Just as Angeline sits locked away forever in prison, so is Tony locked away in a prison of his own making. Of his numerous mistakes, the one from which he will never be set free is the one which results in his loss of love.

TWAIN: SEE: IRENE (RITA) TWAIN

UDO: SEE: TOMMY UDO

VADER: SEE: DARTH VADER

VICTOR MAITLAND

Film Source: *Beverly Hills Cop*
Release Date: 1984
Director: Martin Brest
Production Company: Paramount Pictures
Color
Running Time: 105 minutes
Performed by: Steven Berkoff
Additional Performers: Eddie Murphy (Axel Foley), Lisa Eilbacher (Jenny Summers).

Physical Description: Victor Maitland is a person of distinct characteristics, robustly handsome, with gray hair and a wide, expressive mouth. He speaks with a smooth British accent. He wears high quality suits and ties, and knows how to dress for the best effect. His bright gaze and engaging manner have a hard edge to them.

Character Analysis: Nothing in Victor Maitland's suave, genteel outer persona is as it seems to be. He is an art dealer who has distinguished himself in his career. He is serene and composed, with the polished sophistication required for a man in his profession. His slow, deliberate manner of walking and talking mirrors his character, since he takes time in contemplation of his actions. Yet his real livelihood is far less commendable, consisting of shady dealings with violent endings. The bonds and drugs Maitland smuggles are far more lucrative than art work, and his Beverly Hills mansion reflects his true calling. It is an armed fort, surrounded by tall gates and fences and guarded by security officers. Maitland commits a fatal error when he underestimates police detective Axel Foley's quick mind and serious regard for the death of a friend. Maitland insults Axel at a "members only" restaurant where he advises the detective to "crawl back" under the "little stone" from which he came; later he tells the manager of his art gallery, Jenny Summers, to "Shut up," when he confronts her with her close friend Axel. These examples of rudeness more precisely typify Maitland than his outward display of good manners amongst friends and business associates, and they escalate until he finds no compunction in using Jenny as a human shield in the interests of his own survival. Murder, to Maitland, is comparable to the art he sells—since it has a price to be paid. In the end he is killed in a gun battle with Axel and his back up from the Beverly Hills police. Although Maitland had threatened to "squash" Axel like a bug, it is he who is destroyed. It did not matter whether he financed his career in art by using funds from smuggled drugs and bonds—or if his work as an art dealer led him into more illicit concerns. All the same, Victor Maitland was a criminal, not the proper gentleman he pretended to be. He wanted more than the legitimate rewards he could expect from a respectable occupation. Violence, hidden from public view, epitomized him, and allowed him to reap the materials rewards he desired. The price of such rewards was high, however, costing him not only the respect he had won over the years as an art dealer, but his own life as well.

VILOS COHAGEN

Film Source: *Total Recall*
Release Date: 1990
Director: Paul Verhoeven
Production Company: Caroloco Productions
Color
Running Time: 113 minutes
Performed by: Ronny Cox
Additional Performers: Arnold Schwarzenegger (Doug Quaid), Michael Ironside (Richter), Rachel Ticotin (Melina).

Physical Description: Vilos Cohagen has striking eyes, short reddish-gray hair, and a tall, slender physique which enhances his stylish suits.

Fifty-something, he looks fit. A southern accent softens his rich baritone voice.

Character Analysis: Vilos Cohagen rules Mars under absolute martial law in the year 2084. Workers brought in from Earth to mine the Red planet live under constant fear for their lives due to Cohagen's threats. Doug Quaid enters this cozy den of iniquity after undergoing "total recall," a process which has enabled him to remember an alternate existence as Hauser, a government operative who had infiltrated Cohagen's empire. Cohagen knows exactly who Doug is, since he was the one responsible for erasing Doug's memories and replacing them with new ones. Doug, as Hauser, had discovered that Cohagen had knowledge of hidden reactors beneath the planet's surface that could provide Mars with all the air it needs, a precious commodity, currently in short supply. A tight grip on the Martian economy has enabled Cohagen to squeeze a vast fortune from the miners and other inhabitants, and he refuses to consider relinquishing his monopoly and losing control of the people he rules. Doug won't be "handled," however, and Cohagen sends his trusted enforcer, Richter, after him. Doug kills Richter, and Cohagen, in desperation, cuts off the oxygen supply, threatening to "blow up" the planet in the process. Doug confronts him, and in the ensuing battle, Cohagen is sucked out through a vent onto the Martian surface, where he dies horribly. The reactors kick in, flooding Mars with breathable air, just in time to save Doug and his lover Melina from extinction. Cohagen has ruled Mars ruthlessly and without compassion, relying heavily on his tightly-held reign, until it, and his life, slip through his grasp.

VLADIMIR HARKONNEN

Film Source: *Dune*
Release Date: 1984
Director: David Lynch
Production company: De Laurentiis
Color
Running Time: 137 minutes
Performed by: Kenneth MacMillan
Additional Performers: Kyle MacLachlan (Paul Atreides), Jürgen Prochnow (Duke Leto Atreides), Francesca Annis (Lady Jessica), Alicia Roanne Witt (Alia), Sting (Rabban).

Physical Description: Baron Vladimir Harkonnen's grossly overweight body, encased in a suspension suit, hangs from an artificial hoist which assists in his mobility within his compound. The Baron's flat ugly face is a mass of ulcerated boils, and his sparse, red hair contrasts strangely with his bushy, arched eyebrows. Adding to his garish appearance, his fingernails and toenails have been painted black. Harkonnnen's loud irritating giggle permeates his quarters as he swoops about in his harness, like some horrific, giant bird of prey.

Character Analysis: Baron Harkonnen, the autocratic patriarch of his evil clan, discusses his plans for greater control over his dominion with his nephew, Rabban, as his physician goes about the disgusting task of draining his ulcerous postules. Harkonnen's dreary, lifeless chamber reflects the polluted gloom of Giedi Prime, his home planet. The Baron is delighted when a youth is ushered in to his presence. Harkonnen falls upon the unfortunate young man like some wild beast, wrenching something from the youth's chest which, splattered with blood, he enjests with great relish. The Baron's primary concerns are self-indulgence and power. He is not satisfied with merely conquering the Atreides, his rivals for dominance, but he must torment them as well. He spits in the face of the Lady Jessica, concubine of Duke Leto Atreides, his contempt turning to exultation when he deals directly with the Duke himself. The Baron directs that Arrakis, the desert world known as "Dune," be crushed into submission and, in fact, Harkonnen's utter disregard for the people of Arrakis mirrors his attitude towards everyone. He longs to hold sway over the lucrative trade in "Spice," the most precious commodity in the galaxy, and he is as irascible as a child throwing a tantrum, shouting at everyone in his whiny voice, to make sure he gets his way. His plans go awry, however, and he is called into the presence of the Emperor, who demands that Harkonnen explain himself. He cowers in fear, altogether unprepared for this sudden jeopardy into which he has fallen. None of the problem is his fault, the Baron argues, but he is confronted by Paul Atreides' young sister, Alia, who takes revenge for her people by stabbing him. Harkonnen is propelled into the open jaws of a Sandworm, the Gargantuan, native lifeform which produces Spice. The monster which devours the Baron is far greater than he is. It is a fitting conclusion for a man whose rapacity thus far has known no bounds.

WALKER: SEE: MATTY WALKER

WHORFIN: SEE: JOHN WHORFIN

WILSON: SEE: JACK WILSON

COUNT ZAROFF

Film Source: *The Most Dangerous Game*
Release Date: 1932
Director: Ernest B. Schoedsack
Production Company: An RKO Radio Picture

GEORGETTE S. FOX

B&W
Running Time: 63 minutes
Performed by: Leslie Banks
Additional Performers: Joel McCrea (Robert Rainsford), Fay Wray (Eve Trowbridge), Irving Pichel.

Physical Description: Count Zaroff, cigarette pressed between his lips, and dressed in formal attire, has the dignified mien of a refined gentleman. He assumes a much different appearance in black hunting gear, however. His dark hair, moustache and beard set off brooding eyes. Zaroff's husky voice, delivered in a thick Russian accent, serves to further deepen his disconcerting mystique.

Character Analysis: Count Zaroff is a virtuoso at the piano, but he reveres his hunting skills with idolatrous zeal. Zaroff has been affected by stressful occurrences and thoughts of passion—heralded when Zaroff strokes the scar near his temple, a mark he earned while hunting in Africa. He fled Russia at the time of the Bolshevik Revolution, maintaining his fortune through a quick wit and firm determination. His constant search for more provocative hunts has culminated in his undiminished boredom. Zaroff dwells in the foreboding confines of his restored family castle on an island, "no bigger than a deer park," noted hunter Robert "Bob" Rainsford declares. As a demonstration of his private credo, he has placed on his door a knocker in the form of a wounded centaur carrying an unconscious woman in his arms. The Count, a tenacious adherent to a repugnant doctrine of bestiality in human relationships, discusses his views on passion and his exploits as a hunter with Rainsford, his shipwrecked dinner guest. His one "feminine guest," as he calls her, is Eve Trowbridge, whom the Count desires. Glancing at Eve, he shares with Bob his belief in making love after "the blood is quickened by the kill." This persuasion he repeats as he sends Bob and Eve into the jungle as the "game" for his next hunt. From reading Bob's narratives of his adventures the Count has concluded his illustrious guest shares his own distorted opinions on hunting, and discloses his own frightful, nauseating memorial in a trophy room lined with human heads. Assuring Bob he will not kill Eve because, in his words, "one does not kill the female animal," Zaroff allows Rainsford a day's start before setting out in pursuit. Once he believes Bob to be dead, Zaroff takes Eve back to his fortress. Before he can make good his views on passion, however, Bob returns. Outwitted, Zaroff offers Bob and Eve their freedom, then suddenly pulls a gun from his jacket. Bob stabs the Count with an arrow, causing Zaroff to lose his balance on a window ledge and fall into the jaws of his snarling dogs. Although approved by many, hunting down and killing animals has long disquieted caring individuals. Zaroff's father had been a "sportsman," although he was not a murderer of men. His son sees

162

himself as a "great hunter" in the family tradition who has simply made his favorite activity more interesting, justifying his pursuit of human "game" as a means of quelling his *ennui*. But Bob understands that the Count, by releasing his more savage instincts, has become a "madman" who must be stopped at all cost. Zaroff's chamber of trophy head horrors remains after his death, a repulsive testament to the hunting of his "most dangerous game."

GENERAL ZOD

Film Source: *Superman II*
Release Date: 1980
Director: Richard Lester
Production Company: Warner Bros.
Color
Running Time: 127 minutes
Performed by: Terence Stamp
Additional Performers: Christopher Reeve (Clark Kent/Superman), Margot Kidder (Lois Lane), Sarah Douglas (Ursa), Jack O'Halloran (Non), Gene Hackman (Lex Luthor).

Physical Description: General Zod resembles a raven as he takes to the air, attired in shiny black trousers and shirt, and defying Earth's gravity. He is a native of the planet Krypton, and, like Superman, he possesses superhuman abilities, including extraordinary strength and heat vision. His perfectly groomed hair, moustache, and beard match his jet black clothing. His glistening raven-like eyes miss nothing. Of medium height, and slight of build, he appears deceptively vulnerable. When talking or deliberating, he strokes his beard. Uttering his words as one might a soliloquy, the General compliments his bass viol pitch with resplendent elocution.

Character Analysis: General Zod is a learned individual, erudite and shrewd, and had well-served his own world of Krypton once. Now Zod, his lover, Ursa, and his henchman, Non, have been set adrift in an other-dimensional prison for crimes against their home planet, until they are accidentally released by Superman, their Kryptonite jailor's son. They murder a team of astronauts on the moon, and fly to Earth to take their revenge on Superman. Zod's dream of ascendancy on his own world has been foiled, and he now revels in the discovery of another, more malleable world he can "lead." Following a daunting display of their powers, the General preens before the TV cameras. Leaving death and destruction in their wake, the three begin their march on Washington and the White House, where Zod takes command of the Oval Office after firing on Secret Service and military guards. Zod's pleasure in taking control of the Earth soon wanes and he grows bored, until criminal genius Lex Luthor enters the scene. Zod first orders him killed, but soon reverses this decision after Luthor discloses Superman's true identity and offers to help Zod conquer the Man of Steel. Power over Earth is not the General's greatest wish after all. Until Superman kneels at his feet, his victory is incomplete. In the meantime, Superman has made a reversal of his own, choosing a human existence in order to consummate his love for reporter Lois Lane. The weaknesses he thus assumes have enabled Superman to feel more compassion for the human condition than his superhuman powers ever could. The pain, fear, and insecurity Superman now experiences enlighten him and furnish him with a private reserve of decency and self-respect, which far outweighs Zod's contempt for "these Earth creatures." Regaining his abilities, Superman meets Zod and his cohorts in a battle on and above crowded city streets. Leading his foes away from the city, Superman treats Zod and the others to the same process by which he temporarily became human. Dreams of power brought Zod imprisonment, but eagerness for revenge has vanquished him. His years in prison have increased his wrath, but have taught him nothing about the humans he now encounters. Had Zod sought it, he might have acquired the same respect for humanity and humility as Superman did, but Zod's single-mindedness and narrow perspective have entrapped him as no stockade walls or prison bars ever could. See also: LEX LUTHOR.

ZOLO

Film Source: *Romancing the Stone*
Release Date: 1984
Director: Robert Zemeckis
Production Company: Twentieth Century fox
Color
Running Time: 106 minutes
Performed by: Manuel Ojeda
Additional Performers: Kathleen Turner (Joan Wilder), Michael Douglas (Jack Colton).

Physical Description: General Zolo's thick, dark moustache, hair and eyebrows enhance his piercing eyes. He speaks fluent English with a disarming Spanish accent, utilizing his rugged, sonorous voice to influence others. His physical strength is understated by a medium build and height. General Zolo is rarely without a hat, whether attired in a suit, or military uniform. He skulks as he walks, resembling a leopard trailing its prey.

Character Analysis: General Zolo's worship of power engenders an addiction which is both inescapable and dehumanizing. He feels most at ease when unquestioning, dutiful men are carrying out his every order. Although he is known and feared by many in his own country, Zolo is a stranger to Joan Wilder, the American romantic fiction author who is safeguarding a valuable treasure map for her sister who is being held for ransom by South American smugglers. Joan's apartment is ransacked and her building superintendent is murdered under Zolo's orders, but the map remains hidden with Joan's latest manuscript. Fearing for her sister's safety, Joan flies to Cartajena, where she is tricked into taking the wrong bus. The bus crashes into a blockade set up by Zolo's army, and he demands Joan hand over the map at gun point. Joan is rescued by adventurer and American ex-patriot Jack Colton. Jack and Joan elude Zolo's men in a hair-raising race through the jungle. They successfully follow the map to find the treasure, but it and they are captured. Zolo threatens to toss them into a pit of raging crocodiles. but Jack throws the jewel away. Attempting to retrieve it, Zolo loses both the stone and his hand into the jaws of a crocodile. In a ferocious maneuver, he throws Joan on top of the crocodile pit. Sarcastically repeating a line from one of her books, he poses the question of how fast she is going to die. Joan, in a burst of novel genius, burns him with his own cigar, and Zolo tumbles into the pit alone. Zolo's one goal in life is the acquisition of power—and he has foregone all personal relationships in order to pursue his goal. Harnessing the efforts of weaker minions for his many nefarious schemes, he sets himself up as the ultimate authority figure. Zolo enjoys torturing his victims, and he has mastered the most effective methods of administering pain. Killing is not an avoidable horror, it is, quite simply, just a part of what he does. Zolo has structured his life into a succession of ruthless acts. Now, under conditions he himself has put into motion, Zolo's death fits neatly into the same morbid pattern he has established for himself.

NOTES

[1]*The Basic Writings of C. G. Jung*, ed. Violet S. Lazlo. New York: Modern Library, Random House, 1959, p. 462.

[2]Temira Pachmuss. *F. M. Dostoevsky: Dualism and Synthesis of the Human Soul*. Carbondale, IL: Southern Illinois University Press, 1963, p. 17.

[3]Francis Bacon. "Of Revenge" in *The New International Dictionary of Quotations*, ed. Hugh Rawson and Margaret Miner. New York: New American Library, 1986, p. 315.

[4]Clive Barker. *The Thief of Always*. New York: HarperCollins, 1992, p. 114.

[5]Juvenal. "Satires" in *The New International Dictionary of Quotations*, ed. Hugh Rawson and Margaret Miner. New York: New American Library, 1986, p. 315.

[6]Erich Fromm. *The Anatomy of Human Destructiveness*. Greenwich, CT: Fawcett Publications, 1973, p. 322.

[7]George Orwell. *Nineteen Eighty-Four*. New York: The New American Library, 1961, p. 220.

SELECTED ANNOTATED BIBLIOGRAPHY

Amberg, George, ed. *The New York Times Film Reviews: 1913-1970.* New York: Times Books, 1913- . A seven-volume set containing complete cast listings and reviews of nearly sixty years of films.

The American Institute Catalog, Feature Films: 1911-1920, Volume F-I Berkeley, CA: University of California Press, 1988. Complete A-to-Z titles, with full entries on each film.

Andrew, Geoff. *The Film Handbook: Director.* Boston: G.K. Hall, 1989. An A-to-Z commentary with biographies of major international film directors. Some photographs and lists of directors' credits.

Armstrong, Richard B. and Mary Willems Armstrong. *The Movie List Book: A Reference Guide to Films, Themes, Settings, and Series.* Jefferson, NC: McFarland, 1980. More than 400 alphabetical entries with commentaries on characters and film subjects. Includes table of contents.

Beck, Calvin Thomas. *Heroes of the Horrors.* New York: Macmillan, 1975. Six concise biographies of important performers from terror and fantasy film history, including Lon Chaney, Bela Lugosi, Peter Lorre, and others.

Champlin, Charles. *The Flicks: or Whatever Became of Andy Hardy?* Pasadena, CA: Ward Ritchie Press, 1977. Comments on the changing face of cinema over several decades. Includes many photographs. Foreign and American films are discussed. Looks at television as both competition for, and a separate medium from, films.

Clarens, Carlos. *Crime Movies: From Griffith to* THE GODFATHER *and Beyond.* New York: W. W. Norton, 1980. An in-depth look at the gangster and crime film from its earliest inception through modern cinema. Photographs and commentary chronicle this genres' development. A bibliography of related titles is included.

Daniels, Les. *Living in Fear: A History of Horror in the Mass Media.* New York: Charles Scribner's Sons, 1975. An overview of horror, containing discussions of films from the silent era until the present.

Deutelbaum, Marshall, ed. *Image: On the Art and Evolution of the Film: Photographs and Articles from The Magazine of the International Museum of Photography.* London; New York: Dover Publications and International Museum of Photography, 1979. Contains photographs and much information on early films. Includes interviews with actors and technical artists, as well as studies of such films as D. W. Griffith's *The White Rose* and King Vidor's *The Crowd.* Indexed.

Drake, Douglas. *Horror.* New York: Macmillan, 1966. A study of horror films and connection with works of literature.

Essoe, Gabe. *The Book of Movie Lists.* West Point, CT: Arlington House, 1981. Motion picture memorabilia and trivia, with photographs and index.

Everson, William K. *The Bad Guys: A Pictorial History of the Movie Villain.* Secaucus, NJ: Citadel Press, 1964. Fully illustrated with numerous photographs from a variety of films.

Florescu, Radu R. and Raymond T. McNally. *Dracula: Prince of Many Faces.* Boston, MA: Little, Brown, 1989. Covers the legend of Dracula,

169

as well as the factual life of the historical figure upon which the legend is based.

Franklin, Joe. *Classics of the Silent Screen: A Pictorial Treasury*. Secaucus, NJ: Citadel Press, 1959. Four hundred photographs, seventy-five screen personalities, and fifty movies are covered, including *Dr. Jekyll and Mr. Hyde* and *The Phantom of the Opera*.

French, Phillip. *Westerns: Aspects of a Movie Genre*. New York: Viking, 1973. One chapter of this Western film study focuses on the character of the villain as an integral part of the genre.

Fromm, Erich. *The Anatomy of Human Destructiveness*. Greenwich, CT: Fawcett Publications, 1973. A psychological examination of the forms of aggressive behavior as they relate to human development. Complete with clinical studies.

Garbic, Adam and Jacek Klinowski. *Cinema, the Magic Vehicle: A Guide to Its Achievement. Journey One: The Cinema Through 1949*. Metuchen, NJ: Scarecrow Press, 1975. Short commentaries on international cinema from 1913 to 1949, with indices of directors and films.

Gehring, Wes D., ed. *Handbook of American Film Genres*. New York: Greenwood Press, 1988. Scholarly discussions of genre films, including gangster, comedy, horror, and more, contributed by various critics from the field of cinema. Filmographies, bibliographies, and index included.

Glut, Donald F. *The Dracula Book*. Metuchen, NJ: Scarecrow Press, 1975. Comprehensive look at the legendary vampire in motion pictures and literature.

Golden, Chistopher. *"Cut!" Horror Writers on Horror Film*. New York: Berkley Books, 1992. A series of essays on the horror film genre by famous horror writers and others, illustrated with black-and-white photographs from various films.

Hadley-Garcia, George. *Hispanic Hollywood: The Latins in Motion Pictures*. New York: Carol Publishing Group, 1993. A comprehensive and historical look at Latin American actors in motion pictures complete with photographs index, and brief biographies.

Huss, Roy Gerard. *Focus on the Horror Film*. Englewood Cliffs, NJ: Prentiss-Hall, 1972. Photographs and bibliography of related works.

Katchmer, George A. *Eighty Silent Film Stars: Biographies and Filmographies of the Obscure to the Well Known*. Jefferson, NC: McFarland, 1991. Actors and actresses of the silent era with filmographies, photographs, extensive biographies. Includes index.

Katz, Ephraim. *The Film Encyclopedia*. New York: Harper Perennial, 1994. More than 1200 items of information on actors and actresses, cinema terms, producers, and directors.

Kilday, Gregg. "Hail the Conquering Villain," in *Vogue*, August, 1989. Article on differing interpretations of screen villains both past and present.

King, Stephen. *Stephen King's* DANSE MACABRE. New York: Berkley Books, 1983. An overview of the horror genre. Includes photographs, appendices on films and books, and an index.

Kracauer, Siegfried. *From Caligari to Hitler: A Psychological History of the German Film*. Princeton, NJ: Princeton University Press, 1974. Photographs, index, and bibliography of related titles. In-depth study of silent and sound film making in Germany and the films themselves up to the rise of Adolph Hitler. Short discussion of the cinema in Nazi Germany.

Lieberman, Susan, and Francis Cable. *Memorable Film Characters: An Index to Roles and Performers, 1915-1983*. Westport, Ct: Greenwood Press, 1984. Covers over 1500 characters and performers.

Longman, Larry. *Encyclopedia of Film Comedy*. New York: Garland, 1987. Actors and roles listed in alphabetical order with photographs. Includes a bibliography of sources.

Magill, Frank F., ed. *Magill's Survey of the Cinema: English Language Films*. Englewood Cliffs, NJ: Salem Press, 1980. First in a series of seven volumes containing comprehensive entries on films.

Manchel, Frank. *An Album of Great Science Fiction Films*, rev. ed. New York: Franklin Watts, 1982. Covers several of the most remarkable films of this genre from early motion pictures to the present. Also has a detailed filmography.

———. *Terrors of the Screen*. Englewood Cliffs, NJ: Prentice-Hall, 1970. Discusses terror films from their earliest beginnings through the 1960s. Extensive bibliography and many photographs.

Manuell, Dr. Roger, ed. *The International Encyclopedia of Films*. New York: Crown, 1972. Extensive biographies and photographs of actors and actresses. World cinema reviewed and technical terms defined.

Martin, Mick; and Marsha Porter. *Video Movie Guide: 1995*. New York: Ballentine Books, 1994. Categorized alphabetical listings of more than 15,000 films available on videocassette with comments and ratings on each entry. Includes alphabetical film, cast, and director indexes and a listing of Academy Award winners.

Mast, Gerald. *A Short History of the Movies*, rev. by F. Kawin. New York: MacMillan, 1992. Historical consideration of film and its development throughout the world. Illustrated with both color and black-and-white plates.

McCarty, John. *Psychos: Eighty Years of Mad Movies, Maniacs, and Murderous Deeds*. New York: Saint Martin's Press, 1986. A study of psychotic behavior on film, this book delves into madness and its attendant mayhem as portrayed throughout movie history. It contains a complete bibliography and filmography of the genre.

Michael, Paul, ed. *The Great American Movie Book*. Englewood Cliffs, NJ: Prentice-Hall, 1980. Extensive coverage of films with many photographs.

Mulay, James J., Daniel Curran, and Jeffrey H. Wallenfeld, eds. *Spies and Sleuths: Mystery and Suspense Films on Videocassette*. Evanston, IL: Cine Books, 1988. Indexed reviews of detective and mystery films on videocassette.

Pachmuss, Termira. *F. M. Dostoevsky: Dualism and Synthesis of the Human Soul*. Carbondale, IL: Southern Illinois University Press, 1963. A study of Dostoevsky's works and the recurrent theme of duality intrinsic to them.

Parish, James Robert. *The Great Gangster Pictures*. Metuchen, NJ: Scarecrow Press, 1976. An encyclopedic overview of the ganster film.

———. *The Great Western Pictures*. Metuchen, NJ: Scarecrow Press, 1976. An encyclopedic overview of the Western film.

———, and Michael R. Pitts. *The Great Gangster Pictures II*. Metuchen, NJ: Scarecrow Press, 1987. An encyclopedic overview of the gangster film. Contains a synopsis, photographs, and production information on many films from all eras.

———. *The Great Hollywood Musical Pictures*. Metuchen, NJ: Scarecrow Press, 1992. Photographs and complete biographies and listings of Hollywood musicals from *The Jazz Singer* through the 1980s.

———. *The Great Western Pictures II*. Metuchen, NJ: Scarecrow Press, 1988. An encyclopedic overview of the Western film. Contains a synopsis, photographs, and production information on many films from all eras.

Peary, Danny. *Cult Movies 2: Fifty More of the Classics, the Sleepers, the Weird, and the Wonderful.* New York: Dell, 1983. Covers all eras from silent films to sound. Contains many photographs.

____. *Cult Movies 3: Fifty More of the Classics, the Sleepers, the Weird, and the Wonderful.* New York: Fireside, 1988. Extensive coverage of silent and sound films. Contains many photographs. *Blue Velvet* and *Body Heat* are discussed.

____.' *Guide for the Film Fanatic.* New York: Simon and Schuster, 1986. A concise, well-rounded look at over one thousand films.

Pickard, Roy. *Who Played Who in the Movies, An A-to-Z.* New York: Schocken Books, 1981. An alphabetical listing of film characters and the actors and actresses who portrayed each one. Includes an index and many photographs.

____. *Who Played Who on the Screen.* New York: Hippocrene Books, 1989. Contains a listing of a variety of characters and the actors and actresses who portrayed them.

Pitts, Micheal R. *Horror Film Stars.* Jefferson, NC: McFarland, 1981. Short biographies and film credits on several film performers.

Ray, Robert B. *A Certain Tendency of the Hollywood Cinema, 1930-1980.* Princeton, NJ: Princeton University Press, 1985. An ideological study of the technology and form of motion pictures for fifty years. Contains an extensive bibliography.

Roud, Richard. *Cinema: A Critical Dictionary: The Major Film-Makers.* New York: Viking, 1980. An A-to-Z listing of noted individuals in film history. Includes an index.

Rovin, Jeff. *The Encyclopedia of Monsters.* New York: Facts on File, 1989. Contains hundreds of photographs, movie biographies, etc. on various characters of the genre in encyclopedic form.

Scheuer, Steven H., ed. *Movies on TV and Videocassette: 1993-1994.* New York: Bantam Books, 1992. Alphabetical listings of films available on videocassette with comments and ratings on each entry.

Scott, Jay. *Midnight Matinees: Movies and Their Makers 1975-1985.* New York: Linger Publishing Co., 1985. Discusses films and film-makers of the cult film genre.

Shadoian, Jack. *Dreams and Dead Ends: The American Gangster/Crime Film.* Cambridge, MA: MIT Press, 1977. An indepth look at .American gangster and crime film, from early examples through the first two *Godfather* movies.

Sklar, Robert. *Film: An International History of The Medium.* New York: Harry N. Abrams, 1993. An exceptional overview of the history of world cinema and film production. Contains many color and black-and-white photographs as well as a bibliography, glossary of terms, filmography, and an index.

Stanley, John. *John Stanley's Creature Feature Movie Guide: An A-to-Z Encyclopedia to the Cinema of the Fantastic; Is there a Mad Doctor in the House?* Pacifica, CA: Creatures at Large, 1981-. A series of books cataloging film credits on a yearly basis. Contains photographs and short biographies.

Thomas, Tony, and Aubrey Soloman. *The Films of Twentieth Century Fox,* rev. ed. Secaucus, NJ: Citadel Press, 1985. Contains an alphabetical listing of films with short summaries, photographs, and historical documentation.

Timpone, Anthony, ed. *Fangoria's Best Horror Films.* Avenel, NJ: Cresent Books, 1994. Contains an index, many photographs, information on several recent, as well as older films and interviews with Vincent Price and Clive Barker.

Twitchell, James B. *Dreadful Pleasures: An Anatomy of Modern Horror.* New York: Oxford University Press, 1985. Horror's growth and change in the media. Comprehensive bibliography.

Willis, Donald C. *Horror and Science Fiction Films: A Checklist.* Metuchen, NJ: Scarecrow Press, 1972. Complete listings for many movies.

____. *Horror and Science Fiction Films II.* Metuchen, NJ: Scarecrow Press, 1982. An A-to-Z listing with information on 2,350 films.

Willis, John, ed. *Screen World.* New York: Crown Publishers, 1949-present.

Wolf, Leonard. *Horror: A Connoisseur's Guide to Literature and Film.* New York: Facts on File, 1989. Complete with photographs, this book entry takes a look at horror on film and in literature. Also contains alphabetical listings of films and books.

Wright, Gene. *Horrorshows: The A-to-Z of Horror in Film, TV, Radio, and Theater.* New York: Facts on File, 1985. Complete with bibliography, this book is a study of all forms of horror in the cinema, as well as other media.

Zinman, David. *Fifty Grand Movies of the 1960's and 1970's: The American Film Institute.* New York: Crown, 1986. Contains a cast listing and synopsis of each film discussed and many photographs.

INDEX

Directors

ABOUT THE AUTHOR

GEORGETTE S. FOX says:

FROM THE TIME I COULD READ AND WRITE I have loved working with the written word. Two poems written during my third grade year were published by a Corona, California newspaper, and later I served as a reporter on my high school newspaper for two years. Since 1987 I have published numerous articles, short stories, poems and film reviews in such magazines as *Dream International Quarterly* and *Dead of Night*. In 1995 I received an award for one of my poems from a poetry society in Los Angeles.

I have a Bachelor's Degree in History and a teaching credential from the University of California, Riverside. After teaching for five years I worked as a library clerk for another ten years.

My husband and I have been married for more than twenty years. We live in Riverside, California with our son.

This book is a culmination of my long fascinatioin with the cinema, both as entertainment and as an art form, and with film history in general. My interest was rekindled with an "Art of the Cinema" course taken in college, but my love of motion pictures actually began at the age of four, when my parents took me to see *Elephant Walk* at a local drive-in theatre.

Recent Publications

"Warder" (poem), in *The Gargoyle* (March/April, 1994).

Film review of *Ladyhawke*, in *The Gargoyle* (March/April, 1994).

Film review of *Tale of a Vampire*, in *Dead of Night* (July, 1994).

Film review of *Fortress*, in *Dream International Quarterly* (Spring/ Summer, 1995).

"Dragons in the Sky" (poem), in *Dream International Quarterly* (Spring/ Summer, 1995).

"Midmost" (poem): Award of Recognition, Famous Poets Society, 1995.

"Woven Fabric: Dream Talk with Dr. Robert Van de Castle" (article): *Dream International Quarterly* (Winter, 1995/96).

"Dark Night" (story), in *Dream International Quarterly* (Winter, 1995/ 96).